D1626098

Power Grab

For rulers whose territories are blessed with extractive resources – such as petroleum, metals, and minerals that will power the clean energy transition – converting natural wealth into fiscal wealth is key. Squandering the opportunity to secure these revenues will guarantee short tenures, while capitalizing on windfalls and managing the resulting wealth will fortify the foundations of enduring rule. This book argues that leaders nationalize extractive resources to extend the duration of their power. By taking control of the means of production and establishing state-owned enterprises, leaders capture revenues that might otherwise flow to private firms, and use this increased capital to secure political support. Using a combination of case studies and cross-national statistical analysis with novel techniques, Mahdavi sketches the contours of a crucial political gamble: nationalize and reap immediate gains while risking future prosperity, or maintain private operations, thereby passing on revenue windfalls but securing long-term fiscal streams.

PAASHA MAHDAVI is Assistant Professor of Political Science at the University of California, Santa Barbara. His research on energy governance and political economy has appeared in *Comparative Political Studies*, *Nature Energy*, and *World Politics*, among other journals, and has received media attention from *The Financial Times*, *The Wall Street Journal*, and *The Washington Post*. Mahdavi earned his M.S. in Statistics and Ph.D. in Political Science from UCLA. He has held fellowships at the Initiative for Sustainable Energy Policy, the Payne Institute, and the World Economic Forum, and currently serves as Term Member at the Council on Foreign Relations.

Business and Public Policy

Series Editor

Aseem Prakash, *University of Washington*

Series Board

Sarah Brooks, *Ohio State University*
David Coen, *University College London*
Nathan Jensen, *University of Texas, Austin*
Christophe Knill, *Ludwig-Maximilians-University, Munich*
David Konisky, *Indiana University*
David Levi Faur, *Hebrew University, Jerusalem*
Layna Mosley, *University of North Carolina, Chapel Hill*
Abraham Newman, *Georgetown University*
Leonard Seabrooke, *Copenhagen Business School*
Mike Vandenberg, *Vanderbilt University*
Edward Walker, *University of California, Los Angeles*
Henry Yeung, *Singapore National University*

This series aims to play a pioneering role in shaping the emerging field of business and public policy. *Business and Public Policy* focuses on two central questions. First, how does public policy influence business strategy, operations, organization, and governance, and with what consequences for both business and society? Second, how do businesses themselves influence policy institutions, policy processes, and other policy actors and with what outcomes?

Other books in the series

TIMOTHY WERNER, *Public Forces and Private Politics in American Big Business*

HEVINA S. DASHWOOD, *The Rise of Global Corporate Social Responsibility: Mining and the Spread of Global Norms*

LLEWELYN HUGHES, *Globalizing Oil: Firms and Oil Market Governance in France, Japan, and the United States*

EDWARD T. WALKER, *Grassroots for Hire: Public Affairs Consultants in American Democracy*

CHRISTIAN R. THAUER, *The Managerial Sources of Corporate Social Responsibility: The Spread of Global Standards*

KIYOTERU TSUTSUI & ALWYN LIM (Editors), *Corporate Social Responsibility in a Globalizing World*

ASEEMA SINHA, *Globalizing India: How Global Rules and Markets are Shaping India's Rise to Power*

VICTOR MENALDO, *The Institutions Curse: Natural Resources, Politics, and Development*

JEROEN VAN DER HEIJDEN, *Innovations in Urban Climate Governance: Voluntary Programs for Low Carbon Buildings and Cities*

LILIANA B. ANDONOVA, *Governance Entrepreneurs: International Organizations and the Rise of Global Public-Private Partnerships*

MICHAEL P. VANDENBERG AND JONATHAN M. GILLIGAN, *Beyond Politics: The Private Governance Response to Climate Change*

NATHAN M. JENSEN AND EDMUND J. MALESKY *Incentives to Pander: How Politicians Use Corporate Welfare for Political Gain*

RICHARD W. CARNEY, *Authoritarian Capitalism Sovereign Wealth Funds and State-Owned Enterprises in East Asia and Beyond*par

SARAH BAUERLE DANZMAN *Merging Interests: When Domestic Firms Shape FDI Policy*

Power Grab

Political Survival through Extractive Resource Nationalization

Paasha Mahdavi

University of California, Santa Barbara

CAMBRIDGE
UNIVERSITY PRESS

CAMBRIDGE
UNIVERSITY PRESS

University Printing House, Cambridge CB2 8BS, United Kingdom

One Liberty Plaza, 20th Floor, New York, NY 10006, USA

477 Williamstown Road, Port Melbourne, VIC 3207, Australia

314–321, 3rd Floor, Plot 3, Splendor Forum, Jasola District Centre,
New Delhi – 110025, India

79 Anson Road, #06–04/06, Singapore 079906

Cambridge University Press is part of the University of Cambridge.

It furthers the University's mission by disseminating knowledge in the pursuit of
education, learning, and research at the highest international levels of excellence.

www.cambridge.org
Information on this title: www.cambridge.org/9781108478892
DOI: 10.1017/9781108781350

© Paasha Mahdavi 2020

First published 2020

A catalogue record for this publication is available from the British Library.

ISBN 978-1-108-47889-2 Hardback

To my parents

Contents

List of Figures   *page* xi
List of Tables   xiii
Acknowledgments   xiv

1 The Puzzle of Extractive Resource Nationalization   1
   1.1   What Is Extractive Resource Nationalization?   4
   1.2   The Political Economy of Resource Nationalization   9
   1.3   Summary of the Argument   17
   1.4   Research Design, Methodology, and Measuring Nationalization   31

2 The Theory of Political Survival through Nationalization   38
   2.1   How Does Natural Resource Nationalization Affect Governance?   40
   2.2   The Operational Nationalization Theory   53
   2.3   Initial Empirical Evidence   81
   2.4   Conclusion   89

3 Defining and Measuring Operational Nationalization   91
   3.1   Measuring Nationalization   91
   3.2   Comparisons to Existing Data on State Ownership of Petroleum   99
   3.3   Conclusion   102

4 Why Nationalize? Evidence from National Oil Companies
   around the World   104
   4.1   What Factors Determine Oil Nationalization?   107
   4.2   Data, Methods, and Research Design   113
   4.3   Modeling Nationalizations in the Oil Industry   117
   4.4   Conclusion   132
   4.5   Appendix: Model Specification and Additional Results   133

5 NOCs, Oil Revenues, and Leadership Survival   140
   5.1   Reexamining Theories of Government Revenue and Leader Survival   141
   5.2   Data, Methods, and Research Design   147
   5.3   Statistical Analysis of Nationalization, Revenues, and Survival   158
   5.4   Conclusion   168
   5.5   Appendix: Additional Figures and Tables   171

6 The Dynamics of Nationalization in Pahlavi Iran   177
   6.1   Revisiting the Operational Nationalization Theory in the Context of
         Prerevolutionary Iran   179
   6.2   Case Selection, Data, and Design   182

6.3	Why Did the Shah Opt for an Operational NOC?	184
6.4	Did Operational Nationalization Increase Revenues?	195
6.5	And Yet He Fell	202
6.6	Conclusion	208
6.7	Appendix: BP Projections and Difference-in-Difference Results	209

7 Conclusion: The Implications of Nationalization — **212**

7.1	Nationalization as Opportunism	215
7.2	Oil Nationalizations in the Twenty-First Century	217
7.3	Resource Nationalizations of the Future: Precious Metals, Minerals, and the Energy Transition	223
7.4	Conclusion	225

| *Bibliography* | 226 |
| *Index* | 244 |

Figures

2.1 Oil production before and after operational
    nationalization   *page* 70
2.2 Hypothetical government revenues under different
    degrees of state intervention   72
2.3 Trajectory of annual oil and gas income in Iraq, 1958–1972   87
3.1 Operational oil nationalizations across the world, 1900–2015   94
3.2 State intervention over time: percentage of global oil
    production, 1932–2015   99
4.1 Determinants of operational nationalization: model results
    from Bayesian analysis   118
4.2 Year-to-year changes in predicted probability of operational
    nationalization, 1959–1960 and 1973–1974   120
4.3 Predicted probabilities of operational nationalization for
    selected countries over time   122
4.4 Determinants of operational nationalization:
    revolutionary leadership   123
4.5 Oil production in the 1930–1950 period, Iran compared
    to Saudi Arabia   127
4.6 Ratio of collected oil revenues between foreign and
    host state, Iran versus Saudi Arabia, 1938–1951   131
4.7 Predicted probability of nationalization by autocratic
    regime type   137
4.8 Paired comparison of autocratic regime types
    and nationalization   138
4.9 Predicted probability of nationalization by age of
    the regime   139
5.1 Petroleum income per capita, resource revenues,
    and state capture   150
5.2 Resource revenues (adjusted for real oil price) before
    and after establishing an operational NOC   152
5.3 Leader survival and operational nationalization   155

5.4   Bayesian model results for leadership survival:
      posterior estimates   162
5.5   Bayesian model results for leadership survival:
      predicted probabilities   163
5.6   Conventional model results for leadership survival:
      conditional effects   166
5.7   Predicted probability of autocratic failure and transitions
      to democracy   169
5.8   Resource revenues before and after establishing an
      operational NOC   171
5.9   Predicted probability of autocratic failure using the
      Polity measure   172
5.10 Model results from mediation analysis of operational
      nationalization and resource revenues   175
5.11 Sensitivity of mediation analysis to unmeasured confounders   176
6.1   Iranian government budget operating balance, 1965–1979   193
6.2   Monthly oil production and revenues in Iran, 1970–1975   197
6.3   Actual minus counterfactual monthly oil revenues in Iran   200
6.4   Trajectory of four different BP projections of monthly
      Iranian oil revenue   210

Tables

1.1	Operational nationalization around the world, 1900–2015	*page* 33
2.1	Political outcomes of different state intervention paths in Iran and Iraq	81
3.1	Varieties of nationalization in the natural resource sector	97
4.1	Determinants of operational nationalization: model results from Bayesian hierarchical logistic regression	117
4.2	Interview questions used in eliciting priors for Bayesian analysis	134
4.3	Model results from Guriev et al. (2011) analysis of oil expropriations	134
4.4	Determinants of operational nationalization: model results from OLS and logistic regression	135
4.5	Determinants of operational nationalization: nonaligned movement membership	136
4.6	Determinants of operational nationalization: revolutionary leadership	136
4.7	Determinants of operational nationalization: relative political capacity	137
5.1	Nationalization increases resource revenues collected by the government	159
5.2	Nationalization increases state capture of natural resource revenues	160
5.3	Leader failure, oil revenues, and operational nationalization around the world, 1932–2014	164
5.4	Nationalization increases resource revenues (per capita) collected by the government	173
5.5	Mediation analysis of operational nationalization and resource revenues	174
6.1	Difference-in-difference results using OLS	211

Acknowledgments

My interest in the politics of energy and extractive resources was first sparked by the expropriation of my uncle's metals trading company in Tajikistan and Kazakhstan, back when I was just a young boy. His experience was instructive not only for comprehending the risks undertaken by doing business in autocracies, but also by the sheer political power of leaders in extractive resource economies. By contrast, my two uncles from my mother's side were pioneers in the manufacturing of solar thermal panels for residential water heating in Europe and the United States. They taught me about the wonderful promise of renewable energy, but also its reliance – albeit relatively small – on extractive resources like copper and silicon. This personal connection to the energy and commodities industries has bled into my work ever since then, and this book is in part a reflection of their experiences.

Like many other first-time book authors, I have a long list of people and institutions to thank for all their help, guidance, and support in getting this book from the beginnings of a faint idea all the way to a completed manuscript. But before I continue, I owe the greatest amount of gratitude to my doctoral adviser Michael Ross. His captivating work on natural resource governance inspired me to pursue a PhD in political science and to study under him at UCLA. Michael's mentorship has been the bedrock of my academic career. Our recent work together on fossil fuel subsidies has taught me not only about energy and climate policy but also the art of conducting social science research more broadly. I am grateful and proud to call Michael my advisor, mentor, co-author, and friend.

There is little chance I could have successfully conducted the field and archival research that undergirds the book without the assistance of many contacts, colleagues, and generous acquaintances. In Qatar and the UAE, Robin Mills, Jaafar Altaie, Raya Abu Gulal, Kate Dourian, Siamak Namazi, David Alley, Eithne Treanor, Neha Vora, and Petros Zenieris were wonderfully open with their time in helping me navigate the energy dynamics of the Gulf. Mehboob Sultan in Abu Dhabi was particularly helpful in locating archival materials on the formation of the Abu Dhabi National Oil Company. Several Iranian oil experts and former National Iranian Oil Company (NIOC) officials – who shall remain anonymous given the politically sensitive situation in the Islamic Republic – were essential to helping me understand the politics of oil in Iran. Outside of Iran, Hormoz Naficy, Manoucher Takin, Sunjoy Joshi, Tony Renton, Fereidun Fesharaki, Paul Stevens, and Peter Nolan helped facilitate my research on NIOC and its relations with the Iranian government. The heart of Chapter 6 is based on declassified documents that I was fortunate enough to access at the BP Archives at the University of Warwick in Coventry, United Kingdom, with the invaluable help of Peter Housego. I thank the BP Archives for permission to quote from these documents and to use these materials for constructing the Iranian oil revenues database. I also thank the fantastic staff at the US Library of Congress and the British National Archives, notably Nanette Gibbs and Darren Jones, for helping me to find materials to cross-validate (where possible) the documents used in Chapter 6. I thank Hasnaa Mansour and the members of the Lebanon Parliamentary Committee on Public Works, Transportation, Energy, and Water, for their help in unpacking the debate surrounding the possibility of a Lebanese state-owned oil and gas enterprise, which I review in Chapter 7.

The construction of the national oil company (NOC) database would not have been possible without the generous funding and intellectual guidance of the excellent team at the Natural Resource Governance Institute, most notably Alexandra Gillies and Patrick Heller. A related version of materials in Chapter 4 using the NOC database was published in my 2014 article, "Why do leaders nationalize the oil industry?," in the journal *Energy Policy*. I thank the journal for permission to draw from this work.

The kernel of the argument developed in this book grew out of my irreplaceable training at Stanford's Program on Energy and Sustainable Development, for which I am forever grateful to David Victor. His generosity in taking me on as first-year master's student, and allowing me the intellectual freedom to contribute a chapter on NIOC to his edited volume, along with David Hults and Mark Thurber, was the academic springboard that led to the formulation of several ideas that underpin this book.

These ideas were further nurtured by my fantastic doctoral committee at UCLA – Michael Ross, Daniel Treisman, Michael Thies, Jeffrey Lewis, Miriam Golden, and Mark Handcock in the statistics department. While the book is a far departure from the dissertation on which it is based, several members of the UCLA family provided excellent guidance on the building blocks that formed the thesis, namely Kathy Bawn, James DeNardo, Barbara Geddes, Chad Hazlett, Daniel Posner, Ron Rogowski, Steve Spiegel, Art Stein, Lynn Vavreck, Rob Weiss, and John Zaller.

In many ways, the transition to a book would not have come to fruition without Irfan Nooruddin. His sage-like wisdom was essential in managing the proposal process, as was his role in chairing a book mini-workshop consisting of my former colleagues at Georgetown University. At the workshop, Irfan, Desha Girod, Nita Rudra, Joel Simmons, and James Vreeland provided incisive feedback on the full manuscript that was instrumental in developing a new frame for the book. The book also benefited greatly from feedback by participants of the political economy group at Georgetown (also chaired by Irfan), namely Marc Busch, Raj Desai, Jenny Guardado, Diana Kim, Marko Klašnja, Abe Newman, Ken Opalo, Dennis Quinn, Yuhki Tahjima, Jen Tobin, and Erik Voeten. My McCourt School colleagues at Georgetown provided additionally helpful comments on the project, notably George Akerlof, Mike Bailey, Jacobus Cilliers, Bill Gormley, James Habyarimana, Adriana Kugler, Jon Ladd, Mark Rom, Kent Weaver, and Andy Zeitlin. Raphael Calel was especially helpful, not least of which for crafting the book's title. The later stages of drafting the book were greatly improved by feedback from my new colleagues at UCSB – particularly our crew of junior scholars going through the book-writing gauntlet together, Matto Mildenberger, Julia Morse, and Leah Stokes, as well as Heather Stoll for her thoughtful advice on navigating the production process.

The work on which the book is based also benefited from participant comments at Columbia University, the Graduate Institute of Geneva, the Johns Hopkins School of Advanced International Studies, Oxford University, the Pennsylvania State University, the Collins College of Business at Tulsa University, the University of Maryland, Williams College, the World Bank, Yale University, and ETH Zürich, as well as at panels at the American Political Science Association (APSA), Midwestern Political Science Association (MPSA), and the Society for Political Methodology annual meetings. I especially thank Galen Jackson, Noel Johnston, Anand Rajaram, and Johannes Urpelainen for hosting me at these seminars. I also thank fellow members of the Council on the Future of Energy at the World Economic Forum for their thoughts and ideas on many of the technical aspects of the book.

Several colleagues provided helpful comments on aspects of the book at various stages along the way. For this, I am grateful to Amit Ahuja, Morgan Bazilian, Bruce Bimber, Kate Bruhn, Mark Buntaine, Ruth Carlitz, Andrew Cheon, the late Natasha Chichilnisky-Heal, Jeff Colgan,

Nicole Janz, Noel Johnston, Cynthia Kaplan, Ryan Kennedy, David Konisky, Matthew Kroenig, Paul Lagunes, Renato Lima de Oliveira, Nimah Mazaheri, Brian Min, Francisco Monaldi, Todd Moss, Paul Musgrave, Neil Narang, Jack Paine, David Pellow, Xander Slaski, Roger Stern, Heather Stoll, Chris Warshaw, Rob Weinar, Erika Weinthal, and Johannes Urpelainen. Ben Smith and Arash Davari provided deeply insightful feedback on Chapter 6. Ben also provided excellent ideas and notes on the rest of the manuscript, as well as generally invaluable advice about oil governance, Alaskan politics, and Michelin-worthy cooking recipes. I owe a special debt of gratitude to Victor Menaldo, whose endless generosity in providing feedback on drafts, frames, and my vaguely formed ideas has been irreplaceably helpful. Victor also asked me to join him to lead an intensive workshop at the World Bank, where I not only learned from his stellar research perspective but also refined my own thoughts on where national oil companies fit within the greater political study of natural resources.

Thomas Flaherty, Olivia Cook Prieto, Adam Bouyamourn, JA-Lamar Lyons, Rebecca Lorentzen, and Sydney Bartone provided outstanding research assistance. For their editorial services, I am grateful to Alison Lowander at Hideously Simple and to Letta Page at PageSmithing. I could not have asked for a better series editor than Aseem Prakash, whose advice sharpened the book's argument, tempo, and overall pitch. John Haslam at Cambridge University Press provided excellent guidance throughout the process and, along with Aseem, secured two fantastic reviewers whose feedback greatly improved the manuscript.

Writing an academic book, at least in my view, is simply not possible without the tireless support of friends and family. For countless morsels of wisdom on surviving graduate school, I remain grateful to Jesse Acevedo, Soumi Chatterjee, Arash Davari, Sebastian Garrido de Sierra, Galen Jackson, Felipe Nunes, Steve Palley, Lauren Peritz, and Ryan Weldzius. And in more ways than I could count, I would not be here without the unconditional support of my brother Paymohn and my sister Pardis, in whose footsteps I am humbled and deeply delighted to follow.

For the smiles, laughter, and love they bring me every day, I am grateful to Megan and our beautiful son Darius. Megan has been on this journey with me from the very start, back when I was combing through the oil history volumes at Stanford Library. Her countless readthroughs on drafts and outlines, her astute insights, and her unwavering support have made my research better in every possible way. And to my parents, for everything they have done and sacrificed so that my siblings and I could live our dreams. For this, and for so much more, I dedicate this book to them.

1 The Puzzle of Extractive Resource Nationalization

If political rulers' first struggle is gaining power, strategically securing the means to accrue and retain that power is a close-run second. For rulers whose territories are blessed with extractive resources – such as petroleum, metals, minerals, and other precious commodities – converting natural wealth into fiscal wealth is key. Squandering the opportunity to secure these revenues will guarantee short tenures, while setting a timeline for sustainable extraction, capitalizing on windfalls, and managing the resulting wealth will fortify the foundations of enduring rule. Libya, Venezuela, and the Democratic Republic of Congo all provide instructive cases.

On September 1, 1969, a twenty-seven-year-old rebel upstart named Muammar Qaddafi deposed the Sanusi monarchy and seized power over the Kingdom of Libya.[1] As chairman of the nascent Revolutionary Command Council (RCC), Qaddafi initially promised stability to the twenty-one American and European oil firms on the ground in this, the world's fifth largest oil-producing country. But he quickly realized the firms' disunity gave him leverage, and Qaddafi began expropriating their assets one by one, starting with British Petroleum's Sarir oil field in December 1971.[2] By 1973, the Libyan government had nationalized all foreign firms in the country and placed operations in the hands of the Libyan National Oil Company (Linoco). On the eve of the global oil shock, Qaddafi's government controlled enormous resources.

[1] This vignette relies on the political history of oil in Libya as recorded in First (1975), Simons (1993), Vandewalle (1995, 1998), Bamberg (2000), and Pargeter (2012), as well as in materials documented in the *Foreign Relations of the United States, 1969–1976*, Volume XXXVI: Energy Crisis, 1969–1974. Libya's ranking in world oil production is drawn from the United States Geological Survey (USGS) *Minerals Yearbook Area Reports: International 1969*.

[2] The disunity in this case refers to the split between major oil companies like BP, Shell, and Exxon, and independent oil companies like Occidental, Marathon, and Amerada. Qaddafi knew he could play one off the other by first pressuring smaller firms like Occidental into giving Libya higher returns and then by observing that major firms did not come to Occidental's aid in its time of need. For more on the 1970 negotiations, see Yergin (1991, 577–580).

It had accumulated over $2 billion in gold and foreign exchange reserves from petroleum sales in the first nine months of 1973 alone. In the words of political historian Dirk Vandewalle, nationalization of the oil sector had given Qaddafi "financial resources that would soon expand beyond already heightened expectations – in a political system that, like the monarchy, had no mechanisms for ensuring accountability" (Vandewalle, 1998, 77).

In the heyday of Libya's oil boom, the mid-1960s, Qaddafi's prede-cessor King Idris al-Sanusi and his Cyrenaican elite circle had absolute control over the local economy and its distributive institutions. Idris was less concerned with the short-term problem of consolidating his regime and more concerned with the long-term problem of the country's economic and political development. During 1965 negotiations that resulted in foreign oil firms keeping the lion's share of oil rents, the king was content not to risk future losses and Western retaliation to reap immediate gains from nationalization. His successor was not so forward-thinking. In his early years, Qaddafi faced so many countercoup attempts by his fellow RCC members that historians predicted Libya would be subject to "an endless coup syndrome" (First, 1975, 256). Where Idris's perceived strength prompted restraint with multinational oil firms, Qaddafi's perceived instability led him to "launch a frontal attack on the oil industry,"[3] gambling with nationalization. The gamble paid off: the immediate revenue boost laid the foundation for Qaddafi's forty-two-year dictatorship. Within his first eight years, he established the *jamahiriya* – a military-style revolutionary republicanism – and dedicated vast government expenditures, funded by oil revenues, to militarizing Libyan society and establishing himself as absolute ruler. Qaddafi could afford to spend frivolously on massive defense projects and stock his increasingly bloated military bureaucracies with political allies.

Venezuela's case is much more puzzling. The petro-rich Bolivarian Republic is currently among the most impoverished states in the Western Hemisphere. The nation's food shortages, public health disasters, mass unemployment, rising epidemic of criminal violence, and mounting political instability largely stem from the collapse of its oil sector, which funds over 90 percent of overall state expenditures. How did one of the world's largest and richest oil producers end up in crisis?

Throughout the early 2000s, then-president Hugo Chávez renational-ized oil production by expropriating international oil firms with little to no compensation and placing their seized assets in the hands of

---

[3] Oasis petroleum consortium (Amerada, Continental, and Marathon) internal memoran-dum, September–October 1969. Cited in First (1975, 200).

the national oil company, Petróleos de Venezuela, S.A. (PdVSA). This maneuver allowed Chávez to reap enormous gains from a rise in global oil prices (2001—2008). In turn, his government used petrodollars to fund broad social programs, to purchase international support, to buy off elites, and to imprison or exile opposition leaders (see Hults, 2012b). The increasing value of Venezuela's natural resources allowed Chávez to centralize power and build a lasting socialist dictatorship (assumed by his appointed successor Nicolas Maduro upon Chávez's death in 2013). Yet Chávez's management of the nationalized oil sector was extremely short-sighted. His government ran PdVSA into the ground by promoting unqualified political appointees, stripping many of its most lucrative assets, and deliberately failing to invest in exploration and future oil production. The company was saddled with billions of dollars in foreign debt.[4] As a result, less than two decades after Chávez's "transformation" of the oil industry, Venezuela is on the brink of collapse. An oil sector led by an anemic state-owned enterprise has now seen production dwindle from a high of 3.2 million barrels per day before Chávez came to power to just under 0.6 million barrels per day in October 2019.[5]

A third instructive case on the strategic use of natural resources is the Democratic Republic of the Congo (DRC). In the fast-moving global cobalt market, all eyes are on the DRC, where in March 2018 President Joseph Kabila forcibly renegotiated higher taxes on multinational producers.[6] Cobalt – a crucial element in the superalloys needed for power plants, wind turbines, and the batteries that power consumer electronics and electric cars – is primarily produced in the DRC by multinational corporations (MNCs) like Glencore and FreeportMcMoRan. Amid insatiable global demand, supply struggles to keep pace. Now, Kabila is pondering whether to go further than raising taxes: he seems poised to seize control over the production of this precious commodity.[7] In all but a few applications, cobalt cannot be chemically substituted for another metal, and 70 percent of the world's known cobalt reserves are located within the DRC (see Olivetti et al., 2017). If the state nationalizes cobalt production, it will wreak havoc on global trade, send shockwaves across crucial industries, and stymie the clean energy transition.

[4] Simon Romero, "Chávez seizes assets of oil contractors," *The New York Times* May 8, 2009.
[5] Brian Scheid, "Venezuelan oil output could be halved without Chevron waiver extension: Analysts," *S&P Global Platts* October 14, 2019.
[6] "New DRC mining code will not alter positive outlook," *Mining Review Africa* March 13, 2018.
[7] While Felix Tshisekedi assumed the presidency in January 2019, Kabila still controls the mining sector. Pauline Bax and William Clowes, "Don't be in a rush to do business in world's top cobalt producer," *Bloomberg News* June 18, 2019.

Why did Qaddafi nationalize oil operations when his predecessor maintained private foreign production? Why did Chávez take back control of Venezuela's oil, and how has this paved the way for industry and possibly governmental collapse? Why is the DRC considering nationalizing cobalt? *In general, why do governments nationalize extractive resources?* This book argues that leaders nationalize to extend the duration of their power. By taking control of the means of production and establishing state-owned enterprises (SOEs), their governments capture revenues that might otherwise flow to private firms.[8] Leaders use their increased capital to buy political support and to deter potential challengers. Using a combination of within-country, over-time case studies, and cross-national statistical analysis with novel techniques, I will sketch the contours of a crucial political gamble: nationalize and reap immediate gains while risking future prosperity, or maintain private operations, thereby passing on revenue windfalls but securing long-term fiscal streams. For those whose days in power may be numbered – politically weak resource-rich leaders – nationalization is a risk worth taking. But for those who foresee long, lasting rule – strong resource-rich leaders – the returns may be too costly. This argument therefore highlights the endogeneity of survival to the nationalization decision-making process: initially weak resource-rich leaders seek to survive by seizing revenues via nationalization, while initially strong rulers pass up these opportunities but risk losing their grip on power.

1.1   What Is Extractive Resource Nationalization?

The answer to the question of why leaders nationalize extractive resources is critical to understanding both the specific architecture of natural resource markets and the broader dynamics of state intervention in the economy and opportunistic behavior in general. In some markets, nationalization – the forced acquisition of privately owned assets by the state, either with or without compensation (Wortley, 1956) – is the norm, and state-owned enterprises dominate the sector. Consider that nearly 90 percent of global oil reserves and 94 percent of global natural gas reserves are held by SOEs in the form of national oil companies

---

[8] For simplicity I use the term "private firm" to refer to any entity that is not the host country's SOE; examples include outside MNCs like international oil and mining companies or domestic private firms. This could also include, for instance, cases in which a foreign state-owned company produces oil in the host country, such as Malaysia's national oil company, Petronas, operating oil fields in Iran. For more on these "international national oil companies" see Cheon (2015) and Jones Luong and Sierra (2015).

(NOCs). In terms of production, SOEs oversee 75 percent of the world's oil, 60 percent of all coal, 51 percent of all aluminum, and just under two-thirds of all tin. Yet in the realm of copper and iron, MNCs have almost complete control over both reserves and production, with notable exceptions in Chile and China.[9] This is also the case for the metals and minerals that will fuel the next energy revolution. Palladium – a key component of hydrogen fuel cells and energy storage – is handled primarily by private firms like Anglo Platinum or minority-state-owned companies like Russia's NorNickel or South Africa's Impala. Nearly all of the world's production of lithium – the primary ingredient in the batteries that will make large-scale renewable energy viable – is managed by just four private firms: Sociedad Quimica y Minera de Chile (Chile), Chemetall (Germany), FMC (United States), and Talison (Australia).[10] As these commodities rise in prominence, leaders will be more and more tempted to seize control of production for the state.

In the petroleum, metals, and minerals sectors, nationalization comes in many shapes and sizes (Jones Luong and Weinthal, 2001; Marcel, 2006; Tordo et al., 2011; Victor et al., 2012; Victor, 2013; Hughes, 2014; Sarbu, 2014; Heller and Mihalyi, 2019). On one end of the spectrum are leaders that opt for complete control over the sector. This was the case for Mexico's infamous expropriation of Royal Dutch Shell and Standard Oil in 1938, whereupon President Lázaro Cardenas established the national oil company, Petróleos Mexicanos (Pemex), with monopoly rights over the entire oil industry. On the other end are leaders that choose to nationalize but in effect leave operations and management of production to private firms. The prototypical example in the petroleum sector of this type of nationalization is Nigeria, where the national oil company, NNPC, serves primarily to collect taxes, fees, and sales revenue from Chevron, Shell, Total, and the other firms operating in the oil sector.

These two ends of the spectrum are captured effectively by Jones Luong and Weinthal (2010)'s concepts of "state ownership with control" and "state ownership without control." I build on their pioneering approach, introducing an important innovation: the distinction over whether a state has control is not determined de jure, as in Jones Luong and Weinthal (2010, 7–9), but rather is determined de facto. That is, the important dimension of state ownership is not whether the state can

---

[9] These statistics come from Tordo et al. (2011) and Victor et al. (2012), along with author's own NOC database.

[10] Terence Bell. "An overview of commercial lithium production." *The Balance* May 15, 2017.

legally operate the resources sector, but whether it actually can and does operate and produce resources.[11]

Why is this distinction important? Consider again the case of Nigeria: legally, NNPC is charged with operations in the form of partnerships and joint ventures with outside firms.[12] From the perspective of an outside observer, it would seem that NNPC is involved in operations, though it may be sharing these duties with private companies. But in practice, NNPC rarely produces any oil from its assigned fields (Thurber et al., 2012); instead, private firms manage operations and pay the government back in the form of "equity oil" – crude that is produced by private firms and shared with the government after firms recover their operating costs.[13] Conversely, in Indonesia the government stripped monopoly rights from its existing national oil company, Pertamina, in 2001 and legally restructured it into a limited liability company in 2003 (Hertzmark, 2007, 3). Yet Pertamina continues to operate as the country's primary NOC, actively producing 15 percent of Indonesia's oil and indirectly producing the rest through production-sharing contracts (PriceWaterhouseCoopers, 2016, 10).[14]

This juxtaposition leads to two different types of nationalization in practice. The first occurs when the state nationalizes operations and establishes an SOE that undertakes exploration, discovery, development, and production of natural resources. This SOE allows the state to have a direct say in how resources are produced, even if private firms operate alongside the SOE. The alternative is when the state nationalizes the sector but leaves all operations in the hands of private firms. An SOE may exist in these cases, but is only involved in oversight of operating

---

[11] This is not to say that the de jure classification is an incorrect approach. Indeed, for the purpose of determining the signaling effects of nationalization – particularly to domestic elites – the legal documentation of ownership structure is immediately relevant. But for the purposes of determining the fiscal effects of nationalization, the de facto nationalization of operations is more salient than any legal classification.

Considering all oil producers over time, this distinction leads to a 31 percent difference in how these cases are coded compared to Jones Luong and Weinthal (2010). Specifically, there is an overlap of 2,320 country-years with the Jones Luong and Weinthal (2010) dataset since 1900 (the first year of my database). Of these, we differ in the coding of 725 country-years. I provide more details in chapter 3.

[12] *Nigerian National Petroleum Corporation Act.* Laws of the Federal Republic of Nigeria, Chapter 320 (1990): 5(1)(a).

[13] See OpenOil, 2015, "Oil contracts: How to read and understand them," for an introductory overview about different types of payment structures in the petroleum sector.

[14] At the other extreme are cases in which the SOE becomes so powerful in the context of domestic politics that it can overstep its legal boundaries regarding operations. Such was the case with PdVSA in the 1980s, as the NOC overpowered the relatively weak ministry of energy to take on whatever operations the company saw fit (Philip, 1982; Hults, 2012b).

firms, collection of taxes and fees, and in some cases management of the contract- and license-awarding process. My focus is on the former case, in which the state has a direct and active role in production, which I refer to as *operational nationalization*.

The political implications of this market architecture are profound. In commodities like oil and gas, many of these SOEs are behemoths both at home and in the global market. The oil company Saudi Aramco, for instance, accounts for half of Saudi Arabia's economic production and 85 percent of export revenues.[15] With fifteen times more reserves than ExxonMobil (the largest private oil company in the world), Aramco is internationally valued at just over $2 trillion.[16] Because all of the company's revenues are technically under state control,[17] the Saudi monarch can use this wealth as he sees fit – by reinvesting in the oil sector, channeling it to diversify the nonoil economy, or doling it out to his allies and potential challengers to bolster his rule. In Russia, what had once been a petroleum and mining oligopoly held by a band of private investors (*siloviki*) was subsumed piecemeal by the state. Today, Rosneft and Gazprom – the state-owned giants of the "commanding heights" of Russia's economy – now account for 51 percent of the government's revenues and are crucial instruments of President Vladimir Putin's power.[18] These SOEs are the main depositors to the Reserve Fund and the Russian National Wealth Fund, through which the government funnels its resource wealth for co-optation and consolidation. Resource revenues flow both to individuals in Putin's inner circle, like Rosneft CEO Igor Sechin and FSB head Nikolay Patrushev (the new *siloviki*), and to developing security forces like the National Guard to counter protesters and would-be revolutionaries.[19]

---

[15] OPEC. (2017). *Annual Statistical Bulletin*. Vienna: Organization of the Petroleum Exporting Countries.

[16] "Saudi Aramco's IPO is a mess." *The Economist* October 19, 2017.

[17] In practice, there is variation in what percentage of NOC revenues ultimately end up in the state treasury. While companies such as Saudi Aramco, Ecuador's Petroamazonas, and Chad's SHT transfer 80 to 100 percent of all revenues directly to the state, others such as PetroChina and Ukraine's Naftogaz transfer between 10 and 20 percent to the state's coffers (Heller and Mihalyi, 2019). I return to this issue in Chapters 5 and 6.

[18] Oil and gas revenues constituted 7.4 trillion rubles in the consolidated state budget of 14.5 trillion rubles in 2014. See "Russia economic report: The long journey to recovery." The World Bank Macroeconomics and Fiscal Management report no. 35 (April 2016).

[19] "Igor Sechin, head of Rosneft, is powerful as never before." *The Economist* December 15, 2016. See also "Wheels within wheels: How Mr Putin keeps the country under control." *The Economist* October 22, 2016. For more on the *siloviki*, see Treisman (2007).

Given the book value of their natural resource reserves, these SOEs can also provide a last-resort option for raising revenues in the form of partial privatization. Some states have collected a much-needed cash infusion by listing minority shares of SOE ownership on public exchanges, as in the case of Bolivia's Yacimientos Petrolíferos Fiscales Bolivianos (YPFB) in 1996 or Brazil's Petrobras in 1997. Others have privatized indirectly by allowing foreign investment into SOE extractive ventures, exemplified by the 2015 Mexican energy reforms or the Algerian commercialization of the national gas company, Sonatrach, in 2005. Consider again the case of Saudi Arabia, where in 2017 the government floated the idea of opening up Saudi Aramco in an unprecedented IPO. Although a complete IPO may not come to fruition,[20] the strategy further underscores the country's need for quick revenues – a desire that likely stems from changing leader perceptions of survival based on a potent combination of fiscal pressures, creeping conflict with Iran, and the impending succession to Crown Prince Mohammad bin Salman (see Sulaimani, 2018). But with transparency requirements of a publicly listed company and the long-term uncertainty of retaining sufficient state control over resource rents, opening Aramco to outside investors is a risky means for the ruling monarchy to finance its expenditures. In general, much like operational nationalization, the partial liberalization of extractive resource markets fits in with the broader set of fiscal choices that reward leaders with immediate revenues at the expense of long-term profits.

Cases like these illustrate the importance of nationalization to the state. They provide an initial glimpse into why leaders want control over their natural resources and how this control impacts their survival. To answer these questions, I develop and test an argument that incorporates leadership survival as endogenous to the nationalization process, in which a leader's probability of survival is both the cause and consequence of nationalization. When faced with the choice of nationalization, weak rulers discount the long-run costs of state intervention to seize its short-term gains; by contrast, strong leaders maintain the status quo of privately run operations to ensure long-term gains from private production. The building blocks for this argument are two important but untested claims that I address. First, the choice of nationalization occurs when leaders gain information on negotiated terms between operating firms and host governments. Second, nationalization of

---

[20] David Gardner, "Shelving Saudi Aramco IPO is a blow to crown prince," *Financial Times* August 28, 2018. See also Gordon Platt, "Saudi Aramco's $12 billion issue commands low yields," *Global Finance* May 9, 2019.

operations – whereby leaders establish SOEs that directly operate their countries' oil fields and minerals mines – provides an immediate boost to government collection of resource wealth, which ultimately fosters stronger and more durable dictators and democrats.

1.2   The Political Economy of Resource Nationalization

The conventional wisdom from political economists considers nationalization the inevitable culmination of an escalating negotiation between states and firms. This argument is captured by Raymond Vernon's "obsolescing bargain" in which firms have the greatest leverage in the initial investment phase, but see this erode over time as the state takes advantage of firms' sunk costs and fixed assets to renegotiate higher and higher shares in profits (Vernon, 1971).[21] The argument for why the state desires expropriation typically rests on either revenue-maximization (Kemp, 1992; Guriev et al., 2011; Hajzler, 2012; Warshaw, 2012) or the duty to control the "property of the state" (Wenar, 2007, 2015). This duty stems from the notion that natural resources ultimately belong to citizens and should be protected against the whims and desires of private companies, especially for industries that are, as Colin Robinson puts it, "too important to be left to the market" (Robinson, 1993).

If nationalization is indeed inevitable, then why is it the case that not all extractive resources are nationalized? The chief constraints to expropriation come in the form of three types of costs. Nationalization can provoke international retaliation in the form of either arbitration, embargoes, military action, or the loss of foreign direct investment (FDI) as potential investors are scared off by the threat of future expropriation (Kobrin, 1979; Jensen and Johnston, 2011).[22] The domestic political costs can be acute if state intervention does not cure the purported ills of a natural resource economy run by private firms (see Jensen, 2008; Li, 2009). And the technical inability to develop new reserves or to produce efficiently when operations are under the control of the state can stymie long-term revenues (Boardman and Vining, 1989; Al-Obaidan and Scully, 1992; Bohn and Deacon, 2000; Eller et al., 2011). As

---

[21] This argument can alternatively be interpreted from the lens of a cyclical explanation. For any given individual investment, firms have mobility in the early stages, but see this decline once firms commit to a project that then becomes a fixed asset to be held hostage by the government during negotiations. The cycle then repeats as firms seek new investments in other projects. See also Mikesell (1971); Moran (1973).

[22] Retaliation could also involve the withholding of valuable technology in the future by MNCs, if private companies come to a shared agreement not to disseminate technical advancements with companies in countries in which expropriation has occurred. See Manzano and Monaldi (2009).

the Venezuelan case illustrates, these technical inefficiencies are further damaging to long-run fiscal balances if the government fails to reinvest in exploration and future production by the SOE.

With these costs in mind, scholars in the revenue-maximization camp aver that high commodity prices prompt leaders to nationalize (see Guriev et al., 2011). This action stems from both the gains of reaping enormous rents during high-price periods and the financial cover that high prices provide to offset the costs of nationalization. Conversely, low prices – especially across prolonged periods – spur privatization (or maintain the private-sector status quo) in the face of fiscal pressure. Expropriations in the oil industry tend to follow this pattern: peaking during the oil booms of 1973–1979 and then declining during the busts of 1985 and 2014. But this perspective cannot explain major nationalizations in the 1920–1972 period, when commodity prices were low and relatively stable, including the Mexican, Iranian, and Libyan oil nationalizations of 1938, 1951, and 1972, respectively. Nor can it explain the lack of nationalization in nonoil commodities like copper, lithium, and palladium despite periods of high prices.

What makes such revenue-maximizing behavior different for states intervening in the extractive resource sector as opposed to other sectors of the economy? In other words, why don't we see governments expropriating publicly traded firms when stock prices are high or when companies are reeling in record profits? Part of the answer lies in the fact that extractive resources offer what are known as "appropriable quasi-rents." Technically speaking, the quasi-rent is the value of an asset that is above its operating costs and its salvage value, which is how much the asset is worth if it is sold on the open market (Williamson, 1979).[23]

---

[23] To modify the example of an appropriable quasi-rent that is offered by Klein et al. (1978, 298), imagine an oil platform owned and operated by an MNC. The host government can enter into a purchasing agreement such that the firm produces oil on behalf of the government at a contracted rate of $11,500 per day based on the well's production and an expected oil price of $30 per day. The amortized fixed cost of the platform on a daily basis is $4,500 and the daily operating costs are $7,000. Although the platform is tailored to a specific oil well (i.e., it has high asset specificity), its parts can be transferred and rented out with a salvageable value of $500 per day. (These are hypothetical estimates, but they conform to industry standards for an offshore rig costing $25 million amortized over 15 years with a daily operating cost ranging between $5,000 for a standard rig to upwards of $35,000 per day for high-tech/high-horse-power rigs.) The quasi-rent would be $4,000 per day, or the difference between the contracted rate and the sum of the operating cost and the salvageable value. The firm's net income in this case would be $0, while the government's would be $4,500. However, the government knows that there exists no second party that is able to enter into a purchasing agreement with the firm. It can therefore bully the firm into accepting a much lower offer, specifically anything just above $7,500, knowing that the firm will be forced to accept its terms to cover its existing costs. (The alternative if the rate is exactly

This is in addition to classical "differential rents" that result from the gap between world market prices and local production costs, plus return to capital. Differential rents can be quite large for extractive commodities, as market prices tend to exceed production costs due to a combination of perceptions of scarcity (Hotelling, 1931), oligopolistic control of supply (Marshall, 1890; Marx, 1894) and, for some producers, advantages in ease of extraction (Ricardo, 1871).

In extractive industries like petroleum and mining, the potential for large quasi-rents exists not only because operating assets like oil platforms and mine shafts have low salvage rates and high sunk costs – which is the key characteristic that underpins the obsolescing bargain – but also because of the wedge between short- and long-run operating costs. After exploration and initial production, the costs of extracting oil and minerals are quite low compared to the operating costs of nonextractive industries. Once an oil field is discovered and a well is developed, for example, producing each barrel of oil is relatively cheap. In the early stages of the production cycle, the high underground pressure of the reservoir (compared to pressure at the surface) means that extraction is as straightforward as turning on a pumpjack that has minimal labor and maintenance requirements. But in the later stages, the pressure of the reservoir declines as more oil is brought to surface; operating costs significantly increase because new capital is required to recover each additional barrel. Firms expect these dynamics and therefore include future recovery costs in their initial costs to maintain economically viable production over time. The differential rent in this case is the producer surplus that results when market prices exceed these realized costs. The quasi-rent, then, is the difference between short-run operating and long-run recovery costs, and is large in the early stages of production but disappears as the two costs converge. Nationalization viewed from this framework allows the state to appropriate these quasi-rents that firms would otherwise have used to finance long-term operations. Even if differential rents are low – as would be the case for complex extraction like deepwater offshore oil or deep-shaft copper mining – quasi-rents can still be high because of the gap between contemporaneous and future operating costs.

$7,500 is for the firm to salvage its platform for $500 and take a net loss of $4,000 per day to cover its amortized fixed costs.) The difference between the two contracted rates is the appropriable quasi-rent, which in this example is the entire $4,000 per day. Such would be the case in the event of expropriation with compensation, where the compensated amount to the firm would be the lowest possible contracted rate that the firm would accept before salvaging its assets.

But nationalization may not just be about maximizing government revenues. In its guidelines for corporate goverance of SOEs, the Organization for Economic Cooperation and Development lists the top rationales for state ownership as "maximiz[ing] value for society" and "in the interest of the general public" (OECD, 2015, 17). If nationalization is interpreted as the state fulfilling its duty to protect public resources, the timing of state intervention depends on two disparate factors. The first applies primarily to states with colonial legacies of natural resource extraction. In these cases, leaders nationalize immediately after postcolonial independence to assert their sovereignty over what the public perceives as "excessive foreign influence" (Stevens, 2003, 5). The most likely to act on these perceptions to nationalize foreign-held assets are leaders whose rise to power was built on either casting out the colonial powers themselves or overthrowing so-called puppet regimes loyal to the colonial powers. Broadly speaking, revolutionary leaders – whether specifically toppling colonial regimes or generally coming to power through domestic revolution – in resource-rich states are known to engage in more aggressive and belligerent foreign policy (see Colgan, 2013). Although this line of thought is focused on the increased likelihood that revolutionary leaders will go to war, such as Saddam Hussein's invasion of Kuwait, outright expropriation of foreign-held assets is another manifestation of aggressive behavior. Indeed, one of the "revolutionary foreign policy" cases employed by Colgan (2013, 210–214) is Hugo Chávez's renationalization of the Venezuelan oil industry in the 2004–2007 period.[24]

The postcolonial era also saw the emergence of nascent leaders jockeying to fill the leadership vacuum left by departing imperial powers. In the Middle East, for example, the birth of Arab nationalism was built on the void that developed from the erosion of the Ottoman Empire (Gelvin, 1994). This nationalism would rise again as British and French powers fought for control over the post-Ottoman states and found a permanent footing once the Anglo-French dominance of the region began to wither during the Cold War. Egyptian President Gabel Abdel Nasser's nationalization of the British-held Suez Canal in 1956, for example, paved the way for Nasser as the de facto leader of the

---

[24] I do not code these efforts as operational nationalization since the state was de facto involved in production since 1960 and the founding of the Corporación Venezolana del Petroleo (CVP; replaced in 1976 with PdVSA). Although foreign companies worked alongside the NOC throughout the post-1960 period, the state maintained an operational presence in each exploration and production endeavor – even during "la apertura petrolera" of the 1990s when PdVSA was almost fully privatized. For more on the Venezuelan case, see Hults (2012b) and Manzano and Monaldi (2009).

posits that weak fiscal regimes are the result of nationalization while strong fiscal regimes emerge when the state plays a smaller role in the resource sector – primarily through private ownership – ultimately leading to a robust tax regime in the broader economy. Since there is little doubt that a strong fiscal regime will promote economic development, state capacity, and good governance (Tilly, 1975; Levi, 1989; North and Weingast, 1989), which ownership structure leaders choose to manage their resource wealth clearly has important political and economic impacts. But leaders facing an uncertain future are more interested in fiscal strength in the short term than state capacity and economic development in a future they may not be party to. And from the perspective of leaders looking to secure their continued rule, a small pot of money that is managed efficiently, stably, and with strong institutions looks much less attractive than a large swath of revenues that accrue to state coffers under weak fiscal regimes. This underscores the need for research on two unanswered questions. How does nationalization impact fiscal strength? And how does this affect the choice of whether to nationalize extractive resources?

This book thus represents a departure in how the effects of nationalization on politics are characterized. It casts doubt on the survival-enhancing assumption of private ownership that the production of extractive resources by private firms should lead to higher revenues for resource-rich governments. Instead, by directly assessing whether state intervention increases short-term resource revenues, I build a theory that nationalization is a strategy through which leaders maintain their hold on power. This theory thus makes leaders' beliefs about survival probabilities mutually endogenous with their decision to nationalize extractive operations. In doing so, it not only engages with the causal mechanisms driving resource nationalization but also identifies an explanation for why resource-rich leaders like Qaddafi and Putin survive while others like King Idris and the Shah of Iran fall from rule.

1.3   Summary of the Argument

The decision to nationalize the production of extractive resources affects and is affected by the probability of leadership survival. If leaders seek to maximize their time in power – with maximization of state revenues as the key conduit – they must balance this desire with the costs and risks of nationalization. If they nationalize early, leaders may be faced with costly retaliation in the short term and diminishing returns in the long term. If they nationalize late, leaders may forgo sorely needed revenues in the short term and thus may not be around to reap the long-term benefits.

The key factors in this decision, then, are the perceived technical and retaliatory costs and the immediacy of the need for government revenues.

In the early stages of resource development, the state opts against nationalization and forgoes the majority of revenues (and profits) to entice firms to invest in developing the country's natural resources. In these stages, the state can sign a lopsided revenue-sharing agreement in favor of the firm and is content with whatever revenues it receives – especially if the state has reason to suspect that without the firm, no resources will be extracted and the state's share would effectively be zero. As development progresses and extractive resources reach commercial levels of production and export, both the obsolescing bargain theory and the appropriable quasi-rent theory predict that the state will renegotiate with the producing firm to increase the state's share of resource revenues (Vernon, 1971; Klein et al., 1978). Outright nationalization of production becomes a possibility in these renegotiations if the state learns that the firm is offering more attractive deals to the state's competitors or if the firm is withholding or inaccurately reporting the true profits of production. Without this information, the state will continue to accept the status quo of taxing private operating firms, believing that this is the best possible outcome for maximizing revenue and political survival. But with new information about potentially better deals to be had, the leader now faces a choice: nationalize operations, and reap the benefits of increased resource revenues now but suffer from lower returns in the future; or maintain the status quo of private operational firms while increasing taxes, and secure long-term revenues with the knowledge that it will lose out on the opportunity to appropriate immediate returns.

This juncture prompts the leader to update her beliefs about the probability of survival. Although there are myriad other opportunities to renegotiate agreements that a state has with private firms – for example, trade agreements, land rights, labor laws, and corporate income taxes – the agreement over who controls operations of extractive resources holds enormous sway over a leader's political calculus given the potential for capturing revenues in the form of quasi-rents, higher taxes on SOEs, and the ability to ramp up production. Securing a larger share of resource revenues through nationalization thus offers the leader an opportunity to immediately improve her survival odds. But over time, the operational inefficiencies of SOEs compared to private firms (Boardman and Vining, 1989; Wolf, 2009) will lower the overall amount of resource revenues accrued by the state, thereby potentially decreasing the leader's probability of survival in the long run. Even absent operational inefficiencies, the long-term quasi-rents from extractive resource production may be sufficiently negative – assuming that average operating costs increase over time if new fields and mines are not developed – such that the net realized value of quasi-rents is less than zero.

With diffused information about the viability for a better deal, the choice to nationalize extractive industries depends on the leader's existing beliefs about the probability of survival. A strong leader that foresees a lasting regime – like a monarch or a single-party dictator (see Geddes, 2003) – will choose *not* to nationalize operations. This is based on the likelihood of a negative net present value in the long run relative to maintaining private operating firms. By contrast, a weak leader foreseeing an early exit for whatever reason – like a revolutionary leader or a nascent dictator facing credible threats of coup d'etat (see Colgan, 2013; Wilson and Wright, 2017) – will choose nationalization, knowing that whatever risks and costs this decision carries will not manifest for several years. Because of this shorter time horizon, the weak leader weighs the immediate boost to the treasury that nationalizing extractive resources provides more favorably than the long-term loss of revenues given nationalization's operational inefficiencies over time.[29] This is no different from the general logic of autocratic leaders that highly discount the future going after "easy-to-collect" revenues, thereby sacrificing any long-run development these revenues would have fostered (Levi, 1981; Cukierman et al., 1992; Olson, 1993; Albertus and Menaldo, 2012).

While the choice to nationalize depends on perceived survival probabilities, it is constrained by technical capabilities. Nationalizing operations necessitates having a workforce with the technical skills to explore for and produce resources (Bohn and Deacon, 2000; Nolan and Thurber, 2010; Victor et al., 2012). In natural resource sectors like oil, gas, coal, minerals, and deep-shaft metals, exploration and production are highly complex endeavors. Most exploration efforts are risky and typically fail, and the odds of profitable production decline as geological complexities increase (Selley and Sonnenberg, 2014; Heller, 2017). Exploration and extraction also require highly skilled human capital to operate extractive machinery, particularly in the early development phase of production. Hence, leaders of countries with limited experience with operations – whether because of timing (e.g., being a new producer),

---

[29] I consider time horizons as given, but the factors driving the variation in leaders' discount rates could be incorporated into the argument explicitly. One relevant factor is institutionalization: more institutionalized regimes will have longer time horizons and so will be less likely to nationalize operations. By contrast, leaders in less institutionalized regimes will face greater pressures to nationalize operations given higher discount rates. For the connection between institutionalization and time horizons, see Simmons (2016a).

insurmountable geological complexities, or the lack of human capital – will be unable to nationalize operations, even if the above benefits outweigh the costs.

As constructed, the argument effectively makes a leader's perceived probability of survival endogenous to the decision to nationalize. Weak leaders – who perceive their ouster as imminent and thus need the infusion of revenues to survive – will gamble on nationalization despite its risks and long-term costs. But this decision pays off with an immediate increase in resource revenues for the state, making weak leaders stronger as a result. In this way, the initial perceived probability of survival affects the decision to nationalize, which then impacts future odds of leadership survival. Paradoxically, it is weaker leaders that nationalize and thus become stronger, while strong leaders eschew this option but ultimately lose out on the opportunity to capture revenues from operating firms.

1.3.1   Diffusion of Negotiating Information Leads to Greater Nationalization

One implication of the argument is that leaders are more likely to nationalize when information is diffused about terms of negotiated agreements for other host governments. This follows from the first step in the leader's political calculus about the probability of survival. In the initial stages of resource production, leaders choose private operators as this will lead to increased revenues for the state compared to the alternative of no resource extraction. Once they learn of the possibility of a better deal to be had, leaders update their chances of survival in deciding whether to pursue better terms via nationalization. If leaders indeed make this choice based on how new information updates their survival probabilities, then it should be the case that acts of nationalization are preceded by instances of information diffusion.

When leaders gain information that competitors – governments of countries with similar geological endowments and similar roles in the international market – are receiving better deals over how revenues are shared with firms, they will want to renegotiate the terms of their own arrangements with producing firms. For example, in 1971 the Shah of Iran came to an agreement with Western oil companies to increase their income tax rate to the Iranian government. At the time, the Shah was not fully satisfied with the new deal but still felt it was fair in light of what other oil-exporting governments received. Yet the ink was still drying when the oil companies struck a separate agreement with Saudi Arabia, Iraq, and the UAE that promised an even better deal for the Arab states.

Upon hearing Saudi Arabia's oil minister brag on the radio that its new deal was "four times better than the Shah's," the Shah was incensed and angrily demanded a new arrangement (Bamberg, 2000, 472). As negotiations escalated, the Shah ultimately seized complete control over operations and renationalized the oil sector in 1973 – an event that forms the core of Chapter 6.

Knowledge diffused by competitors also includes more details about the true costs of extraction by private firms, which could spark an awareness that firms are overreporting costs to host governments to capture higher rents. If this information diffuses across borders, leaders are more apt to pursue greater state intervention in search of improved government take. Broadly, renegotiations will result in maintaining private operations but with higher tax rates or choosing to vest operations in state-owned enterprises. One extreme of the latter is complete takeover by the state: there is no better deal in the eyes of a leader than sharing revenues one-hundred-to-zero in favor of the state, instead of dealing with arrangements like fifty-fifty contracts. This describes the rationale behind the wave of oil nationalizations in the 1970s by host governments that, as David Victor writes, "saw huge asymmetries in information and feared that foreign operators were appropriating too much of the benefit from oil production for themselves" (Victor, 2013, 449).

Prior to receiving such information from international competitors, leaders may be content with their share of resource revenues compared to the take-home revenue for operating firms. In these cases, leaders will pursue private ownership and management of resource wealth as well as gentle forms of state intervention in which SOEs play nonoperational roles. This behavior would fall very much in line with the conventional wisdom from legal scholars and social psychologists on bargaining divergence after informational exchange. Absent information about how profits are truly shared, individuals will converge on satisfactory negotiations; but once information about imbalance is revealed, individuals will seek renegotiation or walk away from the bargaining table altogether (see Thompson and Loewenstein, 1992; Loewenstein and Moore, 2004).

This logic underpins one component of the domino effect of oil nationalization in particular, whereby the act of expropriation in one state prompts expropriations in other states given increased incentives for greater returns (and also diminished risks of retaliation) (Kobrin, 1985). If leaders have complete information about the agreements other leaders reach with operating firms, then anytime a new deal is signed it will spur renegotiations across the board. In the oil sector, this "leapfrogging effect" was a key fear of the Seven Sisters – the seven petroleum

MNCs that dominated global oil markets[30] – in conducting individual negotiations with host governments, as they knew that each agreement would set off a new chain reaction across the producer governments (Yergin, 1991, 580–582).

While the oil sector is far from a market with complete information, the level of information sharing between host governments has improved over time. The advent of OPEC, for example, allowed a forum in which leaders could openly discuss their terms of agreement with the Western oil companies (see Doran, 1980). The Tehran and Tripoli meetings in February 1971, for example, were particularly instrumental in diffusing specific negotiating positions used by the Algerians – who successfully expropriated French-owned oil operations that month – that contributed to the first wave of nationalizations in Libya in December 1971 and Iraq in April 1972 (Dietrich, 2017). Efforts in the 2010s to increase transparency in oil and minerals contracts has led to online repositories where anyone can view the exact terms of how revenues are shared between host governments and operators.[31]

In the following chapters, the diffusion of information is operationalized with two different approaches. In cross-national analysis of oil nationalizations, the act of joining OPEC is used as a proxy for information diffusion in the terms of agreements between host governments and the Seven Sisters. Colgan (2019) shows how OPEC fostered a meeting environment in which leaders could reduce transaction and information costs associated with negotiating unilateral agreements with international oil firms.[32] Although joining OPEC is itself an outcome of the desire for leaders to take control of oil operations (Jones Luong and Weinthal, 2010, 314), the timing of joining the organization can nonetheless be used as a measure of when leaders became exposed to new information about the opportunity for better terms of agreements with the Seven Sisters.[33] In a single-case analysis of oil nationalization in 1973 Iran, archival records on negotiations between Iran and BP in

---

[30] BP, Gulf Oil, Royal Dutch Shell, Standard Oil of California, Standard Oil of New Jersey, Standard Oil of New York, and Texaco.

[31] For example, the multilateral Extractive Industries Transparency Initiative (EITI) and the NGO Publish What You Pay (PWYP) encourage both firms and governments to release public information about the fiscal, social, and environmental terms of resource agreements. In addition, the OpenOil initiative maintains an online repository of roughly 800 oil and gas contracts in 73 countries covering 20,000 fields (or, more accurately, "blocks" and "concession areas"). See Kyle Cohen (2015) for a review of the political implications of contract transparency in the oil sector.

[32] This builds on the general effects of international organizations on reducing transaction costs. See Keohane (1984).

[33] In Chapter 4, I also use membership in the Nonaligned Movement as an alternative proxy for a forum in which information is diffused across borders.

light of information spread by the Saudi oil minister allow for greater precision in identifying the effects of information diffusion.

Yet in other sectors, such information is not widely shared – and MNCs go to great lengths to protect the terms of their agreements. In the lithium and palladium industries, for instance, there are no host-government cartels nor any online contract repositories; indeed, even obtaining price information about lithium in advanced markets like Chile is challenging (Maxwell, 2015). Information on production costs in established industries like copper is also hard to obtain, even for long-time producers like Zambia (Manley, 2017). One might expect, then, that the diffusion of information about how revenues are shared in these sectors will shift over time; such a change could spark greater state intervention as more information is revealed to host governments about the potential size of foregone profits.

This aspect of the argument can shed light on why some natural resource sectors in a given country are subject to heavy state intervention, while others remain largely in the hands of private firms. Consider again the case of Chile, a 30-year-old democracy in which state capacity is generally strong and political contestation is high, with several alternative sources of export revenue other than extractive resources. Existing explanations about nationalization would predict that state intervention in the country's natural resources would be one of little or limited state control. Although this prediction is borne out in the lithium sector, where the private company SQM controls production, it misses the mark in the copper sector, where state-run Codelco dominates production and foreign firms play only a minor role in operations. Puzzles like these therefore necessitate a theory that incorporates both state-level and sector-level determinants. In this way, incorporating the concept of information diffusion about revenue-sharing into existing theories advances the understanding of why leaders choose nationalization in different natural resource sectors at different points in time.

1.3.2 Nationalization Fosters Fiscal Strength

Scholars have long known that the commodity boom-and-bust cycle is one reason why resource-rich countries suffer maladies like unpredictable fiscal deficits, low economic growth, and representative governance (for a review, see Frankel, 2010). On the one hand, when commodity prices are high, leaders can make grand commitments to public goods and to development-enhancing projects (Beblawi and Luciani, 1987; Chaudhry, 1997; Karl, 1997; Ross, 2012). They can use this wealth to shore up support at home and to build up defenses militarily (Bueno de Mesquita and Smith, 2010; Cuaresma et al., 2011). On the other hand, when prices are low, these expenditure commitments must be rolled back – often in politically painful ways – or else the government must suffer increasing international debts (see Nooruddin, 2008; Kretzman and Nooruddin, 2011).

In this cycle, who actually collects these windfalls during booms and who suffers these losses during busts is consistently under-appreciated. In times of plenty, does this wealth accrue to state treasuries or to foreign corporations? In times of want, does the state bear the load or are the losses suffered by outside firms?

The degree of state intervention is the key piece to understanding this problem. If leaders choose to nationalize operations in the sector and place production in the hands of SOEs, then the state will reap the greatest rewards during high prices but suffer the most during low prices. If instead leaders choose to allow private firms to do most of the lifting, the state will be unable to capitalize fully on price upswings, but will share any incurred losses during downswings with private firms.

Yet for leaders who are faced with instability when they first take power or who do not expect – for whatever reason – their rule to last, the risks of nationalizing operations may be worth taking (see Olson, 1993). If the choice to nationalize extractive operations will lead to greater revenues for the state in the form of appropriated quasi-rents and higher government take from SOEs, then leaders can use this wealth to increase their odds of survival through placating elites and fending off usurpers (see Wright et al., 2015; Liou and Musgrave, 2016). Leaders that choose not to nationalize may benefit in the long run, but cannot seize the moment if prices suddenly rise, instead losing out on these foregone revenues. This wealth ultimately accrues to the shareholders of MNCs like Rio Tinto or Royal Dutch Shell, rather than to the shareholders of the state. And those that nationalize but still allow private firms to operate will end up somewhere in between. These leaders will have limited ability to capture revenues during booms (but also limited exposure to busts), while also suffering from nationalization's negative externalities of reduced foreign investment in other sectors.

The argument that nationalizing operations will increase revenues and, ultimately, the durability of leaders, rests on three mechanisms: information asymmetry, production elasticity, and operational efficiency. Keep in mind that the alternative ownership design is taxation of private operators, which is also the case when the sector has been nationalized but production is still in the hands of private firms.

Information Asymmetry. The first mechanism is based on a classic principal-agent problem: when the state is not directly involved in operations, an information asymmetry regarding revenues arises between operating firms and the host government (van der Linde, 2000; Mommer, 2002; Warshaw, 2012). The government lacks information about the true revenues generated by the resource sector, which are known only to the producer; the firm can thus decide to share this knowledge with the government either accurately or inaccurately. In most cases, MNCs will opt for the latter, taking advantage of host governments' lack of technical knowledge by withholding accurate information about production and extraction costs (Menaldo, 2016, 140, 167).

In the oil industry, a private firm in charge of operations can hide the cost and quantity of crude oil produced in the host country, given the complex nature of petroleum extraction (see Victor, 2009; Readhead et al., 2018). When it comes time to pay taxes and royalties – both of which are typically assessed as percentages of oil sales minus costs – the firm has a strong incentive to underreport production quantities and overreport production costs. Even in the context of nationalization without seizing operations, where the sector includes a state-owned enterprise involved in oversight rather than production, the state must accept whatever operations-related figures that are reported by producing firms. In this case, the asymmetry of information about extraction figures will lead to the state collecting less oil revenue than it is due.

By contrast, SOEs involved in operations reduce this informational gap from the state's perspective. Based on their experience in day-to-day operations, these companies are "in the know" when it comes to extraction figures and estimates (Grayson, 1981; McPherson, 2003, 2010; Marcel, 2016; Heller, 2017). In the oil sector, a firm operating alongside an NOC with production capacity will be hesitant to misreport quantities and costs, knowing that the state has enough information to dispute these reported figures. The NOC itself will also find it harder to hide information from the state, given its formal ties to government oversight agencies and the preponderance of government-appointed personnel loyal to the leader rather than to outside shareholders. In other words, the government is better able to monitor the SOE compared to the MNC.[34]

---

[34] In practice, some NOCs grow autonomous from government oversight over time and become known as a state within a state – and thus no different from the oil MNCs in hiding revenues from the government. A prominent example is Angola's Sonangol (Heller, 2012).

Nationalization of operations, then, allows the state to reap greater revenues compared to the alternative ownership structures of nationalizing without seizing operations or maintaining private ownership. In effect, the government is now able to capture foregone revenues that would have been collected by firms without the state's full knowledge.

Production Elasticity. The ability to adjust production in response to changing international prices allows an operator to capture greater profits as prices increase. When prices decline, this ability allows the operator to conserve its resource reserves to protect future revenues when prices rebound; this is pertinent for all the commodities considered here, which are finite (and thus scarce). Control over production levels also allows the operator to dictate its own depletion strategy (Tsui, 2011; Stevens, 2012; Menaldo, 2016). For producers with low discount rates, the optimal strategy is to minimize year-to-year volatility in production while maximizing the number of years producing. For those with high discount rates, the optimal strategy is to hit maximal production levels early on, with less concern for the ability to produce in the long term.[35]

From the perspective of the host government, having control over the elasticity of production to changing prices is crucial if private operating firms are not willing (or able) to adjust production levels in response to price changes. With operations vested in the SOE, the state can ensure that the optimal levels of natural resources are extracted – whether optimal means maximal production to capitalize on a high-price environment, or steady production to ensure the availability of long-term supply.

But in the context of maintaining private operators, the state is at the mercy of whatever production levels private firms deem fit. On the one hand, short-term profit-maximization to appease shareholders will lead firms to also capitalize during price spikes with increasing production, which leads to higher taxes collected by host governments. On the other hand, firms in extractive industries have historically acted as price-setters, keeping production steady in an attempt to stabilize prices and profits (see Yergin, 1991). Today, while these firms lack such cartel-like powers, they are highly multinational and must balance increasing production levels in one country with decreasing production levels in others.

These two reasons could be why private oil firms do not adjust production to changing prices. Looking at four of the largest private oil

---

[35] In the oil industry, extracting oil at above-optimal rates early in the production process can not only expedite the decline in reserves, but also sufficiently damage the reservoir to prevent any future extraction.

firms in the world – ExxonMobil, BP, Chevron, and ConocoPhillips – the data reveal that skyrocketing prices (from roughly $30 per barrel in 2001 to over $100 per barrel in 2008) did little to alter supply. Production levels remained largely flat at ExxonMobil, for example, declining slightly from 2.5 million barrels per day in 2000 to just under 2.4 million barrels per day in 2008.[36]

Production elasticity also works in both directions. States with control over large reserves can attempt to manipulate international prices by intentionally altering production levels. The classic case is Saudi Arabia's use of the oil weapon to drive up prices by withholding production during the 1973 Arab-Israeli War and to force prices downward by flooding the market with oil in 1985 to punish other OPEC members for breaking quotas. Put together, nationalizing production and operations allows resource-rich governments to control their fiscal destinies, particularly if private firms are producing at politically or economically suboptimal levels.

Operational Efficiency. In the long run, operations managed by SOEs are less efficient when compared to private firms. Classical economic theory suggests that, all else equal, output from state-run enterprises will be lower than private companies (Stigler, 1971). Other economic theories posit that SOEs involved in operations maximize short-term revenues at the cost of long-term efficiency, given the technical gaps between private and state-run firms (Boardman and Vining, 1989). In the oil sector in particular, theory and evidence falls along the same lines, such that NOCs are found to produce at suboptimal rates compared to the Exxons and Shells of the world (see Hartley and Medlock, 2008). One study, for instance, finds that outside of the OPEC countries, NOCs produce 24 percent less than comparable private oil companies, and nearly 50 percent less when OPEC NOCs are included (Wolf, 2009).

However, the degree to which these operational deficiencies manifest themselves depends in large part on where a country's resource production falls along the extraction cycle (Nolan and Thurber, 2010). Risks are highest and technical expertise is essential in the early stage of operations, when resources are first discovered and production is ramped up to commercially viable levels. Nationalizing at this point in the production cycle (and placing operations in the hands of an SOE instead of keeping private firms in charge of production) will almost certainly

---

[36] "Exxon Mobil – Your best investment … The growth story." *Seeking Alpha*. May 1, 2016. Accessed October 22, 2017 from https://seekingalpha.com/article/3969951-exxon-mobil-best-investment-growth-story.

lead to lower levels of extraction. But in the middle stages of operations these risks are minimized, and any reasonably competent operator can maintain high levels of extraction. In the oil industry, this stage can span decades – depending on a country's reserves – and at the very least can last roughly ten years without major reinvestments. In the final stages of operations, risks return as the need for extracting remaining reserves often requires highly complex methods and technologies. In these latter stages, private firms are again more likely to produce at higher levels than SOEs. SOE operational inefficiencies are thus most prevalent in the early and late stages of extraction. Although the state can expect relatively efficient production from its SOE during the middle stages of extraction, inefficiencies are inevitable as time progresses, making the decision to keep operations in the hands of an SOE harder to justify in the long term.

From the vantage point of the quasi-rent theory described by Klein et al. (1978), the production inefficiencies of SOEs will further decrease the long-term realized value of nationalization. Consider the example of a hypothetical MNC that owns and operates an oil platform contracted by the government through a purchasing agreement. In the short run, there exist appropriable quasi-rents because the government knows that it can offer low compensation for the firm's assets, given the minimal salvageable value of its equipment and low marginal costs of operation. Assume that in the early postdiscovery stages of production, operating costs are $7,000 per day. These relatively low costs can last for the first several years of a well's lifespan. But when reservoir pressure declines, these costs can reach upwards of $40,000 per day for some of the leanest and most technically advanced private firms – and will be much higher for SOEs lacking such operational savvy. If the firm is expropriated, the appropriated quasi-rent adds up to roughly $10 million in the first seven years of the platform's life; but over its entire fifteen-year lifespan, the net realized appropriated value becomes a staggering *negative* $62 million if long-run costs are not incorporated up front.[37] And considering that nationalization may entail hundreds of operational-asset seizures, its long-run costs can be significantly damaging to the government's bottom line if new fields are not discovered and developed.

---

[37] See footnote 23. This assumes a realized value of production at $11,500 per day, based on a fixed market price, and a salvage rate of $500 per day. Operating costs are assumed to be $7,000 per day for the first seven years and then rise linearly to $40,000 by year fifteen. Assuming a constant oil price, the cumulative quasi-rents for the first seven years are +$10,220,000, and −$72,817,500 for the remaining eight years. The scenario assumes that the state appropriates all quasi-rents from the SOE after nationalization such that no long-run operating costs are recovered.

In the short term, these three mechanisms link nationalizing operations to greater fiscal strength. Nationalization allows the government to get a bigger piece of the revenue pie by reducing information asymmetries and by allowing for production elasticity, but because of operational inefficiencies the size of the pie will shrink over time. For leaders with short time horizons – whom I argue are the most likely to nationalize operations – the initial revenue influx is the prize that justifies the gamble of nationalization. These leaders are not yet concerned with recuperating long-run costs that are incurred when addressing resource depletion. But for leaders with longer time horizons, these immediate gains are not worth the loss of long-term profits or the negative realized value of appropriated quasi-rents. As such, they choose not to nationalize and will instead keep operations in the hands of MNCs and will continue to tax resource rents. From a strictly contract-theory perspective, nationalization is an irrational decision by leaders given its long-run costs; but from a political perspective, these long-run costs are justified by the short-run gains from surviving another year or more in power.

1.3.3   Nationalizing Operations Increases Leadership Survival

For those in power, greater fiscal strength in general will foster more durable leaders (see Levi, 1989; Haggard and Kaufman, 2016). This is particularly true for government revenues generated by SOEs, not only because of the sheer size of these windfalls but also due to the opaque nature of SOE budgets (Marcel, 2006; Stevens, 2008; Gillies, 2009; Heller, 2017; Vreeland et al., 2017). This opacity allows leaders to siphon off revenues discreetly for co-opting elites and financing repression before directing resource revenues to more visible expenditures like public goods and services (see Ross, 2012).[38] In Angola, for example, $32 billion (roughly equal to one quarter of the country's GDP) went unaccounted for during the 2007–2010 period; the culprit was the state-owned oil company Sonangol, and the missing funds have been linked to media censorship, the use of force against protesters, and the establishment of foreign escrow accounts for then president José Eduardo dos Santos's inner circle.[39]

---

[38] Note that not all types of government revenue can be used for regime-strengthening activities like repression and co-optation; resource revenues carry a host of properties that allow for more effective expenditures on these activities than nonresource revenues. See Morrison (2015); Girod et al. (2017).

[39] "Angola: Explain missing government funds." *Human Rights Watch* December 20, 2011. Accessed October 27, 2017 from www.hrw.org/news/2011/12/20/angola-explain-missing-government-funds.

Indirectly, this aspect of the argument helps to explain the rise and fall of dictators in contexts that remain unexplained by existing theories of authoritarian politics. Focusing on how different intervention pathways affect state revenues shows how seemingly well-financed leaders like the Shah of Iran can unexpectedly collapse, while seemingly cash-strapped dictatorships like early Ba'athist Iraq can endure – a comparison I describe in greater detail in Chapter 2.

For now, consider again the consolidation of a young Qaddafi's regime in 1977 Libya as a corroboratory example. To achieve early goals of the republicanism he espoused to his followers and to the masses, Qaddafi embarked on an extensive spending program that militarized Libyan society while rapidly expanding educational and health services across the country. As the political historian Alison Pargeter writes, "these grand schemes were all bankrolled by the country's vast oil reserves ... (and) made it possible for him to enforce conformity and to stamp his personality on the country to an extreme degree" (Pargeter, 2012, 111). But this would not have been possible without state control of the sector: of the roughly $10 billion of oil export revenues in 1977, for example, over $7.5 billion remained in the government's hands, care of Linoco.[40] The rest would be paid out to companies like Occidental, Mobil, and AGIP of Italy, operators working alongside the NOC with a 20 to 25 percent minority stake in production. If Qaddafi had not seized control of the sector and had continued the ownership structure of the deposed King Idris, the Libyan state would only have collected half this amount – leaving the bulk of total oil revenues in the hands of Western oil companies instead.[41]

Putting this all together, the argument that leadership survival is endogenous to nationalization suggests several empirical implications to be tested. When information on revenue sharing is not diffused across countries, leaders are likely to maintain the status quo – for nearly all extractive resources, this involves private firms in control of operations. By contrast, the diffusion of information about competitors' agreements will prompt leaders to pursue operational nationalization, conditional on the technical capacity to do so. The direct consequence of this choice is fiscal strength: government take of revenues from natural resources are higher where leaders nationalize operations. These revenues are lower where leaders establish an SOE without nationalizing operations, and lowest where leaders choose to maintain private ownership. The survival

---

[40] USGS 1977. "The mineral industry of Libya." The $7.5 billion number is an estimate based on what the government controlled as per the 1976 Revenue and Financial Law.

[41] This is a rough estimate based on the earlier fifty-fifty profit-sharing (but not revenue-sharing) agreement under the the the Petroleum Law of 1965.

of leaders is thus the indirect consequence of this choice: with higher revenues from nationalized operations, leaders will endure; with lower revenues from operations in the hands of nonstate firms, leadership turnover is more likely.

1.4 Research Design, Methodology, and Measuring Nationalization

The chapters ahead develop this argument and test hypotheses derived from its core implications using a mixed-methods approach. Case-comparative methods provide insights into how differing characteristics of nationalization affect authoritarian survival in cases that remain unexplained by existing theories. Archival methods allow for a microlevel analysis of the decision to nationalize in a single context, which effectively traces the causal process in a sequential manner. Statistical tools used on cross-national data allow for a macrolevel analysis of nationalizing operations in a way that is generalizable across both time and countries. Integrating these methods thus provides a holistic approach to studying nationalization.

The empirical workhorse of this book is state intervention in the oil industry, though I also consider cases of nationalizations in the coal, copper, and natural gas industries as well. My choice to focus on oil in particular rests on both the global importance of this commodity – oil is the most traded natural resource by revenue, is the world's leading fuel for consumption, and despite low prices the industry generates roughly $1.5 trillion annually – and the rich variance in types of state intervention in the sector.[42] It is the most broadly nationalized of all natural resources, as every major oil producer in history except the United States has at some point nationalized its oil industry. The near ubiquity of nationalization means that there are ample opportunities for different types of intervention, ranging from full operational nationalization in Saudi Arabia, to partial nationalization of operations in Russia, to nationalization of nonoperational functions in Nigeria, to full private ownership in Belize.

Kobrin (1980) was the first to quantify nationalization cross-nationally, with the creation of a database that measured every act of oil-related expropriation in a given country and year. Since then, most cross-national quantitative studies on oil nationalization have used and updated this measure (Kobrin, 1984; Minor, 1994; Bohn and Deacon, 2000; Li, 2009; Guriev et al., 2011; Hajzler, 2012; Wilson

---

[42] These figures from Colgan (2013) and the BP Statistical Review of Energy.

and Wright, 2017). The notable exception is Jones Luong and Weinthal (2010), who analyze domestic ownership structure as a measure of nationalization that is related to the idea of the establishment of SOEs.[43] While the existing data on acts of expropriation are helpful in measuring the causes and effects of individual instances of expropriation, these measures do not capture institutional characteristics of nationalization as manifested in the differing frameworks of SOEs across resource-producing countries.

For these reasons, and others I consider in Chapter 3, I code the oil sector of a given country as nationalized if an operational NOC exists in a given year.[44] A full listing of the timing of all operational oil nationalizations is presented in Table 1.1, sorted by year of operational NOC establishment. In Chapter 3, I describe in detail the categorization of whether the NOC has a de facto role in production: those that do are counted as operational nationalizations, and those that do not reflect production controlled by private operating firms (even if an NOC exists in the sector).

I analyze these data with a variety of tests and models. Each draws on new analytical techniques to overcome two methodological challenges: (1) the level of statistical imprecision associated with so-called small data and (2) the ability to compare outcomes to viable counterfactuals. The first impairs studying the causes of nationalization, since these are relatively rare and sticky events. States typically set up NOCs only once throughout their oil histories, with limited examples of privatization and subsequent nationalization (see Hughes, 2014). I address this problem using Bayesian methods, which combine qualitative and quantitative data to calculate relationships with representative uncertainty intervals even in small-N samples. The qualitative data used with these methods

---

[43] In addition, McPherson (2010) proposes a new dichotomous measure based on state participation, whereby sectors with greater than 30 percent state participation (either through ownership of an SOE or participatory contracts with MNCs) are considered "nationalized."

[44] Importantly, operationalizing nationalization using NOC establishments relies on a process that is well-documented and objectively measurable, given there is precise information about when an NOC is established and the conditions under which a sector becomes nationalized. These data are coded from a comprehensive review of every oil nationalization using primary and secondary sources: 25 petroleum laws and executive decrees, 80 United States Geological Survey (USGS) *Minerals Yearbooks* published annually since 1932 (United States Geological Survey, 1932), and roughly 100 scholarly accounts of individual countries' oil histories including examples like Philip (1982); de Oliveira (2012); Victor et al. (2012); Zahlan (1998) and Grayson (1981). The full bibliography of sources, along with country-specific oil histories, is available online at http://dataverse.harvard.edu/dataverse/paasham.

Table 1.1. *Operational nationalization around the world, 1900–2015*

Country	Year	Country	Year	Country	Year
Argentina*	1911	Syria	1968	Ghana	1985
Soviet Union	1917	Algeria	1969	Vietnam	1985
Bolivia*	1936	United Arab Emirates	1971	Ecuador	1990
Brazil	1938	Iraq	1972	Russian Federation	1991
Mexico	1938	Libya	1973	Azerbaijan	1992
France*	1941	Peru	1973	Uzbekistan	1992
Albania	1945	Iran*	1974	Thailand	1993
Poland	1945	Oman	1974	Jordan	1995
Romania*	1948	Qatar	1974	Kazakhstan	1996
Italy*	1949	Saudi Arabia	1974	Sudan	1996
Chile	1950	Trinidad & Tobago	1974	South Africa	1997
Colombia	1951	Bahrain	1975	Yemen	1997
Iran*	1951	Canada*	1976	Bolivia	2007
Austria*	1956	Egypt	1976	Equatorial Guinea	2008
India	1956	United Kingdom*	1976	Congo	2010
Indonesia	1957	Angola	1978	Tunisia	2010
Turkey	1958	Malaysia	1979	Argentina	2012
Cuba	1960	Iran	1980	Cameroon	2013
Venezuela	1960	Norway	1981	Gabon	2013
Kuwait	1961	Suriname	1982		
Pakistan	1968	Denmark	1984		

*Note: *refers to states that later privatized their oil sectors or reversed operational nationalization but continued to maintain a national oil company. Two of these states renationalized after privatization (Argentina in 2012 and Bolivia in 2007). Sources: see footnote 44.*

in part consists of interviews conducted with international oil consultants and former officials at NOCs in the Middle East.

The second problem besets nearly all observational studies of politics. The analysis of nationalization is no different. When assessing the effects of nationalization, it is difficult to make definitive claims by simply comparing each case to other countries that did not undertake these choices. Instead, what is needed are reliable and defensible counterfactuals, which are hard to come by in the absence of experimental conditions. I address this challenge by leveraging corporate projections of outcomes of interest, in this case oil revenues, and compare these to actual outcomes after nationalization of operations. The viability of the counterfactuals rest on the assumption that these projections were made without prior knowledge that nationalization would occur.

I test this assumption and collect data for this analysis by drawing on archival records for the case of renationalization in Iran in 1973. Specifically, I utilize archival documents on the dynamics of negotiations between the Shah of Iran, his advisors, and the group of international oil companies led by BP, coupled with quantitative data on actual and projected amounts of revenue transferred between these oil companies and the Shah's government in the 1960s and early 1970s. Importantly, these records indicate that while preparing projections of oil revenues to be paid to the Shah, BP had no knowledge of the Shah's sudden announcement to reform the NOC by nationalizing production in January 1973. These projected revenues can be used as a counterfactual for what happened to oil revenues after nationalization of operations.

The case of Iran, which is extensively used throughout the book, is an ideal testing ground for my theory given that Iran experienced rich temporal variation in the degree of state intervention across its 109-year history of oil production. Iran has been at the center of global energy politics ever since, from the 1951 oil nationalization that prompted the infamous coup of Iran's first democratically elected leader, to the 1979 revolution that rocked international oil markets, to decades of sanctions over its nuclear program. Opening up the black box of Iranian politics – a case rarely used in political science and public policy – will not only shed light on the inner mechanics of nationalization, but will also be deeply interesting to scholars of international politics.

1.4.1   Chapter Outline: A Road Map for the Rest of the Book

In Chapter 2, I begin by outlining how and why nationalization is central to the politics of resource-rich countries. It opens with an examination of extant theories on natural resource wealth and nationalization in political science, economics, and public policy, and then describes why existing theories are unable to answer the questions this book seeks to answer. With these questions in mind, this chapter presents the book's central theory of why leaders nationalize and how leader survival shapes and is shaped by the choice of nationalization.

After describing empirical implications of the argument, the chapter offers initial evidence to support these claims in the form of exploratory case studies of Iran and Iraq. These are two of the most polarizing cases in the study of natural resource politics. In Iran, the shocking collapse of the Shah in 1979 defied the West's notion of the "island of stability" in the tumultuous Middle East. In Iraq, the fall of the Hashemite monarchy in 1958 ushered in a decade of instability until the unexpected Ba'athist consolidation in 1968, when Hassan al-Bakr established a single-party dictatorship that would last thirty-five years until his successor Saddam Hussein was removed from power following the American invasion of 2003.

In these brief case studies, I draw on political histories to explore how and why leaders in each case pursued state intervention in the oil sector. In particular, each case highlights the important role of information diffusion regarding revenue-sharing agreements. Negotiations between the Shah of Iran and the BP-led consortium in the late 1960s culminated with a satisfactory agreement in 1971 that staved off outright nationalization. This was a short-lived truce as information about better deals across the Persian Gulf prompted the Shah to nationalize operations in 1973. By contrast, government dealings with the Western-backed Iraq Petroleum Company (IPC) were rife from the start with economic grievances and antagonism for imperialistic terms of extraction, culminating with nationalization and transfer of production rights to the Iraqi National Oil Company in 1972. The case comparison also provides an example of leadership stability under nationalization. The case of Ba'athist Iraq is particularly illustrative: despite the constancy of oil wealth, political instability in 1958–1968 and stability in the post-1968 period remains unexplained by existing theories. These are precisely the types of outcomes in which the book's theory predicts nationalization should affect the rise and fall of dictatorships.

In Chapter 3, I describe the nationalization dataset in detail. The chapter begins by defining SOEs with de facto control of operations as a measure of operational nationalization. After describing how operational nationalization is measured, the chapter explains the coding and construction of the 187-country, 116-year dataset of NOCs based on primary and secondary sources of each country's petroleum history. Only 70 of these countries are major producers, but for completeness the full sample includes all sovereign countries with populations greater than 200,000 in 2000. This chapter includes several brief examples of NOC varieties, cases of NOC reforms and privatizations over time, as well as varieties of nationalization in nonoil sectors like copper, coal, zinc, cobalt, and lithium. The chapter also discusses how the database compares with existing nationalization datasets.

In Chapter 4, I empirically assess the veracity of the argument on why leaders nationalize their oil sectors and establish operational NOCs. To test hypotheses derived from the theory's implications, I use a method of statistical analysis that combines the cross-national NOC dataset with information elicited from structured interviews with oil experts. This technique – Bayesian statistics – allows for a holistic analysis of the determinants of nationalization that incorporates both quantitative and qualitative evidence on NOC formation. The results show the importance of information diffusion and perceptions of leader survival in the decision to nationalize the oil sector. I then present a case comparison of Iran and Saudi Arabia in the 1940s to show how information diffused to a strong regime led to maintaining private ownership in Saudi Arabia in 1949, while knowledge about revenue sharing diffused to a weak regime led to nationalization in Iran in 1951.

In Chapter 5, I present a series of longitudinal empirical analyses of nationalization to test its primary effects on revenues and secondary effects on leadership survival. The chapter begins by assessing the claim that nationalization of extractive operations will foster greater government take of resource revenues compared to maintaining operations by private firms. This is perhaps the most important implication of the broader argument: if nationalization does not increase the state's fiscal strength, then the risks of nationalizing operations will heavily outweigh the benefits – and thus provide no insight into why leaders nationalize extractive resources. But if indeed nationalization increases resource revenues collected by the state, leaders can use this fiscal boost to improve their chances of survival in power. Without nationalization, leaders lose out on the immediate opportunity to provide higher revenue capture for the state and to secure their rule.

The chapter then examines whether operational nationalization corresponds to a lower probability of leader failure specifically and regime failure generally. If nationalization increases state capture of resource revenues, then it should be the case that leaders use this wealth to consolidate power and prevent ouster. Beyond the survival of political leaders, it should also be true that political regimes in general will be stronger if resources are nationalized. These hypotheses are tested using the complete cross-national NOC dataset in conjunction with existing data on government revenues, the breakdown of authoritarian (and democratic) regimes, and leadership survival. The empirics support both hypotheses: nationalization increases state capture of resource revenues and increases the likelihood of survival of leaders and their political regimes. The results suggest that nationalizing operations explains why resource-rich leaders survive in some countries but not others.

In Chapter 6, I examine the causal mechanisms of how nationalization of operations increases government revenue using the case of oil politics in prerevolutionary Iran. Here I analyze production elasticity and reduced informational asymmetries after the Shah of Iran nationalized the oil operations of BP and its partners. The chapter draws on a combination of conversations documented in archival records and quantitative analysis of historical fiscal data from the BP Archive in Coventry, UK. The first half of the chapter describes and explains the Shah's surprise decision in January 1973 to reconfigure the country's NOC, the National Iranian Oil Company, from its role as a passive observer to a fully operational oil company able to set production levels and prices. This analysis provides further evidence for the information diffusion argument.

The second half of Chapter 6 is devoted to estimating the revenue-increasing effects of nationalizing operations. To this end, I use BP's revenue projections as counterfactuals to estimate the causal effects of the Shah's decision with respect to (1) whether NOC reform increased government take of oil revenues in 1974–1975 and (2) whether revenues collapsed after retaliation by international oil companies in 1976 to strip the NOC of its ability to sell oil on the global market. The chapter illustrates the importance of the nuances in operational nationalization as well as the consequences of operational versus nonoperational NOCs for fiscal strength.

In Chapter 7, I discuss the scholarly and policy implications of the argument and findings presented in the book. In the context of research on natural resource politics, the book casts light on why leaders in some resource-rich states thrive while in others they fail. Considered from a broader view of leader survival, the argument implies that leaders that pursue predatory and opportunistic behavior are not as likely to fail as the conventional wisdom suggests; these leaders have little option to survive in power other than by seizing assets instead of building growth-enhancing institutions.

In terms of policy, this chapter provides a road map to how extractive resources will be managed in the future for oil and for commodities that have thus far avoided nationalization. The examination of future oil nationalizations will be particularly relevant for states considering their ownership options in light of new discoveries. This chapter highlights two such cases: Lebanon, which is considering establishing an NOC with the ability to take operational control in the future, and Guyana, which has thus far eschewed vesting operational control in the hands of its NOC. But not all extractive sectors have experienced the wave of nationalizations that swept across the world's oil and gas operations. At the time of writing, minerals and advanced materials that are involved in the production of renewable energy facilities and energy storage – namely cobalt, lithium, and palladium – have largely been produced by private firms. If and when the production of these materials is consolidated under the aegis of the state, these nationalizations will have profound impacts not only on the leaders of producing countries, but also on the world that relies upon these resources to sustain the coming industrial revolution in clean energy.

2   The Theory of Political Survival through Nationalization

The central premise of *Power Grab* is that leaders nationalize operations to strengthen their hold on power. I argue that operational nationalization – state control over the physical production of resources – increases the amount of revenues that the state accrues from the extraction and sale of natural resources. This revenue is crucial to a leader's survival because it provides the means to purchase popular support, co-opt elites, and ward off would-be challengers. Where leaders opt against nationalization, they fail to capture the lion's share of rents, which instead typically flow to bank accounts and shareholders of multinational corporations (MNCs) like Royal Dutch Shell and Glencore. But nationalization is a gamble: it entails technical risks, it can elicit retaliation from international investors, and it is less operationally efficient in the long run compared to production by private firms.

Existing arguments based on the theory of the predatory state (see Olson, 1993) would predict that leaders who choose to capture such fiscal spoils at the expense of future gains will be less likely to survive in office. And theories of state ownership over natural resources (see Jones Luong and Weinthal, 2010) contend that leaders who nationalize operations cultivate the foundation for weak fiscal regimes, compared to leaders that instead invest in building institutions that foster long-term economic development. This line of argument further posits that nationalization is a path chosen only by leaders who are strong enough to withstand its political costs. However, I demonstrate that the empirics do not support the conventional wisdom. Not only is nationalization a choice made by weaker leaders – specifically, those who perceive lower odds of future survival – but the rewards that it brings allow these leaders to consolidate power and increase their survival odds. For such leaders, nationalization is akin to a down payment on their future success. Even though nationalizing operations is a risky endeavor – and one that classical models predict entails a negative long-term expected value (see Stigler, 1971) – leaders who perceive their days in office are numbered may not have a future in which to suffer these losses if they cannot find a way to immediately secure their rule. Paradoxically, leaders whose very survival is in question are the ones who take on the risks of nationalization and are rewarded with the fiscal means to endure in power. Those whose survival is assured will eschew this choice, but in doing so will pass up on the opportunity to capture wealth that otherwise flows to outside firms.

This chapter describes the theory that underpins these claims. The argument for why leaders nationalize operations begins with an explanation based on information diffusion as the spark for this decision. The historical production cycle of every extractive resource includes a period in which the host government lacks information on the true size of potential revenues – which are better understood by private firms actually producing these resources – and on the feasibility of alternative pathways to collect these revenues. The diffusion of information on the details of firm-state negotiations in other countries presents a leader with the leverage to earn greater revenues through renegotiation and, ultimately, nationalization. Armed with this information, the leader may still lack the ability to nationalize even if the desire and opportunity to do so is apparent. This reflects the costs of nationalization, which range from the political – international embargoes, withholding of foreign investment, domestic-elite backlash, and distributional conflict – to the technical. The latter includes the production inefficiencies of nationalization in the long run as well as technological barriers in the short run, given potential geological challenges to extraction. Even if leaders are willing to take on the political costs of nationalization, it may still be a risky option if the technical hurdles to nationalizing operations are difficult to clear.

What are the fiscal rewards of accepting both the political and technical risks of nationalization? The theory posits that, in addition to the initial seizure of quasi-rents, the windfalls of operational nationalization result from the state's ability to reduce information asymmetries on the costs of production and to adjust production levels at will. By gaining control over the extraction of natural resources, a leader obtains an upfront infusion of revenues in an ideal form for consolidating power; this fiscal windfall is opaque, discretionary, and not derived from domestic assets. This last characteristic follows from the fact that extractive resource operations prior to nationalization are typically handled by outside firms and MNCs.

I begin this chapter with a review of existing knowledge about natural resource wealth and nationalization from the literatures in political science, economics, and public policy. I then explain why current arguments are unable to answer the questions this book seeks to address. With these questions in mind, this chapter describes my central theory of why leaders nationalize operations and how leader survival is endogenous to the decision-making process. The discussion begins with the role of information diffusion as the spark for nationalization. This provides the groundwork for the unified theoretical framework of how nationalization increases state capture of resource revenues via the mechanisms of information asymmetry, production elasticity, and operational efficiency. The final section of the theoretical discussion offers the ultimate punchline that operational nationalization prolongs leader survival by increasing the government's fiscal strength. After laying out the theory's testable empirical implications, the chapter presents prima facie evidence in the form of brief case studies of Iran and Iraq. The comparison shows that leaders are most stable when operations are nationalized, but are vulnerable when outside firms control operations and thus capture the bulk of resource profits.

2.1   How Does Natural Resource Nationalization Affect Governance?

Natural resource wealth presents a development paradox. On the one hand, it can bring a country out of poverty with the dramatic amount of money that resources like oil, coal, metals, and precious minerals create for governments lucky enough to reside above resource reserves. On the other hand, it can wreak havoc on a country's other economic sectors, gender equity, governance, and the propensity for violent conflict.[1] How the state manages its resource wealth – whether through direct production by state-owned enterprises (SOEs) or by regulating private firms – plays a critical role in the country's political development. Greater intervention in natural resource sectors leads to weaker fiscal institutions but also stronger fiscal balances, ultimately resulting in more durable leaders. But the decision on how to manage the sector is far from exogenous; instead, the politics, economics, and geology of a country's resources shape the state's choice of how much to intervene in the sector. This section traces the existing scholarship that underpins each of these claims, with consideration to the intellectual contributions made by political scientists, economists, historians, and international business scholars.

---

[1] In this section, I focus on the prevailing theories and arguments about resource effects on governance in particular, leaving out discussions of how resource wealth has influenced economic growth, patriarchy, and wars.

2.1.1 Theories of Natural Resource Wealth and Political Development

The pioneers of the theory of the "political resource curse," Terry Lynn Karl and Michael Ross, began with the assertion that oil is bad for governance, with Ross focusing the field on the distinction between democracy and non-democracy (Karl, 1997; Ross, 2001; Jensen and Wantchekon, 2004; Aslaksen, 2010; Ramsay, 2011). Although the causal pathways for why oil hinders democracy remain disputed (Herb, 2005; Dunning, 2008; Haber and Menaldo, 2011; Brooks and Kurtz, 2016; Menaldo, 2016), the typical explanation rests on fiscal channels for oil's deleterious effects on democracy.

The most recognized of these explanations is based on a simple idea: "No representation without taxation" (Beblawi and Luciani, 1987; Ross, 2004). This clever play on the American Revolution's slogan is the mantra of the rentier state theorist. Where other governments must tax their citizens to support the state's role as public goods provider, a rentier state – that is, a state that generates income by collecting an external rent, whether it be foreign aid or revenue generated by natural resource sales – has no need for taxing its citizens (Mahdavy, 1970; Beblawi and Luciani, 1987; Chaudhry, 1997). Rentier states, therefore, do not depend on the complicity of their citizens when making fiscal decisions. Instead, according to rentier state theory, this type of state plays the role of *l'état providence*: political leaders buy support using these rents by spending it on public goods and patronage, buying off more people with larger packages of money than their non-rentier state counterparts (Beblawi and Luciani, 1987).Thus the existence of an external fiscal-revenue source, such as sales of any natural resource or even foreign aid, widens the gap between citizens and their government. In the words of the father of rentier state theory, Hussein Mahdavy, "a government that can expand its services without resorting to heavy taxation acquires an independence from the people seldom found in other countries" (Mahdavy, 1970, 466). It was not until thirty years after Mahdavy's treatise that Michael Ross recognized this causal mechanism as the reason for why so many of the world's resource-exporting states have remained authoritarian despite the wave of democratization that hit autocrats from 1974 to 1990 (Ross, 1999, 2001).

Scholars then began investigating not just authoritarian tendencies of resource wealth but also its stabilizing effects for those in power. That is, not only do natural resources hinder democratization, they also reduce the likelihood of transitioning to another dictatorship (Wright et al., 2015). Along similar lines as rentier state theory, the updated argument that "oil hinders leadership instability" has its roots in fiscal and economic explanations. Here, Ross (2012), Smith (2004), and Ulfelder (2007) argue that natural resource wealth prolongs leadership survival due to an "allocative strategy" of increased government spending allowed by the collection of resource rents (Luciani, 1990). Robinson et al. (2006), for instance, suggest that in democracies government revenue from natural resources is spent on providing jobs, thereby persuading voters to reelect the incumbent government. The same is true in dictatorships: Wright et al. (2015) contend that oil wealth increases the survival of autocracies by reducing pressures to democratize and by decreasing the probability of coups through military spending. Similarly, Cuaresma et al. (2011) show how revenue from oil production increases the duration of autocratic leaders through increasing payments to elites and "kingmakers."

Generally speaking, any increase in government revenues should positively affect the chances of regime survival, whether that regime is democratic or otherwise. In the context of natural resource wealth, this increase in revenues (and expenditures) occurs without having to resort to institution building or to establishing a strong income taxation system. This is a particularly attractive option for leaders who heavily discount the future and are not concerned with the economic growth-enhancing benefits of establishing a functioning tax base (Levi, 1989). Such is the behavior of the so-called predatory state, wherein rulers prefer the easy option of capturing rents today rather than spend the time and effort to build stable institutions for a robust economy that can be taxed in the future (Levi, 1981; Bates and Lien, 1985; Olson, 1993). These leaders do not have assurances that their rule will survive long enough to reap such future rewards. Grabbing natural resource rents in the present, even if it portends negative long-term consequences for development, is the best way to secure future survival.[2] States led by more stationary rulers, on the other hand, need not risk future development and prosperity by overinvesting in the extractive economy.

2.1.2   Does Natural Resource Wealth Always Hinder Development?

For all of these pernicious effects on politics, there come to mind several examples of resource-producing countries that experience relatively better governance, such as Brazil, Canada, Malaysia, the United Kingdom, and the United States (Mitchell, 2011). Furthermore, the stability-enhancing effects of resource wealth are exemplified by the enduring regimes in Saudi Arabia, Putin's Russia, and Angola, while these effects

---

[2] I thank Victor Menaldo for raising this point.

were absent in Imperial Iran, Mexico under the PRI, and postindependence Nigeria.

This has given rise to a new branch of scholarly work questioning the scale and reach of theories of natural resource politics. Much of this began with Benjamin Smith's work on understanding why regimes like Indonesia were able to survive the boom-and-bust cycle of the 1970s and 1980s, while others like Iran collapsed. Smith (2007) came to the conclusion that the conditions under which oil is discovered matter for oil's stability-enhancing effects, particularly the development of institutions linking the state to civil society. Where oil shaped the very nature of the state, it leads to the negative outcomes commonly associated with resource wealth; but where the state had already reached "late development" – as in Canada and the United States – oil's effects on governance were not as pronounced.

Dunning (2008) continued this line of reasoning to show that resource wealth effects are conditional on inequality and institutional factors that can mediate oil's specific effect on democracy. This accounts for why oil hinders democracy in places like Angola or Algeria but not in Brazil or Venezuela. Indeed, Menaldo (2012) argues that this is why the Middle East has largely avoided the wave of democratization that hit Latin America. A broad-ranging economic analysis of natural resource–wealth effects suggests that these conditions depend on whether "good institutional characteristics emerged prior to the discovery of natural resources" (Lederman and Maloney, 2008, 32). In this way, the debate has been somewhat reframed to an analysis of the factors involved in the "conditional resource curse," whereby some countries seem cursed by resources while others seem blessed by them (Kurtz and Brooks, 2011).

The idea that natural resource wealth is not politically exogenous emerged as a key theme from this line of thought (Haber and Menaldo, 2011). Brooks and Kurtz (2016) assert that resource extraction is endogenous to industrialization: policies that foster industrial development provide the foundation for both natural resource production and the social factors that underpin democratization. Menaldo (2016) examines institutional development as a contributing factor to resource wealth. By illuminating the endogeneity of resource riches to political and economic capacity, Menaldo (2016) avers that a country's reliance on resource wealth is itself an outcome of bad governance, which begets further poor governance outcomes. The conditionality of Menaldo's "institutions curse" thus depends on the level of institutional development prior to extracting natural resources. This explains why resource wealth has been a blessing in countries like Mexico, Indonesia, and the

Gulf states, but a curse for governance in Nigeria, the former Soviet states, and Venezuela.

Beyond this spatial variation, scholars have also pointed to a temporal dimension of the resource curse, finding that authoritarianism endures in petrostates primarily after the 1970s (see Aslaksen, 2010, for a review). Not coincidentally, this is a period "marked by widespread state ownership of resource wealth, which contrasts with ownership patterns earlier in history" (Goldberg et al., 2008, 438). Results from Ross (2012) and Andersen and Ross (2013) point to the strongest evidence of a resource curse in the post-1979 era, while the weakest results for the Haber and Menaldo (2011) argument against a resource curse appear in the post-1973 period (Liou and Musgrave, 2014).[3] These two studies, among others, point out the post-1970s period is markedly different from prior periods, but the explanation as to why this is the case has yet to be tested systematically. My own suggestion that nationalization provides an answer is not a novel one – indeed, Ross (2012), Andersen and Ross (2013), and Menaldo (2016) speculate (but do not demonstrate) that nationalization matters, and Jones Luong and Weinthal (2010) point to the wave of expropriation in the 1970s as a structural shift in the capture of oil rents – but I show why more work is needed to illustrate the validity of this argument.

2.1.3   Theorizing Nationalization within Resource Politics

In their book on the politics of resource ownership, *Oil Is Not a Curse*, Pauline Jones Luong and Erika Weinthal develop a theory that ownership structure – i.e., the degree of state intervention in the resource sector – plays an intervening role in the relationship between oil wealth and weak fiscal regimes. These weak fiscal regimes in turn are "linked directly to poor economic growth, enfeebled states, and authoritarian regimes" (Jones Luong and Weinthal, 2010, 27). Employing a case study approach based on evidence from the former Soviet states, the authors provide empirical support for their theoretical finding that state ownership of the oil sector fosters weak fiscal regimes while private domestic ownership fosters strong fiscal regimes (see also Jones Luong and Weinthal, 2001,

---

[3] Part of the reason for such stark differences (despite using similar data) is that Haber and Menaldo include country-fixed effects in a dynamic model of democratic transition, while Ross employs country-fixed effects in a static logistic model. Furthermore, the interpretation of a treatment effect (oil wealth as the treatment) in Haber and Menaldo's analysis for the post-1970s period is not appropriate, given the lack of a credible control group. See Andersen and Ross (2013) for more detail on these points.

2006; Weinthal and Jones Luong, 2006). And as conventional wisdom posits, the fiscal link – how the government collects revenue and how that revenue is distributed – is the primary linkage between natural resource wealth and political development.

To explain different degrees of state intervention, Jones Luong and Weinthal (2010) begin with the assumption that leaders are sovereignty maximizers and thus prefer, all else equal, to control natural resource production. But leaders must balance this desire with their primary goal of staying in power; hence, despite preferring nationalization, leaders end up choosing different ownership structures based on two disparate political factors. The first is the degree of alternative revenue streams: whether leaders have other commodities or products whose export or sale provides a large share of total government revenues. This is also the case in states with advanced economies, in which corporate and personal income taxes generate the bulk of the government's fiscal revenues. The second is the level of distributional conflict, defined as the degree to which leaders face strong and credible domestic opponents with fiscal autonomy, which includes political parties in the opposition or subnational governments with secessionist demands. Higher political contestation, in other words, implies a stronger level of distributional conflict.

Jones Luong and Weinthal (2010, 301–309) argue that when both factors are favorable to rulers – high access to alternative revenues and low contestation – leaders will opt for nationalization. Because this scenario offers the most assurance to leaders' continued survival in power, they can choose their most preferred outcome: state control over natural resource extraction. But the interesting action in the case of low distributional conflict is how access to alternative revenues shapes the type of nationalization pursued. When leaders lack this access, they choose to nationalize without control over operations (which I refer to as the formation of nonoperational SOEs); when leaders are flush with alternative revenue streams, they choose to nationalize operations (i.e., form operational SOEs). By contrast, when access to alternative revenues is limited and distributional conflict is high, leaders choose their least preferred option of natural resource extraction by private international firms. In this case, leaders are politically constrained and must choose to give up sovereignty over resources in exchange for fiscal support from outside firms. This line of argument therefore implies that politically strong leaders nationalize, while politically weak leaders instead rely on private operating firms.

Yet the data on operational nationalizations show the opposite pattern, in line with earlier work on the expropriation of foreign direct investment (Li, 2009).[4] Leaders who perceive their days in office are numbered are the most likely to nationalize operations, while leaders with greater prospects of survival prefer nonstate firms to control operations. What explains this divergence? I agree that the decision over ownership structures is based on which choice maximizes a leader's time in office, but disagree on which option fulfills this goal. By not incorporating the survival-enhancing effects of nationalization – on which I elaborate in greater detail in the next section – into a leader's decision-making calculus, Jones Luong and Weinthal (2010) assume that private ownership provides greater prospects for political survival. This assumption is based on their empirical finding that private operations foster strong *fiscal regimes*, a finding that I do not dispute. But this misses the more important outcome of *fiscal strength*: the actual collection of resource revenues by governments in resource-rich countries. I argue the immediate fiscal rewards from operational nationalization outpace those from maintaining private operating firms after resources have been initially developed. This stems from a combination of de facto state control over production levels and the ability of the state to narrow the information gap regarding the true costs and profits of resource production. (In Chapter 3, I describe how this component of measuring nationalization differs from the existing approach and why this matters for the broader argument.)

From the perspective of a leader trying to consolidate power to survive, the immediate financial windfall from nationalizing operations is life-saving. Even if nationalization results in a weaker capacity to collect taxes from the broader economy in the future, it is still the choice that will provide the leader with the greatest odds of immediate survival. The conventional theory for why leaders nationalize is thus problematic because it does not take into account the importance of fiscal strength, nor does it explicitly model the endogeneity of political survival to the decision-making process.

2.1.4   Alternatives to *Why Leaders Nationalize: Bargaining, Institutions, and Ideology*

There is a burgeoning literature on why states expropriate in the first place, though there is a lack of consensus on the factors that

---

[4] Note that Li's (2009) findings only held for leaders of autocratic regimes, in which leaders with short time horizons could expropriate foreign direct investment (FDI) without being constrained by strong executive checks and balances.

determine nationalization. Here I summarize the existing scholarship – in addition to the work of Pauline Jones Luong and Erika Weinthal – on determinants of nationalization introduced in Chapter 1.

The starting point for political economists is the theory of the obsolescing bargain, in which nationalization is viewed as the inevitable culmination of an escalating negotiation between states and firms (see Vernon, 1971). Firms have the greatest leverage during the exploration and early production phase since extraction costs are high and exploration is risky. But this leverage diminishes over time. As costs decline and resource discoveries are confirmed, the state takes advantage of firms' sunk costs and fixed assets to renegotiate for greater shares in resource profits. But as long as firms acquiesce to lower and lower shares of revenues, leaders will continue the structure of private ownership. At some point, however, the state's demands exceed what firms are willing to accept to remain profitable and higher tax rates on firms give way to outright nationalization of firms' production.[5]

Building on the foundations of the obsolescing bargain is the argument that expropriations are determined by high commodity prices and weak tax-collection mechanisms (Manzano and Monaldi, 2009; Chang et al., 2010). This is the case for both oil nationalizations and the expropriation of non-oil minerals like bauxite, copper, lead, nickel, silver, tin, and zinc (Duncan, 2006; Warshaw, 2012). The logic behind this argument is that nationalization is costly – either because of international retaliation, reputation costs, or because of lost production during expropriation (Kobrin, 1979; Boardman and Vining, 1989; Bohn and Deacon, 2000; Jensen et al., 2019).[6] When prices are high, the benefits of nationalization outweigh the costs; additionally, high prices can create stronger incentives to nationalize given the larger immediate prize of expropriation, irrespective of its costs (Guriev et al., 2011). But low expropriation costs can also spur nationalization even in times of low commodity prices; this is likely if leaders have reason to believe that FDI will not be impacted by expropriation or if the resulting SOE faces low production inefficiencies (Stroebel and van Benthem, 2013).

[5] Prior work also finds a domino effect that mimics the obsolescing bargain, whereby nationalization in neighboring countries prompts nationalization at home (Kobrin, 1985; Hajzler, 2012; Mahdavi, 2014).

[6] There is evidence that leaders may not care about the reputation or investor costs of expropriation when it comes to nationalization of natural resource wealth since the benefits almost always outweigh the risks. This helps explain why expropriation is much more common in lucrative extractive industries than in manufacturing industries where profit margins are lower. See Jensen and Johnston (2011).

Scholars also agree that weak institutional checks on the executive provide the opportunity for leaders to expropriate without broad consensus. Jensen (2008) began this line of argument by showing that leaders with fewer legislative and judicial constraints are more likely to nationalize, making expropriation more likely under autocratic regimes compared to democracies. Li (2009) took this a step farther by introducing leader time horizons into the equation: political institutions matter primarily because they serve to constrain political incentives to expropriate when leaders highly discount the future. In other words, shortsighted leaders may all *prefer* to behave opportunistically, but they can only *act* on these preferences when facing fewer structural roadblocks like democratic institutions and executive constraints.

Empirical studies of nationalizations in the oil sector corroborate this viewpoint (Jones Luong and Weinthal, 2010; Guriev et al., 2011; Warshaw, 2012). As Wilson and Wright (2017) demonstrate, however, legislative constraints are effective in lowering the risk of expropriation even within autocratic regimes, but only in dictatorships that rely on broader coalitions for support (see Jensen et al., 2014, for a contrasting view). In dictatorships marked by personalist or absolutist control, these legislative institutions merely serve the functions of providing information to the dictator about his elites and offering elites the means to distribute clientelist goods and services (Svolik, 2012).

There is more doubt about the role of political ideology on the likelihood of nationalization. Some argue that left-leaning governments are more likely to seize control of assets for the state (Manzano and Monaldi, 2009), while others find that political ideology is not a motivating factor in resource nationalization, especially in the Latin American context (Berrios et al., 2011). Even expanding the argument to include land and nonresource nationalizations, scholars still find that ideology does not determine nationalization (Albertus and Menaldo, 2012). This would fit in with arguments about how ideology impacts the type of nationalization but not the decision to nationalize in the first place. As Kobrin (1984, 337) writes, ideology and other political considerations "are more likely to affect the circumstances of a takeover – like timing, rhetoric, and negotiating posture – than to determine whether expropriation takes place or not."

In line with the argument that leaders nationalize to consolidate their power, prior work shows how leaders can use SOEs to bolster their rule. In the oil sector, NOCs are often employed as "instruments of control" whereby leaders target clientelistic and universal benefits to buy support (Cheon et al., 2015). The differences in the institutional design of NOCs influence to what extent the state can interfere with demands that the NOC perform noncommercial activities like providing petroleum subsidies, social programs, state employment, and infrastructural development (McPherson, 2003; Victor et al., 2012). But the success of achieving these goals, and thus securing support for the regime, very much depends on the ability to finance these activities.

2.1.5   Time Inconsistency and the Natural Resources Trap

Thus far, I have considered nationalization from the perspective of leaders in resource-producing countries. But how is nationalization viewed from the perspective of operating firms? Do firms have a sense of which leaders will nationalize their assets? If so, why do these firms even enter into contracts with leaders known to engage in opportunism?

Given the high sophistication of extractive resource firms, it is not likely that they are ignorant of the potential risks of nationalization. It is more likely instead that nationalization is an expected outcome that is priced in to the initial contract with the host government (Schwartz and Trolle, 2010). For example, firms could seek to capture as much of the profits up front and in the early years of production as possible, including differential rents but excluding quasi-rents (which are needed for future recovery costs). In the oil industry, this can take the form of tax exemptions, underbidding in the initial auction, and demanding cost reimbursement (Mead, 1994; Baunsgaard, 2001). The latter is a particularly attractive defensive option, whereby the operating firm is guaranteed payment by the state for its incurred preproduction costs prior to evidence of a successful discovery. But, if firms are front-loading much of the profits from resource extraction, then the state almost has no choice but to nationalize as soon as it is feasible. This phenomenon is known as the "natural resource trap," as eloquently described by Hogan et al. (2010, 3):

Because MNCs anticipate expropriation, they will offer a contract that compensates them for the risk. But this forces the (host country) to expropriate; if they do not firms will be rewarded with a windfall gain that may be politically intolerable. It is a double trap, because lack of credibility not only creates a contract that in itself is more vulnerable, but also because it forces even those governments that would prefer to operate in a stable and law-abiding context to fall in the vicious cycle with the rest.

This line of thinking expands the theory of the obsolescing bargain to consider how firms will respond in the face of these risks. In the initial stages of an extractive resource's historical development, one tactic adopted by firms is portfolio diversification. Consider, for example, the international petroleum industry in the period between World War II and the 1973 Arab Oil Embargo. The market was dominated by a handful of major firms, chief among them the Seven Sisters of American and European companies (see Chapter 1), that held assets in nearly all non-Communist countries producing oil (see Yergin, 1991). Expropriation in one state could be offset by ramping up production in another and by increasing exploration efforts to constantly develop new assets (Bamberg, 2000). Today, such diversification by a concentrated set of major firms is the strategy adopted by the Big Four of lithium extraction.

Firm concentration can form a collective front that could punish against expropriating states and implicitly sanction its own members for continuing to invest in a host state that exhibits opportunistic and predatory behavior. This is the same self-enforcing behavior adopted by international lenders in the context of sovereign debt defaults (see Wright, 2002; Tomz, 2007). For example, a bank that is caught lending to a defaulting debtor is punished by other banks in its consortium. This structure provides banks the confidence to lend capital to a borrower in a risky context since they know that any default will have actual reputation costs for the borrower's ability to raise future capital. In extractive industries, MNCs can apply the same tactic to any firm that invests in an expropriatory host state by disbanding partnerships with the firm or excluding the firm from industry associations.

Despite several defensive measures at their disposal, firms still cannot sufficiently prevent expropriation. To date, there is no consensus contract structure or firm behavior that effectively thwarts the threat of extractive resource nationalization. Perhaps contracts and defensive measures exist in the abstract that impede nationalization (see Hogan and Sturzenegger, 2010). But in practice firms have yet to find effective designs to protect their investments in the long run.

With this in mind, another perspective is that firms know they will be expropriated but expect that they will be invited back once the host government realizes it cannot fiscally sustain profitable operations. That is, since expropriation is inevitable and since there is no contract structure that can prevent firms' assets from seizure, firms accept the initial risk with the knowledge that they will return after expropriation – albeit with a lower share of the profits. This would make nationalization more like a renegotiation of the existing market structure in which MNCs extract resources while states collect taxes and fees. I consider this postnationalization possibility later on in the chapter as the outcome of when operational nationalization fails to endure.

2.1.6   Degrees of Nationalization at Different Points in Time

Nationalization is not a one-size-fits-all affair, but rather falls into the two broader categories depicted in Jones Luong and Weinthal (2001) of nationalization with and without control of production. Sometimes this distinction exists because of changes in the production cycle over time within a given country. When resources are first discovered and the government opts for nationalization to form an SOE, it will typically defer control over operations to private firms (Tordo et al., 2011; Victor, 2013). This stems from the government's lack of experience with operating what is a complex industrial process, especially in the oil and deep-shaft mining industries. This expertise develops over time as the SOE works (but does not operate) alongside private firms, allowing the state to obtain information and technical knowledge about the extractive sector (Grayson, 1981). At a certain experiential tipping point, the state will have enough knowledge to allow the SOE to operate the country's fields or mines, culminating in the formation of a full-fledged, operational SOE. In the late stages of the production cycle, when complexities arise anew, the state may choose to partially privatize the SOE and in the process, give back control over operations to private firms.

Yet the distinction between these two types of nationalization is not solely due to technical capacity or production cycles. Klapp (1987) postulates that leaders choose one type over the other based on the bargaining constraints they face at home and from abroad. In emerging markets, leaders are constrained by international lenders who can withhold financing for extractive resource projects; in advanced markets, leaders are constrained by domestic interest groups that would rather see resource production controlled by private firms as opposed to the state. These limitations manifest in a model of SOEs whereby the state avoids direct expropriation of private assets and instead establishes an entity that competes with other firms over extraction. Although the focus of Klapp (1987) is on these types of SOEs – in both developed and developing country contexts – the theory would predict that absent these constraints, leaders will choose a more direct role for the state in resource operations. This would conform to both the Jones Luong and Weinthal category of state ownership with production control and my category of operational SOE. A key distinction, however, is that Klapp (1987) only considers constraints that are external to the leader's circle of power – international banks and domestic interest groups – without bringing the internal constraints that affect a leader's survival odds to the fore.

A critical challenge to leaders' survival prospects is domestic fiscal pressure, which can affect the choice leaders make across different points in time. Periods of large deficits and high levels of debt – a common occurrence in resource-rich states once booms turn to busts (Manzano and Rigobon, 2001; Nooruddin, 2008) – will push both strong and weak leaders to pursue nationalization of operations rather than nationalizing without operational control. The immediate gains to establishing an operational SOE can offset fiscal losses incurred during long periods of debt or economic crisis. These fiscal pressures can also come in the form of ambitious expenditures, even in the absence of low prices. This is often the case in rapidly modernizing states, in which earlier resource discoveries encourage leaders to pursue massive investments in physical infrastructure, education, health, and other public goods and services. As these expenditures ramp up – sometimes exponentially – leaders without access to alternative revenue streams will look to nationalization as a lifeline (contra Jones Luong and Weinthal, 2010). This is particularly acute for leaders who face credible oppositions or those in weakly consolidated regimes that lack strong support from elite coalitions (see Bueno de Mesquita et al., 2003; Bueno de Mesquita and Smith, 2010), but can affect even the strongest and most durable of leaders as well.

SOEs established in the developed world differ remarkably from the SOEs discussed up to this point. These entities were designed not as a means to control foreign-held assets via expropriation but rather, as Llewelyn Hughes writes, as a "vehicle for business-government cooperation" (Hughes, 2014, 31). In early twentieth-century France, for instance, negotiated agreements between the oil sector and the French government set up regulations over market share within national markets. Because the state at the time lacked strong bureaucratic institutions (relative to states like the UK and the US), these negotiations resulted in the formation of the large, diversified state-owned oil firms of Compagnie Française des Pétroles (CFP) and Elf-Aquitaine. This is in contrast to a case like Japan, in which the high quality of preexisting bureaucratic institutions gave the state leverage over firms during these negotiations. This leverage resulted in smaller, less diversified SOEs, like the Imperial Oil Development Corporation and the Japanese National Oil Company (JNOC). As these developed-country SOEs adapted to new market conditions – namely the rise of Middle East oil producers – firm strategies shifted to more liberalization and less state intervention. By the late 1980s, only a handful of advanced-market countries still maintained NOCs, chief among them the Norwegian NOC Statoil (now Equinor).

A softer version of this kind of liberalization is partial privatization through public listing of SOEs. Carney (2018) argues that this allows leaders to maintain some control over operations while also forcing state entities to compete for financing on the open market. These publicly listed SOEs can therefore generate greater returns compared to their prelisting earnings. But since they are typically still majority-owned by the state, leaders can continue using these entities for political gains, according to Carney (2018), to "preserve the power and stability of the incumbent regime." This is an interesting endgame strategy for leaders who inherit aging SOEs; in a sense, public listing allows leaders to squeeze out more revenues from an SOE that is otherwise declining in profitability. But it also serves as a response to international pressures for liberalization, whether during the heyday of the Washington Consensus (Williamson, 1990) or as part of contemporary conditional lending requirements by the IMF (Vreeland, 2007).

Yet despite this assortment of studies, we still do not understand nationalization's (or privatization's) broader consequences. We expect that a strong fiscal regime (Jones Luong and Weinthal, 2010) will promote economic development, state capacity, and good governance (Tilly, 1975; Levi, 1989; North and Weingast, 1989). The choice of ownership structure to manage resource wealth clearly has important impacts. But it is unclear how varieties of state intervention will affect the two most vital considerations for any ruler: how much money the government has at its disposal (fiscal strength) and how long the leader will last in power (leadership survival). We also still lack clarity on why leaders choose one ownership structure over another, especially for cases in which some resource sectors are under the aegis of SOEs while other sectors remain managed by private firms. This is further complicated by changes over time that do not conform with technical dynamics or changes in institutional quality, such that we cannot use existing explanations to answer the question of why leaders choose to nationalize at some points in time but not others. I contend that only by incorporating a leader's perceptions of survival in the decision-making process can we make sense of the empirical patterns that characterize not only the historical context of state-dominated industries like oil and gas, but also natural resources like metals and minerals that will undergo different varieties of nationalization in the future.

2.2   The Operational Nationalization Theory

Prior to developing the theoretical argument, I begin with a brief discussion of state intervention across the natural resource production cycle. Before natural resources are first discovered within their countries, leaders hire nonstate, outside firms to explore for potential deposits. These contracts typically provide the state with up-front royalties in exchange for property rights and promises that exploring firms keep some share of profits from production if resources are discovered. Upon discovery (and sometimes beforehand), leaders set a tax rate on operating firms for revenues generated from the production of developed resources. Typically this arrangement excessively favors the firm, such that the state captures only a minority of profits earned from resource sales. Yet from the perspective of the state, this small share is nonetheless preferred over the alternative of not contracting a firm for operations, which would entail no extraction whatsoever. At this stage of production, then, leaders are satisfied with the status quo of taxing firms since the only other viable option is to exclude operating firms – leading to no production and thus zero revenues for the state.

Leaders consider renegotiating these agreements when they learn about the possibility of effectively earning greater revenues. This knowledge is gained from the spread of information about the agreements of competitors – leaders of other countries with similar resource endowments – that entail higher revenue-sharing terms for the state relative to operating firms. This diffused information serves as an indicator that a higher tax rate is a feasible option. In addition to the desire not to be outstaged by their competitors, leaders will seek to renegotiate their existing agreements to increase the state's collection of resource revenues.

Renegotiation offers leaders two types of choices to boost their take-home revenues. The first comprises maintaining the current framework of outside firms producing natural resources and paying the government taxes, royalties, or any other similar fee structure. To increase government revenues within this option, leaders will renegotiate for higher tax rates, higher production levels, or both. If firms accept renegotiations, then the government achieves its goal of increasing revenues but still faces the existing information asymmetry over accurate reporting of costs and profits. The second type of choice comprises nationalization of operations. This outcome follows from renegotiations that result in either seizure of existing firms' extractive assets (with or without compensation), or takeover of producing fields without asset seizure. In both cases, control over production is transfered to a state-owned entity. Resource revenues generated by this operational SOE are controlled by the state, which can in theory tax the SOE's income at 100 percent without fear of market exit, but in practice chooses an optimal tax rate to ensure effective future production.

How does this choice affect government capture of revenues from natural resource extraction? In Chapter 1, I sketched out three mechanisms for why this might be the case – information asymmetry, production elasticity, and operational efficiency – which I delve into below in greater detail. But for now, take the argument as given that governments nationalizing operations will be rewarded with high revenues early on, but low revenues in the long run, given SOE operating inefficiencies compared to private firms. In addition, nationalization is risky: international investors may retaliate directly with embargoes or litigation, or indirectly by decreasing FDI in the broader economy (Jensen and Johnston, 2011). Nationalization could also fail to materialize if the state underestimates the technical challenges of extraction or cannot clear the financial roadblocks to selling resources on the international market.

By contrast, maintaining private firms means low revenues early on – despite higher taxes after renegotiations – given the asymmetries of information between firm and state on the true costs of production. Over time, however, these firms' high operating efficiency ensures stable returns for the state. This explains why conventional political-economy theories would valuate private operations positively in expectation, and nationalized operations negatively in expectation. But the viability of increasing taxes on private firms as an alternative to nationalization is only attractive in as much as the government can effectively prevent firms from misreporting tax revenues. Technical information asymmetries – specifically, information about the true cost of production and the true level of profits from resource sales – are only one reason for the gap between what the host state is owed in tax revenue and what it actually collects from the operating firm (Beer and Loeprick, 2017). States with weak bureaucratic capacity, for instance, will find it more difficult to enforce proper tax payments from any firm in the economy, let alone an extractive resource firm with informational advantages (Levi, 1989; Brautigam et al., 2008). The ability to sanction firms for evading taxes depends not only on the development of strong tax systems (Bates and Lien, 1985) but also on the strength of supporting institutions like an effective judiciary and statistical agency (Besley and Persson, 2014), and on the political "reach" to monitor all corners of the country's sovereign borders (Kugler and Tammen, 2012).

It could also be the case that the negative political optics of increasing taxation as opposed to nationalizing operations will pose a threat for leaders who lack strong and secure political positions. The decision to increase taxes instead of nationalization could be publicly perceived as the leader's inability to extract higher returns from operating firms or, even worse, as deliberate capitulation to foreign agents. As I explain in Chapter 4, this was a prominently vocalized criticism of the Shah of Iran in 1950. His government's decision to eschew nationalization and restructure contractual agreements with the Anglo-Iranian Oil Company

(AIOC) only compounded his weakening grip on power with the rise of his pro-nationalization prime minister, Mohammad Mossadegh.

Fast forward nearly 70 years to Congolese President Joseph Kabila's decision to renegotiate cobalt contracts in March 2018. Under reforms to Congo's mining law, the government mandated a sharp increase in royalties paid by MNCs like Glencore and Randgold. But serious doubts exist as to whether the companies will not only accept the terms of the new legislation but also comply in good faith with higher payments to the Congolese state. That he did not opt for outright nationalization of cobalt operations is already viewed as a missed opportunity for Kabila to assert sovereignty over what are publicly perceived to be dishonest mining MNCs. The chairman of the state-owned mining firm (which lacks control over operations) has, for instance, criticized Glencore and others for "manipulated costs and production figures, resulting in lower dividends and royalty payments to the Congolese government." This decision could be a gamble for Kabila, whose long-term survival in power – after formally stepping down from the presidency in 2019, but still in control of much of the government – hinges on his future ability to mobilize mass and elite support.[7]

Which choice leaders ultimately make – whether to maintain the status quo, renegotiate to increase taxation, or nationalize operations – depends on which option maximizes their odds of survival. On the one hand, leaders with low odds of survival will gamble on the opportunity to increase their fiscal strength through nationalization even if it means less revenue in the future. These leaders desperately need to consolidate their power – otherwise, they face ouster, exile, imprisonment, and even death. Revenues from nationalized natural resources provide an effective means to buy support and to ward off challengers to ensure leaders' survival in power. Incorporating these political benefits into the valuation, nationalization would thus have a higher expected value for these leaders compared to maintaining operations by nonstate firms. On the other hand, leaders with more assurances of survival will instead opt for renegotiations over higher taxes on operating firms and eschew nationalization. For these leaders, nonstate operations provide the highest rewards in expectation.

---

[7] This vignette of Congo's cobalt governance draws from Leila Hubeaut and Ergen Ege, "Revision of Democratic Republic of Congo's mining code driven by cobalt price rise," *Dentons* July 2, 2018; "Congo mines minister insists no compromise on new mining code," *Reuters* September 12, 2018; David Pilling, "Cut-throat cobalt drama will leave Congolese people the losers," *The Financial Times* May 16, 2018; and Alexandra Wexler and Scott Patterson, "As cobalt prices rise, Congo raises pressure on Western mining giants," *The Wall Street Journal* February 6, 2018. See also footnote 7 in Chapter 1.

In making this decision, leaders will look to the future consequences of each option for their survival in power. For strong leaders who choose not to nationalize, the positive expected value of maintaining nonstate operations will contribute to their continued political survival. If unforeseen challenges to their rule arise, however, these leaders might rue passing up an opportunity to strengthen their power. By opting not to capture the lion's share of rents, which instead are typically forfeited to foreign MNCs and outside firms, this choice prevents leaders from taking full advantage of their resource endowments. Where leaders choose instead to nationalize operations, these rents accrue directly to the state, fostering more durable, lasting leaders. If the gamble of nationalization pays off, in other words, paradoxically it is the weaker leader who becomes stronger because of the fiscal windfalls from nationalizing at a key stage of consolidating power.

This is a paradox because it directly contradicts the conventional wisdom on predatory states (Bates and Lien, 1985; Levi, 1989; Olson, 1993). The "take what you can, give nothing back" behavior of short-sighted leaders should lead to an unstable regime and a relatively quick exit from power. This would also be true of nationalizing operations if one only considers its negative expected value from standard political-economy models. But this viewpoint does not properly incorporate the challenges of hanging onto power for this type of leader and the immediate survival-enhancing benefits of nationalization. By securing an early infusion of revenues, leaders who nationalize operations can distribute this wealth to loyal elites, co-opted opponents, and would-be challengers. Shoring up political support allows leaders to survive in office longer, even if at first glance the act of nationalization hinders their long-term rewards.[8]

This logic leads to the key takeaway of the argument: the probability of survival and the decision to nationalize resource operations are mutually endogenous. Leader perceptions of survival odds influence the choice of nationalizing operations; through its effect on fiscal strength, this choice influences the future odds of survival. In the sections that follow, I describe in detail the argument's three observable implications, which I empirically test in the remaining chapters of the book. First, nationalization is prompted by the diffusion of information that sparks leaders to renegotiate their existing agreements with operating firms. Second, nationalizing operations increases the actual collection of resource revenues by the state relative to maintaining private operating firms. And third, nationalization increases leader survival.

[8] I thank Victor Menaldo for this point.

2.2.1   *Information Diffusion as the Spark for Nationalization*

New information about the potential to garner a better deal from firms producing natural resources prompts a leader to reconsider her options. On the one hand, nationalization of operations can increase a leader's fiscal strength in the short term at the expense of future gains. On the other hand, maintaining nonstate firms in charge of operations limits short-term revenues but offers long-term benefits. Which one a leader chooses depends on which option maximizes her survival odds. In this way, information diffusion serves as a spark for a leader to update her survival beliefs and choose the degree of state intervention – nationalize operations or not – that will satisfy these updated beliefs.

A better deal can refer to improving either the host government's share of profits – for example, moving from a fifty-fifty split with an outside firm to a fifty-five/forty-five split in favor of the government – or the firm's actual payment of its promised share. The latter refers to firms overreporting costs or underreporting production so that the overall size of profits is artificially diminished. A contemporary example of this in extractive resource sectors is "transfer mispricing": firms misreport procurement costs to host governments to pay lower taxes on reported income. For example, mining firms can misreport to governments the true costs of procuring extractive equipment when these transactions occur between the firm and its subsidiary as opposed to on the open market, thus making it challenging for the government to monitor the actual price (Readhead, 2016). With this or any type of misreporting, the government still receives its proper percentage of taxes, but the amount of profits accrued will be far lower than the amount the government is due.

In both cases, new information about the possibility of greater revenues will prompt the host government to renegotiate its existing arrangements, either by increasing its profit share or by increasing enforcement of misreporting. International competitors are one source for this new information. If a leader learns that his competitor – the leader of another resource-producing country with similar geological endowments and working with the same operating firm – is receiving a higher share, then he will see this deal as not only attractive but also attainable. Up until receiving this information, this higher share may not have seemed feasible; forcing the firm to give up more profits to the government could lead to the firm exiting the market and leaving the government empty-handed. But with the knowledge that other leaders have effectively negotiated for a higher profit share *without* losing the operating firm in the process, a leader views renegotiations for a better deal as a viable and achievable action.

Another source for information diffusion is revelation of agreement details by the media. In the pre-OPEC era of petroleum markets, leaders would learn about the terms of their competitors' agreements with international oil companies through newspaper and radio reports. News of the Middle East's first fifty-fifty revenue-sharing plan, signed between Saudi Arabia and the American-owned Aramco, on December 30, 1950, made its way to the Shah of Iran via *The New York Times* three days later and spurred his own call for renegotiations – an event I analyze in detail in Chapter 4.[9] But this is not just a phenomenon of the past. In Tanzania in July 2014, for instance, a leaked gas contract between the government and the Norwegian company Statoil (now Equinor) prompted local media to declare that the Tanzanian government was "fooled" out of almost $1 billion in lost profits because of how production sharing was to be structured over the long term.[10] Such revelations will also prompt leaders to renegotiate existing agreements for a greater share of natural resource profits.

This part of the argument is not attributing a causal effect to information diffusion. Rather, the information diffused serves as a prompt for leaders to update their beliefs about political survival based on their existing revenue-sharing agreements. In this way, the diffusion of information is a spark for leaders to reconsider their choices about the fiscal terms over how natural resources are extracted within their countries; it is simply providing an impetus to update beliefs about future prospects in general. In the context of individual decision-making, this phenomenon is often referred to as Bayesian updating: when an individual with existing beliefs about the world learns something relevant to these beliefs, they will update their belief structure to incorporate this new piece of information (see Box and Tiao, 1973). For a leader contemplating future political survival, new information about the *possibility* of greater revenues from natural resources will be incorporated into an updated probability of survival. Renegotiations with operating firms – either resulting in nationalization or not – turns this possibility into reality.

Without such information, leaders will be content with their share of resource revenues. As long as firms are paying their taxes and royalties consistently and without delay, leaders have no reason to

---

[9] "Saudi Arabia gets half US oil profit; Ibn Saud and Aramco agree to 50–50 sharing plan from January 1, 1950." *The New York Times* January 3, 1951. Page A1; A14.

[10] The Citizen Reporter, 2014, "$1 bn. loss: Who's fooling Tanzanians?," *The Citizen*. Accessed from www.thecitizen.co.tz/News/-1bn-loss--Who-s-fooling-Tanzanians-/-/1840392/2382948/-/ya2a1oz/-/index.html.

suspect that they are being underpaid (relative to the market value of the commodity) or that a better deal could be had without interrupting their income stream. This behavior echoes the conventional wisdom from law and social psychology on bargaining divergence after informational exchange. Absent information about the true costs of production and profit-sharing arrangements that others receive, individuals will converge on satisfactory negotiations. However, once this information is revealed, individuals will try to renegotiate or will walk away from the bargaining table altogether (see Thompson and Loewenstein, 1992; Loewenstein and Moore, 2004).

The argument implies that leaders who are exposed to diffused information about better revenue-sharing agreements are more likely to renegotiate their existing contracts. These renegotiations will result in nationalization for leaders who perceive lower odds of survival, and in maintaining nonstate firms in charge of operations for leaders who perceive higher odds of survival. Empirically, testing this aspect of the argument involves either using a proxy for information diffusion in a broad, cross-national setting or analyzing instances of diffused information in a single case or set of country cases. In the oil industry, the creation of OPEC provided a forum for leaders to meet and discuss pricing mechanisms regarding how the Seven Sisters operated in their host countries. This fostered an environment in which information about different revenue-sharing arrangements was revealed by leaders of countries in the cartel, all in the name of reducing transaction and information costs associated with their prior experience negotiating unilateral agreements with the Seven Sisters (see Colgan, 2019). Leaders whose countries are members of this forum are more likely to be exposed to such diffused information. If the argument about information diffusion and renegotiation is true, then being an OPEC member should correspond to a higher likelihood of nationalization.

Of course, OPEC membership is only a rough proxy for exposure to diffused information. Case studies can help to trace the process of how information diffusion sparks negotiation. The spread of information to a specific leader about better revenue-sharing terms achieved by competitors should lead to renegotiation resulting in either nationalization or maintaining outside firms at higher tax rates (or equivalent if status quo); the alternative (i.e., null hypothesis) is that information diffusion does not prompt renegotiations. One example of information diffusion that I draw on in the chapters ahead is the signing of new agreements between host governments and international oil companies. Leaders learn of the contents of these agreements – specifically, the degree of revenue sharing between government and firm – from either the media or from within an information sharing forum like OPEC or, more recently, networks like the New Petroleum Producers Discussion Group. The argument would predict that with this newfound knowledge in hand, relatively stronger leaders will maintain outside firms but seek to renegotiate their own agreements to increase their governments' collection of resource revenues while relatively weaker leaders will nationalize operations.

Temporally, the diffusion of information about revenue-sharing agreements only advances in time, with no opportunities for backsliding or reversion. In other words, more and more information is diffused as time progresses, suggesting a race to the bottom whereby leaders continually renegotiate until all resource-producing countries have nationalized operations. That the data do not support this characterization reflects not the desire of leaders to choose this option but rather the *capability* to do so.

The choice of an operational SOE necessitates having a workforce with the technical skills needed to explore for and produce resources. In natural resource sectors like oil, gas, coal, minerals, and deep-shaft metals, exploration and production are highly complex endeavors. Most exploration efforts are risky and typically fail: in the oil sector, for example, roughly eight out of every one hundred drilled exploratory wells results in a commercial discovery in "frontier" countries (i.e., those without prior discoveries), while only 36 percent succeed in mature producers (Heller, 2017). Exploration and extraction also require highly skilled human capital to operate extractive machinery, particularly in the early development phase of production. This technical capability thus serves as a kind of precondition for nationalization.

Consider the case of Angola's oil nationalization, when in 1976 the nascent People's Movement for the Liberation of Angola (MPLA) party expropriated Portuguese oil company Angol to form the state-owned Sonangol. The NOC was established during a time of crisis, as most international oil companies fled the country in the face of civil war. Instead of creating a production-capable NOC, the MPLA decided to coerce Western companies back into the country to continue operations, knowing that any Angolan state-run company needed more expertise to engage in exploration and production (Heller, 2012).[11] Not until 1978 did the company begin to engage directly in joint ventures and production-sharing agreements. At this time the state enacted Law 13/78

---

[11] According to Soares de Oliveira (2007), the government promised Gulf Oil, one of the members of the Angol company consortium, that no further expropriations would take place nor would the company be subjected to the violence that had been ravaging the country outside of the strategically (or, fortuitously) well-placed oil reserves in the disconnected Cabinda province.

(known as the 1978 petroleum law) and Sonangol took both de facto and de jure control of 51 percent of the oil fields produced by private operating firms to become an operationally capable national company (Hodges, 2004).

The same technical preconditions must be met outside the oil sector as well. In the case of copper, for instance, the extraction of commercial-grade ore from the ground requires advanced technologies like deep ore underground mining and in situ solution mining, manned and developed by teams of highly skilled engineers and miners. Variation in homegrown human capital is one reason why Chile's nationalization in 1971 culminated with the formation of the operational state-owned Codelco in 1976, while Zimbabwe's copper nationalization in 1980 resulted in the nonoperational state-owned Zimbabwe Mining Development Corporation (ZMDC).[12] In 2019, armed with over thirty years of technical-skills development working alongside MNCs, Zimbabwe is now considering converting ZMDC into an operational SOE that will actively explore for and develop new copper (and other metals) deposits.

Hence, leaders of countries with limited experience with operations – whether because of timing (e.g., being a new producer), insurmountable geological complexities, or the lack of human capital – will opt for nonoperational nationalization even if the above benefits outweigh the costs. Conditional on nationalization and establishing an SOE, low-risk geological environments tend to favor production by the state, whereas high-risk environments necessitate regulation of private firms that carry out the majority of production and operations (Nolan and Thurber, 2010; Victor et al., 2012). As experience is developed or as the geology of new mines and fields eases over time, leaders will consider renationalizing to form operational SOEs. Likewise, if the geology of new discoveries grows more complex or if human capital diminishes for any reason (e.g., because of brain drain during outbreaks of war or economic crises), leaders of countries with operational SOEs will sell off extractive assets and opt for nonoperational SOEs or even outright complete privatization (see Carney, 2018).

In this way, factors like geological complexity and timing in the production cycle – a concept I describe in detail below – serve as *technical* determinants for whether leaders nationalize operations. The

---

[12] Beyond copper, ZMDC is also involved in chromite, gold, platinum, and diamonds. A separate SOE, ZISCO, manages iron ore and steel. Sales of these minerals and metals are managed by the Minerals Marketing Corporation of Zimbabwe (MMCZ), which the World Bank estimates exerts a negative cost to the industry given its inefficiencies and redundancies as an unnecessary middle man. See World Bank (2011) for further details.

key *political* determinant I have argued throughout this book that drives this decision is a leader's perceived odds of survival. Information diffusion serves instead as a spark for leaders to update their survival perceptions and seek to renegotiate existing contracts to increase resource revenues collected by the government. At this decision point, leaders who perceive a long and lasting rule will opt against nationalization to reap the long-term gains of nonstate operations. But leaders who perceive a short rule will opt for nationalizing operations to capture a short-term increase in revenues at the cost of future benefits. A better understanding of the consequences of nationalization as opposed to maintaining nonstate firms in charge of operations will help to make better sense of this choice.

2.2.2 Consequences of Different Degrees of State Intervention

By seizing control of natural resource operations from private firms, states can immediately bolster government revenues by seizing a higher share of differential rents – the gap between market prices and operating costs plus return on capital – and by appropriating quasi-rents. Recall from Chapter 1 that the latter results from the low salvageable value of extractive assets and the gap between short- and long-term recovery costs. Beyond this revenue injection, nationalizing operations via an operational SOE gives leaders the ability to reduce state-firm information asymmetries and provides greater autonomy in production decisions to take advantage of changing prices. Although in the long run these SOEs are less operationally efficient than private firms, I posit that in the short run the operational SOE framework provides higher government revenues from the state's natural resource wealth. I argue that these revenues lead to more durable leaders by allowing rulers to buy support and to ward off challengers with fiscal resources that would otherwise be spent on future recovery or lost to the shareholders of private and often foreign firms.

Nationalizing Operations Reduces Information Asymmetry

When private firms control production, an information asymmetry exists between firms and the host government regarding resource costs and revenues (van der Linde, 2000; Mommer, 2002). The government lacks information about the true revenues generated by the resource sector, which are known only to the producer; the firm can thus decide to share this knowledge with the government (either accurately or inaccurately). By gaining control over production, the state can assert stricter oversight to narrow this gap. As Christopher Warshaw writes regarding the petroleum industry, this allows states to gain "information on the real costs of oil operations, which can help assuage the fear that private 'agents' operating in the oil sector are operating for their own benefit rather than the benefit of the host country" (Warshaw, 2012, 38).

This information gap can be detrimental to a government's fiscal balances when in the absence of SOEs the regulating ministry lacks the institutional capacity to monitor basic operations of private firms. Such is the case in Sierra Leone's mining sector, where the ministry is understaffed and the state lacks strong tax institutions (for example, the country lacked a proper tax court until 2015). Despite an industry that makes up 20 percent of Sierra Leone's GDP, the ministry and the country's tax authority combined only employ six staffers assigned to auditing the mining sector's tax payments. According to a Natural Resource Governance Institute (NRGI) report from April 2017, the deputy minister of mines lamented as such: "We do not have capacity to get involved with legal issues. Companies have the best lawyers; as a ministry we don't have the best lawyers."[13] The complexities of oil extraction make it difficult for governments to ascertain the accuracy of information reported by private firms (Blitzer et al., 1984; Beer and Loeprick, 2017). Firms have strong incentives to underreport production quantities and overrerport production costs in order to minimize taxes and royalties, which are typically assessed as percentages of oil sales minus costs (see Readhead et al., 2018). This is also the case in the context of nationalization without operational control, where SOEs oversee production operated by private firms. In these cases, the state will collect less oil revenue than it is due because of the asymmetry of information about extraction figures.

In Zambia, one of the world's largest copper producers, reports estimate that the government loses up to $2 billion per year (roughly 10 percent of its GDP) because of revenue underreporting and tax evasion by MNCs like Glencore and Vedanta. In 2010, for example, Zambia produced $5.7 billion worth of copper but the government only received $633 million in tax payments from the MNCs. After reforming the tax code in late 2010 to increase the royalty rate and establish a variable profit tax, the government's revenues from copper rose to $1.4 billion out of a total $7.2 billion in production revenues.[14] Yet this increase still fell short of what the government was owed. Aside from

---

[13] "Securing mining revenues: Good practice from Zambia, Tanzania, South Africa." Natural Resources Governance Institute briefing April 17, 2017.

[14] Moore Stephens. *Zambia Extractive Industries Transparency Initiative (ZEITI): Reconciliation Report for the Year 2011*. February 2014, Annex 8; US Geological Survey Minerals Information: Copper, 2012 report.

one mine, the effective tax rate on production paid by copper MNCs averaged a paltry 7 percent, compared to the 25–30 percent tax rates set in Zambian copper contracts.[15] This again highlights that while increasing the tax rate is a viable alternative to nationalization, for leaders looking to pocket as much short-term revenue as possible, it is still a less-preferred option: given informational asymmetries over costs and profits, the state loses out on revenues that are effectively captured by the firm.

Nationalizing operations via an operational SOE can narrow this informational gap. This gap is narrowest where operational SOEs have a monopoly on production. In this case, production revenues are directly extracted from the SOE to the treasury, where the state can then decide how much to send back to the SOE to cover costs and future reinvestments. Such is the case in Malaysia's petroleum sector, where state-owned Petronas's profits are directly transferred to the government via dividends; the state then transfers back funds for cost recovery and exploration investments (Lopez, 2012). In 2012, these dividends accounted for 74 percent of Petronas's net income, leaving the company only $3 billion for reinvestment.[16] This high tax rate highlights one assumption driving the overall effect that government revenues are higher under state control: governments can charge the SOE a higher tax rate than private firms without fear of market exit. For example, the Saudi Arabian government in 2017 set a whopping 85 percent tax rate on the net income of its NOC, Saudi Aramco.[17] The effective government take of NOC revenues in smaller producers like Ecuador's Petroamazonas or Chad's SHT is just as demanding: these NOCs transfer between 80 and 100 percent of all revenues directly to the state (Heller and Mihalyi, 2019). There's no doubt that any private firm charged such a high rate would exit the market. And if such appropriation continues over time, then SOE production will inevitably decline; the lack of reinvestment in exploration hinders the ability to replace existing reserves with new discoveries.

---

[15] "Extracting minerals, extracting wealth: How Zambia is losing $3 billion from corporate tax dodging." *War on Want* Briefing Report. Accessed October 28, 2017 from www.waronwant.org/sites/default/files/WarOnWant_ZambiaTaxReport_web.pdf.
The exception was a mine run by Kansanshi Mining Plc, which is a partnership of the Canadian company First Quantum (80 percent) and the Zambian government (20 percent). The other top-five companies operating in the country produced $4.3 billion worth of copper but paid only $310 million in taxes, compared to the $853 million paid in taxes by Kansanshi on $2.04 billion in production revenues.
[16] *Petronas Annual Report*, 2012, page 36. Converted into USD using the FRED exchange rate of 3 ringit to 1 US dollar. Accessed from www.petronas.com.my/investor-relations/Pages/annual-report.aspx.
[17] "Saudi Arabia, a kingdom built on oil, plans future beyond it." *Washington Post* April 21, 2017.

Where operational SOEs do not have a monopoly on production, these entities are able to identify misreported figures from other firms operating alongside the SOE in the sector. Based on their experience in day-to-day operations, these SOEs are "in the know" when it comes to extraction figures and estimates (Grayson, 1981; McPherson, 2003, 2010; Marcel, 2016; Heller, 2017). In the oil sector, a firm operating alongside an operational NOC will be hesitant to misreport quantities and costs, knowing that the state has enough information to dispute these reported figures. The operational NOC itself will also find it harder to hide information from the state, given its formal ties to government oversight agencies as well as the preponderance of government-appointed personnel who are loyal to the leader rather than to outside shareholders. From the government's perspective, it is relatively easier to monitor its own SOE than it is to monitor MNCs.

In practice, some operational SOEs grow autonomous from government oversight and become known as a state within a state – and thus no different from the MNCs in hiding revenues from the government (Cheon, 2019; Heller and Mihalyi, 2019). A prominent example is Angola's Sonangol, which has considerable fiscal autonomy and is often accused of overinvesting in foreign assets instead of contributing to the domestic economy (Hodges, 2004; Heller, 2012). That said, the government can still track the flow of revenues (or "lost" revenues, as it were) since the treasury or central bank monitors SOE expenditures – thus tracing revenue inflows based on revenue outflows. And compared to private MNCs, the SOE is composed of personnel appointed directly by the leader (or legislative body). This allows the leader to pressure SOE officials to maintain minimal standards of fiscal reporting, either by threatening to replace officials with those who will toe the line or by directly punishing disobedient SOE managers with imprisonment or exile under the pretense of "anti-corruption" campaigns.[18] For both reasons – increased institutional oversight and the ability to sanction malfeasant SOE officials – the state can expect more accurate reporting of costs and revenues from an operational SOE than from a private firm, even in the context of a fiscally autonomous SOE.

---

[18] The former tactic is commonly used in Nigeria, where board members of the NNPC are frequently shuffled by the president. The latter tactic is less frequent in practice, but has occurred in the context of Putin's consolidation of Gazprom and Rosneft, and in Iran during President Ahmadinejad's purge of oil officials in the promise "to end corruption and to deliver oil money to kitchen tables." See Laura Secor, "The rationalist: A dissident economist's attempts to reform the revolution," *The New Yorker* February 2, 2009. On Nigeria and Russia, see Thurber et al. (2012) and Goldman (2008).

How does an SOE reduce these asymmetries in practice? Existing research emphasizes the use of ex-post monitoring tools that allow the SOE to monitor firm decisions after the fact (Mommer, 2002; Hults, 2012a). These are what public administration scholars would consider active governance controls as opposed to more passive tools like ex-ante procedures and incentives (Vining and Weimar, 1990; Vives, 2000). Some of these techniques involve regular audits, frequent inspections of extraction sites, benchmarking, performance reviews, and other forms of information gathering. In the United Arab Emirates, for example, the state-owned Abu Dhabi National Oil Company (ADNOC) performs inspections of offshore platforms operated by its subsidiary ADCO in joint partnerships with BP, ExxonMobil, Shell, and Total. These visits offer the chance not only to ensure compliance with environmental standards but also to oversee and report firms' production levels and extractive processes (Rai and Victor, 2012).[19] Indeed, one of the most common government-directed responsibilities for national oil companies is "effective monitoring of operators and revenue collection" (Heller et al., 2014, 4).

Although a ministry or a nonoperational SOE could in theory perform these same duties, these entities' lack of operational experience prevents them from obtaining accurate information about the extractive process. Regulatory agencies like a country's ministry of mines may indeed be staffed with highly skilled technocrats with experience in mineral production (World Bank, 2011). But without direct experience working the country's own natural resources, there will be a mismatch between the level of knowledge about general production costs held by the ministry and the level of knowledge about country-specific production costs held by the firm. The gap is even larger when the firm uses its own subsidiaries to handle multiple levels of the extractive supply chain, effectively masking the true costs of capital, operations, transactions, and distribution (Readhead et al., 2018). The ministry can still perform inspection visits, audits, and other forms of ex-post monitoring to reduce asymmetries, but will lack the proper baseline or frame of reference to evaluate whether extractive firms are reporting information accurately.

Nationalization of operations, then, should allow the state to reap greater revenues compared to the alternative ownership structures of nationalizing without operational control or maintaining private ownership. Nationalization therefore allows the government to capture foregone revenues that, unbeknown to the state, would have been captured by firms.

---

[19] See also ADNOC, 2012, *Abu Dhabi National Oil Company 2011 Sustainability Report*.

Nationalizing Operations Allows Production Elasticity

The second mechanism at play in the effect of operational SOEs on state revenue collection is production elasticity. This refers to the ability of an operator to adjust production in response to changing international prices. In general, this allows the operator – whether an SOE or a private firm – to capture greater profits as prices increase. When prices decline, production elasticity allows the operator to conserve its resource reserves to protect future revenues when prices rebound. Being able to change production levels at will also allows the operator to dictate its own depletion strategy, measured typically by the reserves-to-production ratio (Stevens, 2012; Menaldo, 2016).

The optimal rate of natural resource depletion largely depends on profit-maximization strategies and discount rates (Hotelling, 1931). For producers with long time horizons, the optimal strategy is to pursue high reserves-to-production ratios and to minimize year-to-year volatility in production; this also maximizes the number of years producing. For those with short time horizons, the optimal strategy is fast depletion: the operator will try to produce at the maximum as early as possible, with little concern for production levels in the future. This strategy is particularly short-sighted in the oil industry, in which extraction at high rates early in the process will not only expedite the decline in reserves, but can also prevent future production by damaging existing reservoirs.[20]

Host government control over the elasticity of production is critical when private firms do not adjust production levels in response to market price changes. Operational nationalization ensures that the state can extract natural resources at optimal levels. This could be maximal production in order to capitalize on high prices; steady production to maintain long-term supply flows; or quota-adjusted production to satisfy external limits (such as OPEC quotas).

But in the context of either nationalization without operational control or maintaining private ownership, the state is at the mercy of whatever production levels private operators deem fit. Short-term maximization of profits to appease shareholders will lead firms to also capitalize during price spikes with increasing production, which leads to higher taxes collected by host governments. But firms in extractive industries historically acted as price-setters, keeping production steady in an attempt

---

[20] This occurs due to rapid reduction of subsurface pressure, which can trap remaining reserves; enhanced oil recovery techniques can be applied in such cases, though because of high costs these reserves are typically left unproduced. See Selley and Sonnenberg (2014).

to stabilize profits (see Yergin, 1991). In the current market, while these firms lack such cartel-like powers, they are highly multinational and must balance increasing production in one country with decreasing production levels in others. As I point out in the previous chapter, this could explain why private oil firms do not systematically adjust production in response to changing prices.

Production elasticity also works in both directions because depletion strategies impact market prices (Hotelling, 1931). States with control over large reserves can attempt to manipulate international prices by intentionally altering production levels. For example, Saudi Arabia withheld oil production in 1973 during the oil embargo and overproduced in 1985 to punish noncompliant OPEC members. In effect, production elasticity allows resource-rich leaders greater control over fiscal returns, especially if private firms produce at politically or economically suboptimal levels.

While state control of operations could result in both upward and downward adjustment of production in response to price changes, we might expect leaders to consistently push for higher production levels with limited examples of deliberate decreases. This would fall in line with the expectation that leaders who choose the operational SOE framework are short-term revenue-maximizers compared with those who choose nonoperational SOEs or to maintain private ownership.

Such is the case in the oil sector: production levels on average *increase* following the establishment of an operational SOE. Figure 2.1 shows oil production in logged metric tonnes in the five years leading up to and the five years after nationalizing production to establish an operational SOE. For example, average annual production – represented by the bold black line – roughly doubles from 0.71 million metric tonnes (13.47 logged units) two years before nationalization to 1.39 million metric tonnes (14.15 logged units) two years afterwards. Part of this increase stems from the expected production elasticity since nationalizations tend to occur when prices rise. However, for nineteen out of the fifty-seven cases plotted, operational SOEs were established during the low-price period of 1931–1971. This suggests that leaders are opting to use their ability to control oil production to squeeze out as much revenue as possible to make up for losses incurred during a low-price environment.

Production Inefficiencies of Nationalizing Operations
Although reducing information asymmetries and unlocking production elasticity increase government revenues from natural resource wealth, this effect is constrained by the likelihood that operations managed by SOEs are less efficient when compared to private firms in the long run.

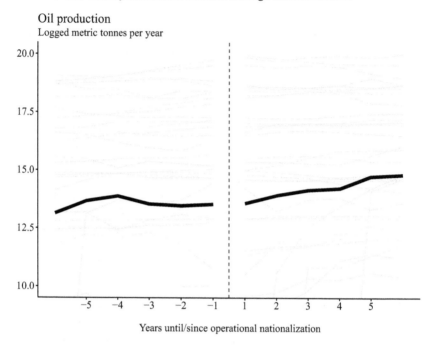

Figure 2.1 Oil production before and after operational nationalization
Note: Production lines are drawn for fifty-seven oil-producing countries in the five years before and after establishing an operational national oil company. Data on operational NOCs comes from the author's database; data on production is collected from the United States Geological Survey (USGS) via Ross and Mahdavi (2014).

Traditional economic theory has studied the relationship between state ownership and firm performance, dating as far back as Adam Smith, who proclaimed that "characters do not exist who are more distant than the sovereign and the entrepreneur" (Smith, 1776; Wolf, 2009, 771, 2643). In particular, theories of economic regulation have shown the relative inefficiency of state ownership and heavily regulated markets compared to perfectly competitive markets and, in some experiences, private monopolies. Posner (1975) shows that public regulation – a general term for state intervention in the market – bears higher social costs than private monopoly, despite the latter's higher consumer prices. Regulation, Posner argues, leads to higher social costs in the form of increased dead-weight loss because firms in regulated markets are more concentrated, and thus are able to easily collude with one another. By contrast, competition in the market will force monopoly-seeking firms to compete heavily against one another, thereby reducing the amount of collusion between firms. This reflects the thought process of Chicago School economists, who emphasize that public regulation is less efficient than privatization of markets, and that state-owned enterprises are more socially inefficient than investor-owned companies (see Stigler, 1971).

Others have shown that SOEs involved in operations maximize short-term revenues at the cost of long-term efficiency, given the technical gaps between private and state-run firms. This stems from the notion that by nearly every standard of corporate and technical performance, state-owned enterprises perform worse than private enterprises. A highly influential study by Boardman and Vining (1989) shows that across the manufacturing and mining sectors, private firms significantly outperform SOEs on profitability measures (return on equity, net income, etc.) and efficiency outcomes (sales per asset, assets per employee, etc.). Weak incentives to innovate and to monitor worker efficiency are often pinned as the culprit for the performance differences between SOEs and private firms (de Alessi, 1974).

SOEs in the oil sector track this pattern: research on NOC production finds that NOCs produce at inefficient rates when compared to major international oil companies (IOCs) (see Hartley and Medlock, 2008). Wolf (2009), for instance, finds that NOCs produce up to 50 percent less than comparable private oil companies. Another analysis provides corroboratory support to find that IOCs are roughly 30 percent more efficient at converting reserves into production than NOCs, controlling for a variety of geologic and geographic conditions, and are generally more efficient in converting reserves into revenue (Victor, 2007). And in terms of discoveries, operational NOCs fare worse than both NOC–IOC partnerships and private companies working without government involvement (Brunnschweiler and Poelhekke, 2019).

Nolan and Thurber (2010) demonstrate that the impact of these operational inefficiencies depends on where a country's resource production lies within the extraction cycle. Risks are highest and technical expertise is essential when resources are first discovered and production is ramped up to commercially viable levels. Any country that nationalizes at this stage runs a high risk of lower levels of extraction compared to keeping private firms in charge of production. These risks are minimized at the middle stages of operations; at this stage, any reasonably competent operator can maintain high levels of extraction without significant production loss due to inefficiency. In the context of petroleum production, this medium stage can last decades (conditional on a country's reserves) and can last roughly ten years at a minimum without major reinvestments in exploration and reservoir maintenance. Risks return at the final stages of operations, given the highly complex

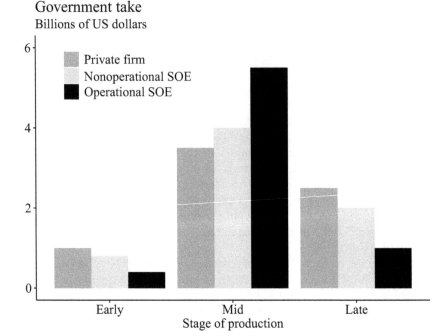

Figure 2.2 Hypothetical government revenues under different degrees of state intervention

methods and technologies needed to extract the remaining reserves from the reservoir or mineshaft. In these latter stages, the efficiency of private firms results in production at higher levels compared to operational SOEs.

The inefficiencies of operational SOEs are therefore most prevalent in the early and late stages of extraction. This is summarized in Figure 2.2 with hypothetical levels of government revenue from natural resource wealth plotted for different intervention scenarios at different stages of the production cycle. The biggest gains from an operational SOE come from the middle stages of extraction compared to private firms and nonoperational SOEs, while the operational SOE performs the worst in the early and late stages. The performance of nonoperational SOEs falls somewhere between the two ends of state intervention, with marginally higher government revenues than private firms in the middle stage of production and marginally lower revenues than private firms in the early and late stages. While the state can expect relatively efficient production from its SOE during the mid stages of extraction, inefficiencies are inevitable as time progresses, making the decision to keep operations in the hands of an SOE harder to justify in the long term.

Differences in the recovery of long-run costs also affect the present value of government revenues across different intervention scenarios. Within the quasi-rent framework for extractive resources, there exists a considerable wedge between short- and long-term marginal costs, given the challenges of later stages of extraction and the investment needed to sustain production in the future. This implies that over time, short-run profits turn into long-run losses as marginal costs begin to exceed market prices.[21] Profits are therefore not sustainable without continuously finding and developing new resources that allow the operator to repeatedly reset the production cycle over time. And even if profits are reinvested in exploration and discovery, choosing the operational SOE framework still poses risks to long-term returns, given performance differences between SOEs and private firms.

Greater Revenues from Nationalizing Operations Foster More Durable Leaders

These choices provide three different institutional types: private ownership, SOEs with control over operations, and SOEs that oversee production by private firms. Following the above argument, these choices will impact the sustainability of government take of revenues from natural resources. At one end is the operational SOE, in which take is highest in the short term but disintegrates over time as low efficiency cripples production. At the other end is private ownership, in which take is lowest but long-term efficiency is highest.

The cases of SOEs without operational control – SOEs with regulatory powers or SOEs with no authority over either production or regulatory oversight[22] – offer lower government take but varying levels of efficiency. In these contexts, MNCs produce a country's resources at largely efficient rates, with stable income accruing to the state over time, conditional on commodity prices and reserves. But because of the existing information asymmetries between host and producer, the amount of revenue collected by the government will fall short of its

---

[21] In an overly simplified scenario, imagine that the market price stays fixed over time such that the price exceeds operating costs early in the extraction cycle. If operating costs rise monotonically, then the quasi-rent – the difference between the price-determined value and operating costs plus salvage value – shifts from positive to negative over time. Without a fixed-price assumption, profits will still turn to losses unless prices rise faster than operating costs over time.

[22] Such is the case of the NOC that is established neither to produce oil nor to regulate those that do produce oil, but instead to collect tax revenues from operators and transfer them to the state treasury. Market capitalists might perceive this institution as ideal since it maintains a very laissez-faire role in the sector.

potential; instead, most of the country's resource revenues will flow to these private firms.

The center column in Figure 2.2 provides a visual summary of these theoretical outcomes for a state that is at the middle stage of resource development and is deciding between maintaining the status quo of private ownership or nationalizing to establish either an operational SOE or a nonoperational SOE. At this stage, the choice of an operational SOE provides the state with the greatest amount of resource revenues compared to the two alternative structures. But as inefficiencies mount up over time, the operational SOE framework provides the government with less revenue than it would receive under private ownership or under a nonoperational SOE overseeing private firms.

Among these pathways, the frameworks that increase government take of resource wealth will allow leaders to reap the full potential of their countries' resources. The high pass-through of revenues to the state treasury will allow the regime to maintain high expenditures (on things like public goods and elite cooptation) without resorting to taxing the income of its citizens. This is the classic case of the rentier state (Mahdavy, 1970; Beblawi and Luciani, 1987), which typifies the strong and stable petrostate.

Those frameworks that do not maximize government take leave leaders unable to take advantage of their natural resource wealth. In the context of the nonoperational SOE–ownership structure, leader endurance is not greatly enhanced by resource wealth since the state is not capturing the bulk of this wealth to use for public expenditures and the purchase of political support. When the state can eschew nationalization altogether and not go down the interventionist pathway, the regime cannot similarly realize its natural resource potential as operating firms will capture most of the country's resource wealth.

This a key distinction: whereas the resource-curse theorist would posit that (conditional on preexisting development conditions) natural resource wealth increases leader survival, the theory here would predict that this is only the case in which the leader has control over operations and production. In its simplest form, the argument thus boils down to a dichotomy: either the state does or does not have de facto control of operations.

Postnationalization Pathways with Operational Control

Although the focus of the argument thus far has been about the causes and consequences of operational nationalization, it is useful to consider how the theory applies to postnationalization choices over extractive governance. There are three general pathways that the state could pursue after taking de facto control over operations. The first is part of what I introduce in the previous section as the natural resource "trap" (Hogan et al., 2010). Firms whose operations are expropriated are invited back if the state comes to realize that the SOE cannot profitably manage production without outside assistance. In effect, operational nationalization becomes a one-time seizure of quasi-rents from outside firms and a temporary increase in government take of the sector's differential rents. Afterward, operations return to being privately controlled and taxed by the state. Note that this does not entail privatization, but merely a transfer of authority over production to outside firms from the SOE, which remains intact as an operating partner, as a regulator, or simply as a tax collector. The second and third pathways result from an operational nationalization "enduring" such that outside firms are not invited back in as de facto operators. Although some leaders choose to foster a well-financed SOE that can recover its long-run costs, other leaders choose to extract maximal rents from the SOE with little regard to long-term reinvestment (see Victor et al., 2012). The former is the state-as-steward model of SOE governance, as exemplified by cases like Chile's Codelco, Malaysia's Petronas, and Norway's Equinor. The latter is the state-as-appropriator model, as illustrated by cases like Mexico's Pemex, Myanmar's Gem Enterprise, and Venezuela's PdVSA.

How do these different postnationalization pathways affect the government's collection of revenues from natural resource development? The first scenario is nearly identical to the prenationalization status quo of taxing private firms – with the exception of a one-time appropriation of quasi-rents and taking a higher share of the sector's differential rents – such that long-term production efficiency and investment is maximized. Fiscally, the state collects an influx of revenues plus what it receives in taxes on a long-term revenue stream, which, as before, can be subject to profit underreporting and cost overreporting by outside firms. The second scenario also entails a one-time influx of appropriated revenues, plus the state's share of postnationalization revenues from SOE production thereafter. Although long-term resource revenues are lower than would be the case under private ownership because of SOE inefficiencies, the state can secure a higher share of this smaller stream because of its ability to tax SOEs at higher rates without fear of market exit. Expectedly, leaders will prefer this pathway to the first scenario when a higher share of a smaller revenue stream is greater than a lower share of a larger revenue stream. The third scenario allows leaders to take an even higher share of the SOEs revenues, but at the direct expense of long-term production. At the extreme, the SOE gives *all* of its revenues to the state without the ability to recover existing costs or to cover exploration and future development costs. The result is a sector in which production is limited to reserves that have been discovered and developed at the time of nationalization, with no ability to sustain production once these reserves are exhausted. In effect, the state repeatedly appropriates the SOE's share of quasi-rents that would otherwise be reinvested to ensure future production given rising marginal costs of operations. In the short- to medium-term, this pathway offers leaders the most revenues when compared to the first and second pathways, but in the long-term this provides declining revenues (at or close to zero in the extreme case).

Given these three distinct postnationalization pathways, what explains why leaders choose one route over another? The operational nationalization theory offers an explanation centered on leader time horizons and perceived information asymmetries between operator and state. All short-sighted leaders would prefer the second and third cases – in which operational nationalization endures – because this provides the greatest revenues up front despite a higher likelihood of lower returns in the future. Those who fail to pull off operational nationalization end up inviting outside firms back in, either due to technical and/or market constraints, unwise postnationalization investment decisions, or political constraints in the form of domestic opposition or international pressure to roll back expropriation. The Argentine expropriation of YPF–Repsol in 2012 is illustrative of this version of the natural resources trap. The failure of the state-run YPF to operate the highly prospective but geologically challenging shale oil fields of the Vaca Muerta, coupled with intense financial and political pressure by the governments of Spain and the United States, led to nationalization backsliding (Maurer and Herrero, 2013; Slaski, 2019). In 2013, the Argentine government was court-ordered to compensate Repsol to the tune of $5 billion, and MNCs like Chevron and Shell were brought in to develop the Vaca Muerta alongside YPF.[23]

Beyond failed nationalizations by short-sighted leaders, inviting MNCs back after nationalization is a deliberate choice made by less-opportunistic leaders who seek to capture a one-time slice of rents, but prefer to keep long-run production in the hands of private firms. In effect, this implies that leaders are not appropriating quasi-rents from firms that can retain the untaxed portion of long-term revenues to help in recovering their initial sunk costs. This is the story of the postnationalization decisions of the UAE's Sheikh Zayed, who

---

[23] Tracy Rucinski, Andrés González, and Kevin Gray, "Spain's Repsol agrees to $5 billion settlement with Argentina over YPF." *Reuters* February 25, 2014.

intentionally retained the core firms of the consortia whose concessions were nationalized first in 1971 and again in 1974. Keeping companies like BP, Exxon, Shell, and Total after nationalization may have been outwardly justified by the lack of ADNOC's capacity to develop the country's oil fields (Rai and Victor, 2012). But my argument would suggest that the choice was driven internally by Zayed's long time horizons to ensure continual oil revenues for the lasting development of the UAE and the stability of the al-Nahyan dynastic monarchy (Herb, 1999, 2014).

The more interesting choice, however, is not whether firms are retained or invited back in after nationalization, but whether leaders opt for the state-as-steward or the state-as-appropriator model of SOE governance if operational nationalization fully endures. Again, much like Olson's predatory bandits, leaders who perceive their time in power is limited will be more likely to choose the option that offers the greatest rewards as soon as possible, even if it comes at the expense of future development (Olson, 2000). Such leaders will then continue appropriating quasi-rents from the newly established SOE, with no incentive to develop sustainable postnationalization production. In effect, the state treats its SOE like an outside firm whose revenues can be seized over and over again until quasi-rents completely disappear – either because existing reserves dry up and the sector is reopened to outside investment, as in posttransition Mexico, or because the sector collapses entirely, as in Maduro's Venezuela (see Addison and Roe, 2018; Stevens, 2018).

But short time horizons are not the only reason to opt for continual appropriation after nationalization. Leaders who feel secure in power but perceive a growing informational gap between the state and its SOE will also engage in opportunistic behavior. Such leaders may begin on the state-as-steward pathway; but as perceptions grow that their SOEs withhold profits or overreport costs, leaders veer toward greater postnationalization appropriation. This is a direct response to the state-within-a-state phenomenon of SOEs becoming too politically autonomous and potentially posing a threat to those in power.

Consider Mexico under the PRI, where the single-party dictatorship in the 1970s had bolstered Pemex with financial support from the state – up to 17 percent of the federal budget – to discover and develop new fields.[24] After the major discovery of the Cantarell field in 1976, what had previously been a low-profile, domestically focused NOC turned into a powerful export-oriented enterprise. In 1982, Pemex Director

---

[24] This brief vignette is based on the history of Pemex in the 1970s and 1980s as recounted in Philip (1982), Philip (1999), and Stojanovski (2012).

General Jorge Diaz Serrano had presidential aspirations, much to the chagrin of the PRI's cabinet ministers, given his lack of government experience and his close ties to the US. The appointment of Miguel de la Madrid, a staunch opponent of Diaz Serrano, to a revamped Secretariat of Planning and Budgeting in 1979 led to an all-out assault on Pemex. The Secretariat publicly denounced the company as administratively secretive and having too much political autonomy. The NOC's profits were gutted by a combination of increasing taxes and low domestic prices, leading to a deficit of nearly $16 million in 1981. By the time global oil prices collapsed in 1986, Pemex was under complete control of the state. Its primary purpose was to serve as a cash cow to directly fund the PRI's expenditures and as a political tool to distribute patronage to the PRI's large clientelistic network.

These diverging postnationalization pathways exemplify a broader pattern of leader behavior when there is the potential to appropriate quasi-rents and traditional profits from economic activity. Opportunism arises when time horizons are short and there is little regard for sustainable long-term development (North and Weingast, 1989; Olson, 1993; Li, 2009; Jensen et al., 2012). But it also emerges when leaders perceive an information gap vis-à-vis an agent – whether a private firm or a state-owned entity – on taxes owed, fees paid, or costs declared. With a sense that such figures are misreported, leaders may engage in opportunistic behavior to recover what they believe to be rightfully theirs. Such actions can start a vicious cycle in which leaders gain poor reputations (Jensen, 2006), subsequently attracting unfaithful investors whose dishonest reporting only further tarnishes leaders' perceptions of information gaps between state and firm.

2.2.3 Implications and Predictions

The theory sketched in this chapter presents numerous implications whose validity can be assessed with empirically tested hypotheses. I articulate four such hypotheses here that I test in the chapters ahead.[25]

---

[25] Note that I do not directly test the hypothesis that short-sighted leaders are more likely to nationalize operations. A leader's own perception of his time horizon is not directly measurable, given that, to use the words of John Mearsheimer and Stephen Walt, it is "a mental state that we cannot observe" (Mearsheimer and Walt, 2013, 433). Instead, I assess the implications of this aspect of the theory using proxy measures for time horizons in Chapter 4 and a descriptive analysis of the Shah of Iran's perceived time horizons in Chapter 6.

Hypothesis 1 *Leaders who are exposed to diffused information about competitors' revenue-sharing agreements are more likely to nationalize natural resource operations.*

This is the key expectation of the diffusion of information argument. Learning that a better deal could be had with operating firms prompts leaders to renegotiate their existing agreements. Not all of these renegotiations result in nationalization – in some cases, leaders will continue to allow private firms to operate the country's fields and mines, either through complete private ownership of the sector or through an SOE that is not involved in operations. But for leaders with lower perceived-survival odds, these renegotiations will end in nationalization of operations, if they are technically capable of doing so given geological constraints. Although not a direct test of the broader argument, the hypothesis that information diffusion is followed by nationalization is an expectation of the argument. If nationalization is one possible outcome of renegotiation, and renegotiation is prompted by the spread of information about competitors' revenue-sharing agreements, then in expectation nationalization should be more likely after such information is diffused. The counter (falsification) of this hypothesis is that nationalization should be less likely or no more likely after information diffusion. In the cross-national analysis presented in Chapter 4, a country's membership in OPEC serves as a proxy for its leader's exposure to diffused information. In the comparative-case analysis in the same chapter, information diffusion is measured by examining the spread of news about the signing of specific oil agreements between host governments and international oil companies in 1948–1950. In Chapter 6, the diffusion of information is directly assessed using archival records of conversations between the Shah of Iran and members of the international consortium of oil companies led by British Petroleum.

Hypothesis 2 *Production will be immediately higher after nationalizing operations.*

If operational nationalization provides the state the ability to dictate production levels at will, then leaders will be expected to increase production to secure higher revenues in the short term. In times of high prices, this is what one typically would see if production is elastic to price. In times of low prices, states may still increase production in an attempt to balance fiscal deficits and pay off debts created by collapsing prices. I test this hypothesis using cross-national data in Chapter 5 and using within-country production projections in Chapter 6. Note that I do not test the long-run operational inefficiency argument directly here;

I eschew this test because it is well-established in the literature that SOEs perform worse on nearly all measures of operational efficiency in the long run compared to private firms (see Wolf, 2009).

Hypothesis 3 *Resource revenues accruing directly to the state will be higher when the SOE has an operational role.*

This assesses the validity of the theory on how nationalization impacts government take. Compared to the nonoperational SOE and no SOE frameworks, the operational SOE will provide production elasticity and will reduce information asymmetries between host government and producer when it comes to reporting accurate figures on extraction costs and quantities. In comparison to nonoperational SOEs in particular, SOEs with operational roles gain valuable financial and managerial experience that helps to increase government return on investment per barrel or ton produced. If these two mechanisms accurately describe the effects of SOE choices, then one should observe greater resource revenues for the state when SOEs control operations. I test this hypothesis in Chapter 5 using multiple measures of annual resource revenues cross-nationally, and in Chapter 6 using verified monthly receipts of oil revenues collected by the Iranian government.

Hypothesis 4 *Leaders in resource-producing countries with nationalized operations are more likely to endure.*

If operational nationalization provides the state with more revenues in the short run compared to when the state lacks operational control, then leaders should be more likely to survive under this framework. With more money in the treasury, leaders can finance a wider range of expenditures to ward off challengers and to buy political support, either directly via patronage and cooptation or indirectly via financing broad economic development (Levi, 1989; Geddes, 2003; Acemoglu and Robinson, 2005). In expectation, leaders should be more likely to survive in power when operations are nationalized compared to leaders of countries without nationalized operations. Chapter 5 provides a direct test of this hypothesis using cross-national data. Chapter 6 offers an interpretation of how this aspect of the theory explains the postnationalization consolidation of power by the Shah of Iran, only to see his regime collapse after the reversal of operational nationalization.

In brief, these seemingly technical choices over management of the resources sector bear important consequences for governance and political stability, both in the short term and the long term. To summarize

Table 2.1. *Political outcomes of different state intervention paths in Iran and Iraq*

Country	Years	Institutional path	Fiscal strength	Durability
Iran	1946–1951*	Private ownership	Low	Low
Iran	1974–1976	Operational nationalization	High	High
Iran	1976–1979	Nonoperational nationalization	Moderate	Low
Iraq	1953–1961	Private ownership	Low	Low
Iraq	1961–1972	Nonoperational nationalization	Moderate	Moderate
Iraq	1972–1981	Operational nationalization	High	High

Note: Operational nationalization *refers to state-run enterprises that extract and produce natural resources.* Nonoperational nationalization *refers to state-run enterprises that regulate and oversee private/outside firms that extract and produce natural resources.*

* *I do not directly address this case here, but provide it as a companion to Iraq's period of private ownership in the pre-1961 period. More details on this period are provided in Chapter 4.*

these predictions, I present a stylization of these institutional pathways and their political consequences – fiscal strength and leader durability – in Table 2.1. Because the book's primary testing ground is the oil industry, I outline each institutional pathway in the specific context of different types of national oil companies. And as I describe in the next section, the cases of pre-1980 Iran and Iraq offer a compelling comparison of different state-intervention pathways in the oil sector.

2.3   Initial Empirical Evidence

The political trajectories of Iran and Iraq exemplify two of the most polarizing cases of leadership failure. In Iran, the shocking collapse of the Shah in 1979 defied the West's notion of the "island of stability" in the tumultuous Middle East. The Hashemite monarchy in Iraq fell forty years prior, but ushered in a decade of instability until Ba'athist consolidation in 1968. Given both countries' vast oil wealth, especially in the 1960–1980 period, their turbulent political histories provide a sharp foil to the conventional wisdom that natural resource wealth increases leader durability (Smith, 2004; Ulfelder, 2007; Ross, 2012; Wright et al., 2015).

A key point, however, is that government collection of oil wealth was not constant throughout this period in either case. Although both countries maintained NOCs, the lack of sustained operational roles of these NOCs allowed foreign companies, instead of the states themselves, to capture the bulk of oil revenues and profits. Matters changed for both cases in 1972–1974 when both adopted operational NOCs. Whereas this change was permanent in Iraq, state control backtracked in Iran by 1976.

Together, these cases offer prima facie evidence for theoretical claims about nationalization and the dynamics of leader survival. It should be noted, of course, that the trajectories below corroborate the theory but cannot serve to explain definitively the rise and fall of leadership in Iraq and Iran in the pre-1980 period.

2.3.1   Pahlavi Iran before the Fall

On January 23, 1973, in a special National Congress to commemorate the tenth anniversary of the White Revolution modernization program, the Shah of Iran outlined his vision for the oil industry.[26] After months of negotiations, renationalization of oil operations was formalized in an agreement signed with the BP-led Consortium of Western oil companies on July 16, 1973, and implemented six months later by parliament. The agreement established that "full and complete ownership, operation and control in respect of all hydrocarbon reserves, assets and administration of the petroleum industry shall be exercised by NIOC."[27] In addition to production control, NIOC was also granted the ability to set prices for oil sold and delivered to the market.

The agreement was a complete restructuring of the industry. From 1954 until the signing of the agreement, NIOC existed as a fully state-owned oil enterprise but it had no commercial role in production or operations, nor did it have any influence over prices and extraction timelines, both of which were completely controlled by the consortium. Even though NIOC legally owned all of Iran's oil, the company had no ability to determine the volume of exports (Bamberg, 2000). After the agreement was signed, the Petroleum Act of 1974 formally heralded the culmination of operational nationalization. Henceforth only NIOC would have complete ownership, production rights, and control over

---

[26] This section is a brief introduction to the book's later chapter on nationalization in 1970s Iran. The chapter draws on primary evidence accessed in June 2016 from the British Petroleum (BP) Archives and the Foreign and Commonwealth Office (FCO) letters at the British National Archives. The BP Archives are housed at the Modern Records Centre of the University of Warwick, UK, with access permission granted explicitly from BP plc. I provide citations to documents from the archives using the archive reference number (e.g., BP 4779 or FCO 96/537), the title of the document, and the date of the document if applicable.

[27] Quoted from BP 14381. "Iran: Sale and purchase agreement and related arrangements, 1973." Preamble, p. 4. © BP plc.

exports and prices.[28] The consortium thus became merely contractors to be paid for their services rendered as assistants to NIOC's operations. With these terms agreed to, this type of NOC implied maximum state control over operations as well as maximum government take from oil revenues.

By seizing control over operations only months before the October 1973 Arab embargo and the subsequent price shock, the Shah put himself in a position to fully control Iran's oil revenue stream. The dramatic upswing in oil rents allowed the Shah to finance his new modernization vision for a "Great Civilization." In doing so, expenditures in the country's Fifth Five Year Plan were revised from $32 billion to $123 billion – a whopping fifty times bigger in real terms than the Fourth Five Year Plan.[29]

In spite of this dramatic increase in revenues in 1973–1975, the Shah's regime collapsed, stunningly, a mere three years later and ushered in the Islamic Republic. This naturally raises the question, why didn't operational nationalization strengthen the Shah?

Tensions grew with the consortium in November 1975 when, as Iran's oil income began declining, it became clear to the Shah that Iran's global petroleum sales did not match its production output. By January 1976, the Shah spared no formalities in meeting with company representatives when he exclaimed that "the Consortium was in breach of the 1973 agreement" for its failure to export as much Iranian oil as promised.[30] At the heart of the problem was a disagreement over "liftings" – which refer to the amount of crude oil produced and sold on the market by the consortium – and that NIOC and the Consortium were producing more oil than was being exported and distributed for consumption. Even though NIOC had full control over production vis-à-vis the 1973 agreement, it did not have control over marketing – that is, control over selling the oil to the world's consumers.

The Shah thus blamed the consortium for his declining oil income – roughly $2.85 billion in foregone revenues – because of BP, Shell, and the American companies' deliberate reduction in liftings.[31] Outwardly, the consortium blamed the post-1973 global recession for reduced demand for crude oil and therefore reduced sales to their consumers in the US and Europe. But internally, conversations among consortium

---

[28] Petroleum Law, National Iranian Parliament, Iran Senate, 1974. Article 3, paragraph 1.

[29] Bank Markazi *Annual Reports and Balance Sheets* (various years).

[30] "Record of the conversation between the Foreign & Commonwealth Secretary and Mr. David Steel, chairman of BP: 1 March 1976." FCO 96/537. British National Archives. Document 51.

[31] "Iran starts new talks with the oil companies." *The Washington Post* April 23, 1976.

members painted a different picture: although it was true that demand had slumped, the bigger reason for the underlifting of Iranian oil was that the American companies had "allowed their liftings to fall to low levels partly as a way of exerting pressure in the negotiations for a new agreement."[32] Exxon, Texaco, Mobil, and Socal had effectively cut liftings to zero in late 1975 and had displaced Iranian crude with oil from Saudi Arabia, which was more profitable to the Americans based on their latest deal with the Saudis. BP even knew that this action by members of the consortium was in violation of the 1973 agreement, but it was reluctant to admit as much and instead preferred "to bluff the matter out with the Iranians."[33] In short, the Shah was right in his suspicions for why the Iranian government was receiving less revenue than was dictated by prices and production levels.

But when the Shah publicly threatened to take over marketing and direct sales to foreign consumers in April 1976, the consortium knew it was all a bluff. NIOC, it asserted to journalists covering the matter, "presently lacks the capability to take on such a vast operation."[34] All in all, this ensured a decline in oil revenues – especially once the global market cooled off and international oil prices turned sour – despite NIOC's new powers over production and prices. After years of consecutive growth, oil revenues dropped 4.6 percent in real terms from their peak (in the 1974–1975 Iranian calendar year) of $18 million to $17.1 million the following year.[35] By 1978, state expenditures continued to increase – based on the Fifth Five Year Plan, which presumed oil revenues would monotonically increase indefinitely. And because the Shah could do nothing to counter the drop in prices by increasing sales, state surpluses turned to widening deficits. Iran would thus not be spared the scenario that is all too familiar to oil-producing countries once booms turn to busts.

So how does the operational nationalization theory provide greater insight into why the Shah's regime collapsed in the face of a popular revolution in 1979? Scholarly explanations for the Iranian Revolution comprise nothing short of a cottage industry.[36] I do not wish to revisit this vast debate in great detail here, but one aspect of these theories that merits discussion is that the Shah was unable to survive because

---

[32] "Mr. Dell's visit to Iran: 31 December 1976." FCO 96/537. British National Archives. Document 73.
[33] "Iran: Negotiations with the Consortium." FCO 96/537. British National Archives. Document 46.
[34] "Iran starts new talks with the oil companies." *The Washington Post* April 23, 1976.
[35] Bank Markazi *Annual Reports and Balance Sheets* (various years).
[36] For an excellent discussion of these theories in a comparative politics context, see Smith (2007).

he lacked an apparatus capable of preventing would-be supporters from turning into members of the opposition.

With greater revenues, perhaps he could have overcome limited institutional capacity by diverting increasing amounts of wealth to the merchant class and to the clergy, just as he did in 1973–1975. When oil revenues began to decline starting in 1976 because of the reversal of nationalization, this meant less money for repression, co-optation, and the political support necessary to prolong his rule. What had allowed the dictatorships of oil-rich countries like the Gulf monarchies, Indonesia, Libya, and Mexico to weather the storm of lower prices and demand in the late 1970s – namely, the ability of the state to control production and exports – was simply lacking in Iran.

2.3.2   Ba'athist Consolidation in Iraq

On July 14, 1958, a group calling themselves the Free Officers overthrew the twenty-seven-year-old Hashemite monarchy of Iraq. Led by Brigadier 'Abd al-Karim Qasim, the revolutionaries established a new Iraqi Republic under the pan-Arab banner of the Ba'athist Party.[37] Once Qasim declared himself as the Republic's first prime minister, he tore the government away from Ba'athist ideologies toward a military dictatorship, alienating (and at times purging) Ba'athist leadership in the process. His rule was to be short-lived: Qasim's nascent regime could not weather the 1963 Ramadan Revolution, which ended with Qasim's execution on February 9, 1963, less than five years after taking power. All told, between 1958 and 1968 the country experienced no fewer than ten military coups. Stability returned once the Ba'athists regained power in July 1968 under the helm of Ahmed Hassan al-Bakr, who ruled Iraq until his death in 1981, with the infamous Saddam Hussein (his kinsman and right-hand man) taking the reins in the late years of al-Bakr's illness.

This case illustrates the rich variation in regime stability within Iraq despite the constancy of oil wealth. During the period of rule under Qasim, oil income per capita in Iraq averaged roughly $750 in real terms – the third richest in the world in per capita terms, following only Saudi Arabia and Venezuela (Ross and Mahdavi, 2014). And yet, the early revolutionaries could not maintain their grip on power while the subsequent regimes of al-Bakr and later Hussein reigned supreme. Although there are several explanations for the country's instability in

---

[37] This section relies solely on secondary accounts of Iraq's oil history. In doing so, it draws heavily from Tripp (2000), Devlin (1991), Farouk-Sluglett and Sluglett (2001), Alnasrawi (2002), and Mikdashi (1966).

the postmonarchy period and its stability under al-Bakr, the role of state intervention in the oil sector has been absent from this discussion.

Applying the nationalization theory here provides greater insight into why Qasim and his immediate successors failed to consolidate their regimes while al-Bakr succeeded. When Qasim first took power, the oil sector was managed by five MNCs (Exxon, Mobil, Shell, BP, and Total) with controlling shares in the Iraq Petroleum Company (IPC). Much like the BP-led consortium in Iran, the IPC had concessionary rights over the country's oil and paid the Iraqi government a royalty and tax based on production levels and operation costs. Qasim championed himself as a liberator of Iraq's oil from the yoke of foreign intervention; in 1958 he achieved much popularity through his repeated promises of kicking out Western powers and restoring the means of production to the people.

But once in power, Qasim did not nationalize the IPC because he was fearful of repercussions from the West, namely the embargo of Iran after Mossadegh's attempt at nationalization in 1951 and his coup in 1953. It was not until intense public pressure on Qasim's regime forced him to move beyond changing the concessionary contracts that nationalization began. To this end, the Iraqi government adopted Law no. 80 in 1961.[38] The first phase of nationalization was a state claim to 25 percent ownership (known in the oil industry as "participation") in IPC in 1961. At this point, operations at IPC remained in the hands of the five-company consortium, with the state only marginally closer to capturing the full potential of its oil wealth.

It was not until after his ouster that the next government formally established an NOC, the Iraqi National Oil Company (INOC), in February 1964. This regime, headed by another member of the Free Officers, 'Abd al-Salim 'Arif, sought to emulate the state economic consolidation of Nasserite Egypt through nationalization. But these efforts resulted in only superficial control of the economy (and of the oil sector in particular) at best. A deal struck between 'Arif's government and the IPC in June 1965 would provide a one-time infusion of oil revenues to the state in return for formally returning 100 percent authority of Iraq's oil to the IPC. In the process, the negotiation effectively killed Law no. 80: the IPC would once again be in full control over Iraqi production and thus, the oil revenues of the Iraqi government.

The back-and-forth between the IPC and each successive Iraqi government continued for the next seven years. Throughout this period, the IPC maintained its grip over Iraq's oil sector, notwithstanding efforts

---

[38] "Defining the Exploitation Areas for the Oil Companies." See Alnasrawi (2002) for details on the law.

Oil and gas income
Billions of constant 2014 US dollars

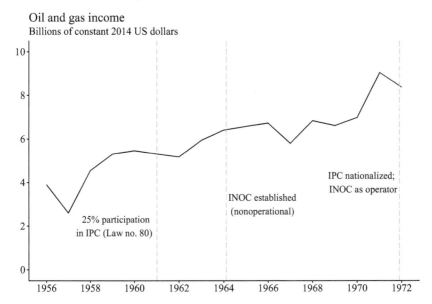

Figure 2.3 Trajectory of annual oil and gas income in Iraq, 1958–1972
Note: Changes in the degree of state intervention are labeled next to vertical lines marking the timing of each event. Data source: Ross and Mahdavi (2014).

by the government of 'Abd al-Rahman 'Arif (al-Salim's brother) and Tahir Yahya to break the IPC monopoly. It was not until June 1972, in the fourth year of al-Bakr's new Ba'athist regime, that Iraq successfully nationalized production from IPC and vested operational control in INOC. A visualization of the timing of each of these ownership structure changes in the 1958–1972 period is presented in Figure 2.3 in relation to the trend of total income from petroleum produced in Iraq.

While overall petroleum income was rising in real terms during this period, much of this wealth was being captured by the IPC and not the Iraqi government. There was a marginal increase in government take after INOC was established in 1964 (compared to the no NOC status quo of 1958–1964). But as I describe in earlier sections, government revenues are only slightly higher when the NOC lacks operational capacity. In particular, the 1965–1972 era would correspond to the nonoperational SOE institutional pathway, given that the IPC had de facto control over the oil sector. It was only after IPC's operations were nationalized and INOC was given production control in June 1972 that the state would be able to sharply increase government take of oil revenues.

The inability to take advantage of the country's oil wealth in the pre-1972 period hindered the consolidation of the postmonarchy regimes of 'Abd al-Karim Qasim, 'Abd al-Salim 'Arif, 'Abd al-Rahman 'Arif, and the short spells of control by the Ba'athist National Guard. The 'Arif brothers, for instance, were constantly fighting off challenges to their rule from the anti-Nasserite Ba'athist contingent, the National Guard, and the separatist Kurdistan Democratic Party throughout the 1963–1968 period. With the exception of the support from a small contingent of military allies loyal to their patrimonial clan – the first manifestation of the infamous Iraqi Republican Guard – each of the two 'Arif leaders could never pacify their challengers nor buy their support. No resources could be spared for creating institutions to foster popular support from civil society, let alone to co-opt elites outside the inner circle. After al-Salim 'Arif's alleged assassination by the National Guard in April 1966, his brother al-Rahman 'Arif was deposed in a palace coup in July 1968 by al-Bakr and 'Arif's own Republican Guard who had, according to historian Charles Tripp, "become disappointed in his patronage" (Tripp, 2000, 208).

Al-Bakr would fare much better in light of increasing fiscal resources to sustain the patrimonial system of his court. After al-Bakr struck a deal with the USSR to explore oil fields in the north in 1969 and INOC's takeover of operational control in 1972, the Iraqi government was in a much stronger position to capture the full potential of the country's oil income. Coupled with the 1973 price shock, the ability of INOC to increase production levels even after prices collapsed in 1975–1976 ensured that al-Bakr could expand his patronage network to the broad and complex quilt of Ba'athist elites. Further, the long-standing conflict with the Kurds (backed by the Shah of Iran) came to an end with the 1975 Algiers Agreement and the inability of the KDP to hold back al-Bakr and Saddam Hussein's renewed military offensive.

Two final points are warranted here. First, I do not intend to explain with the nationalization theory the complex narrative of Iraqi instability in the postmonarchy period. The reasons for al-Bakr's success and his predecessor's failures cannot simply be explained through a fiscal framework alone, but rather through a multitude of theoretical lenses involving political factions, cultural alliances, leadership qualities, and international factors.

Second, the ability to reform ownership structures is by no means exogenous: the weaknesses of the regimes of Qasim and 'Arif were no more evident than in their inability to takeover operations from IPC and vest them into an Iraqi NOC. That said, 'Abd al-Salim 'Arif was successful in establishing a national oil company amidst strong international pressures to maintain private ownership. But that this NOC had no role in operations meant that the lion's share of revenues would continue to flow outside the country: neither he nor his brother could reap the full benefit of Iraq's incredible oil wealth. By contrast, the creation of an operational NOC allowed al-Bakr and Saddam Hussein – powerful enough to consolidate the oil sector under state control – to become even stronger and set the stage for a thirty-five-year Ba'athist dictatorship.

2.4 Conclusion

In the context of research on natural resource politics, the theory I presented in this chapter sheds light on why leaders in some resource-rich states thrive while in others they fail. Nationalization can be viewed as a strategy through which leaders strengthen their hold on power: this seemingly technical choice over who controls operations impacts the amount of revenues that the state accrues from the production and sale of petroleum. Not all nationalizations are alike: while some state-owned entities explore, develop, and produce resources, others are reduced to merely overseeing the sector with little actual role in operations. The former, which I refer to as operational nationalization, enables the state to reap the benefits of its resource wealth, while the latter are in many ways similar to not having nationalized the sector at all. This revenue augments a leader's hold on power, as this money can be used to consolidate his or her regime. Where leaders design SOEs that result in low government take of rents – which instead typically flow to bank accounts and shareholders of foreign MNCs – this choice prevents leaders from taking full advantage of their resource endowments.

This argument helps to explain why seemingly resource-rich leaders collapse where and when we least expect. The early postmonarchy regimes of Iraq, for example, could not leverage the country's increasing oil wealth to ensure their survival. This wealth was largely captured by the likes of Exxon, Shell, and BP, preventing the regimes of Qasim, al-Salim 'Arif, and al-Rahman 'Arif from co-opting challengers and rewarding their inner elite of military leadership. Not until INOC took over operations in 1972 did the government regain control over its oil revenues. This newfound wealth, further propelled by the 1973–1974 oil price shock, provided the foundation for a successful clientelistic machine that fostered the long patrimonial rule of the Ba'athist party under al-Bakr and later Hussein.

In neighboring Iran, the downfall of the Shah in 1979 sent shock waves of surprise across the globe. This "island of stability" in the volatile

Middle East failed to quell a popular revolution amidst what should have been a strong, consolidated regime bolstered by vast petroleum wealth. Instead, without de facto control over all operations, NIOC and the Shah could not sufficiently increase oil exports to balance a dramatically widening deficit in state expenditures. What had once been firmly in control of the state after operational nationalization in 1973 had reverted to the BP-led consortium by 1976. This loss of control over sorely needed oil revenues translated to a lost opportunity for the Shah to shore up his regime three years later when he needed it most.

These case studies serve to provide only prima facie evidence of the mechanisms through which the theory's broader argument reflects the empirical trajectory of resource-rich states. But, together with theory, these cases provide a more precise account of the conditional effect of natural resource wealth on politics. Beyond spatial differences due to prediscovery political institutions or temporal differences due to changing international market conditions, this argument emphasizes the important role that postdiscovery institutional design – specifically, the decision to nationalize natural resource operations – plays in determining whether natural resource wealth prolongs the survival of political leaders, and explains why leaders choose one design over another.

3   Defining and Measuring Operational Nationalization

What constitutes nationalization? How is operational nationalization empirically different from other forms of nationalization? Before turning to tests of the argument that leaders nationalize natural resource operations to increase their odds of survival, I review various existing approaches to how nationalization is measured and present the new database of oil nationalization used throughout the book.[1]

3.1   Measuring Nationalization

Nationalization is the acquisition of privately owned assets by the state, either with or without compensation (Wortley, 1956). In the context of the oil industry, nationalization is not just this acquisition, but also the establishment of a state-backed apparatus to operate these expropriated assets; in other contexts, outright expropriation may not occur, with a state-run entity established to operate and produce resources that are legally under the aegis of the state (Victor et al., 2012). In either case, this state-owned enterprise, or SOE, is commonly referred to as a national oil company, or NOC.

3.1.1   Timing and Duration of Nationalization: NOCs

When measuring oil nationalizations quantitatively, scholars have largely ignored SOE establishments and instead have focused on individual acts of expropriation. Kobrin (1980) was the first to quantify nationalization cross-nationally, with the creation of a database that measured every act of oil-related expropriation in a given country and year. Since then, most cross-national quantitative studies on oil nationalization have used and updated this measure (Kobrin, 1984; Minor, 1994; Bohn and Deacon, 2000; Li, 2009; Guriev et al., 2011; Wilson and Wright, 2017). The notable exception is the work I discuss in Chapters 1 and 2 by

---

[1] The full NOC database and all supporting material, including individual country oil histories, can be accessed at https://dataverse.harvard.edu/dataverse/paasham.

Jones Luong and Weinthal (2010), who analyze domestic ownership structure as a measure of nationalization that is related to the idea of the establishment of NOCs. In addition, McPherson (2010) considers a dichotomous measure based on state participation, whereby sectors with greater than 30 percent state participation (either through ownership of an NOC or participatory contracts with international oil companies, or IOCs) are considered "nationalized."

While the existing data on acts of expropriation are helpful in measuring the causes and effects of individual instances of expropriation, these measures do not capture institutional characteristics of nationalization as manifested in the differing frameworks of NOCs across oil-producing countries. In addition, these data may suffer from overcounting when conceptualizing nationalization as an institutional change in ownership structure of natural resources. For example, the Kobrin (1980) data counts four acts of oil-related expropriation occurring in Qatar during the 1972–1977 period. In practice, nationalization began in 1974 with the establishment of the Qatar Petroleum Company (QPC) as a state-owned oil company upon the expropriated assets of Shell Qatar. All subsequent expropriations are effectively less relevant since the international community had already recognized Qatar as operating a nationalized oil sector as of 1974 (Crystal, 1989). The same is true for Abu Dhabi: after the establishment of the Abu Dhabi National Oil Company (ADNOC) in 1971, any further expropriations by the king, Sheikh Zayed, were state consolidations of private assets (Suleiman, 2008). In other words, the state had already begun its intervention and nationalized the oil sector in 1971, so any consequential expropriations are not salient to the discussion of the initial timing or onset of nationalization.

I begin by considering an oil sector of a given country operationally nationalized if an NOC exists that physically operates the country's petroleum fields. In formal terms, this refers to de facto operational state control. To this end, I created a new data set based on the oil histories of every country since 1900. I extend the time period back to 1900 because the existing data on expropriations do not cover the period prior to 1962, when anecdotal evidence suggests some of the most important nationalizations occurred in the 1930s (Mexico, Bolivia, and Brazil) and 1950s (Iran and Indonesia).[2] These data are coded from a comprehensive review of every oil nationalization using primary and secondary sources: twenty-five petroleum laws and executive decrees, eighty United States Geological Survey (USGS) *Minerals Yearbooks* published annually since 1932 (United States Geological Survey, 1932),

---

[2] The Jones Luong and Weinthal ownership data, however, extend back to 1871.

and roughly 100 scholarly accounts of individual countries' oil histories, including examples like Philip (1982); de Oliveira (2012); Victor et al. (2012); Zahlan (1998); and Grayson (1981). Importantly, coding nationalization using NOCs relies on a process that is well-documented and objectively measurable, given there is precise information about when an NOC is established and the conditions under which a sector becomes operationally nationalized.

This variable is named *operational NOC* in the data and is a dummy variable with the following rule used to code it 1 or 0: if there is an SOE in the oil sector with greater than 50 percent state ownership, then the NOC dummy is coded 1 if the enterprise is actively involved in operations and production, and 0 otherwise. "Actively involved" refers to the NOC's role in upstream petroleum production: the physical exploration, discovery, development, extraction, and recovery of crude oil.[3] It does not refer to the NOC's role in downstream activities like processing, refining, marketing, and distribution. Whether an NOC plays an active role in operations is measured using oil and gas almanacs like the USGS *Minerals Yearbooks* referenced above: if the NOC is listed as an operating company for any given oil field in the country in a given year, with corresponding nonzero annual production and capacity, then it is coded as an operational NOC.

The unit of analysis is "country-year." The choice of calendar year, instead of budget year or fiscal year, is due to the availability of data for the independent variables in the analysis. (I use years instead of quarters, months, weeks, days, etc. for the same reason.) Furthermore, as budget and fiscal years vary widely across countries, using the Gregorian calendar year as the unit of time provides for a more comparable analysis. The trends shown in the top panel of Figure 3.1 are based on this method of coding nationalized sectors.

A similar measure can be constructed based not on majority ownership by the state, but rather state ownership of what is sometimes referred to as a "golden share," whereby the state may not control the majority of shares but retains the authority to outvote other shareholders on key company decisions. There are only three differences between these coding rules: France (1995–2003), Italy (1998), and the UK (1983–1985). The dates refer to periods in which the two coding decisions differ – for example, in France, starting in 1995 the state held

---

[3] In some cases the NOC may undertake upstream operations via a subsidiary: the National Iranian Oil Company, for instance, outsources the physical production of oil to regional subsidiaries like the Iranian Central Oil Fields Company. These instances are still coded as operational nationalization, since the subsidiary is a formal entity of the NOC.

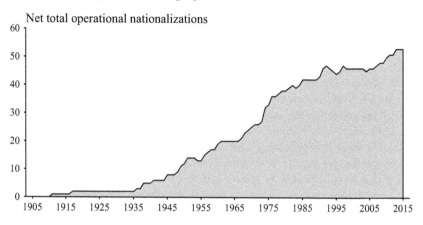

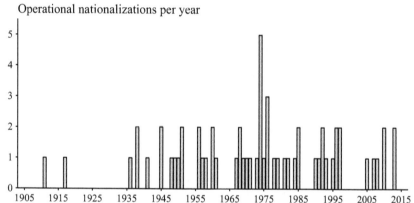

Figure 3.1 Operational oil nationalizations across the world, 1900–2015

Number of states establishing operational NOCs cumulatively over time (top panel) and number of states establishing operational NOCs each year (bottom panel). The top panel accounts for privatizations or reversions to nonoperational NOCs in each year so that the height of each part of the line reflects the total number of states with operational NOCs in a given year.

a minority stake in Elf-Aquitaine (later Total) with a golden share until 2003, at which point the company became fully privatized (though the state continues to own a small proportion of shares). If coding under the majority-ownership rule, these years would be marked 0; if coding under the golden-share rule, these years would be marked 1. Nonetheless, I primarily use a 50 percent threshold for substantive reasons: the government must be the majority shareholder of the company to prevent private investors from influencing key and nonkey decisions.

In terms of the timing of operational nationalization, I construct another binary measure, *nationalization* (short for operational nationalization), based on the *operational NOC* variable. The *nationalization* dummy variable is coded as follows: the first year that an operational NOC is established or the first year that an NOC commences an operational role is measured as the year of nationalization for a given country, coded as 1 for that year, with all other years taking on a 0 value. By this measure, states may only nationalize more than once if a previous NOC was privatized, as was the case in Canada, France, and the UK, or if the NOC reverted to a nonoperational role. (A full listing of the timing of all oil nationalizations is presented in Table 1.1 in Chapter 1, sorted by year of operational NOC establishment.)

Three examples will help to clarify how the *operational NOC* and *nationalization* measures are constructed. Consider Mexico, where Lazaro Cardenas's expropriation of Shell and Standard Oil in 1938 – an event that is still celebrated as a major national holiday (Fiesta Patria) – led to the establishment in that year of Petróleos Mexicanos (Pemex). This NOC was established with full state ownership of the company's shares and de facto operational capacity (Philip, 1982). For the Mexican case, the *operational NOC* dummy is coded 0 from 1900 (the first year in the data) to 1937, and 1 thereafter; the *nationalization* dummy is coded 1 only for the year 1938, and is 0 for every other year.

But not all states form an NOC and nationalize operations in the same year. In the case of Ecuador, for instance, on June 23, 1972, the government created a state-owned petroleum enterprise, the Corporación Estatal Petrolera Ecuatoriana, or CEPE. Because the state knew it lacked the technical expertise to explore and develop new fields, CEPE was not actively involved in operations. Instead, CEPE played a sideline role through production-sharing agreements with operating companies that undertook production and extraction. It was not until 1989–1990, when the company was renamed Petroecuador, that the company began producing and operating the country's fields, with the government taking on a more direct and active role in oil operations. In this case, while an NOC was established in 1972, operational nationalization did not occur until 1990, the first year that the *operational NOC* dummy is coded as 1.

For cases of privatization, consider the coding of Canada, which established an operational NOC by the name of Petro-Canada in 1975–1976, only to privatize the company in 1995.[4] For this case, the *NOC* dummy is coded 1 for 1976–1995 and 0 for all other years, and the

---

[4] Privatization of state shares began in 1991, but the government sold its majority shares in 1995 (retaining 19 percent of the company), with complete privatization in 2004.

nationalization dummy is 1 for 1976 and 0 otherwise. What separates this from the other cases is that for analysis of the timing of nationalization, Mexico and Ecuador are removed from the sample after 1938 and 1990, respectively, since they cannot technically renationalize the industry; Canada, by contrast, reenters the data set following privatization in 1995 since the government can choose to nationalize oil operations again.

3.1.2   Institutional Characteristics: Not All NOCs Are the Same

Beyond the historical trajectory of their NOCs, the institutional pathways of Canada and Mexico are different in important ways. Pemex is an extreme example of an operational NOC: not only is it involved in production and regulation of the sector, but up until 2015 it was also the monopoly operator of Mexico's oil industry and was fully owned by the Mexican government. The company engages in noncommercial activities like social programs, fuel subsidies, and the required use of domestically produced inputs like concrete, steel, and plastics. By contrast, Petro-Canada was just like any other oil company, with the only exception being that 57 percent of the company's shares were owned by the government (making it a Federal Crown Corporation of Canada). The company explored for oil and operated oil fields in Alberta alongside other companies like BP, Mobil, Shell, and Suncor; it was thus not a monopoly producer. It did not engage in noncommercial activities and it played no role in regulating other companies in the sector. Indeed, Petro-Canada had to compete with other companies for contracts that were awarded by provincial governments and their ministries (for example, the Alberta Energy Regulator).

The key institutional difference I emphasize throughout this book is whether the SOE produces and operates resource fields and mines. Regarding natural resources broadly construed, those who do are called *operational SOEs* and those that do not are *nonoperational SOEs*. In the oil industry, this captures an important distinction between states whose NOCs are oil companies in the literal sense versus those who are oil companies in that they manage other oil companies actually involved in production. In terms of my broader argument, this distinction is critical: production capacity matters in an SOE because it translates to more resource revenues for the state than would be possible under private ownership or under SOEs that are merely tax and regulatory entities.

Because time-series data on specific production percentages are not available – even at any point in time for nearly twenty of the roughly seventy oil producers – I use a producer versus nonproducer proxy.

Table 3.1. *Varieties of nationalization in the natural resource sector*

Institutional path	State activities	Examples: oil sector	Examples: metals & minerals sector
Operational SOE	exploration, discovery, extraction, production	Brazil, Iran, Malaysia, Norway, Russia, Saudi Arabia	Chile (copper), China (iron), Ghana (aluminum), India (coal), Morocco (phosphate), Bolivia (tin)
Nonoperational SOE	revenue collection, regulation, tax monitoring	Congo, Ghana, Nigeria, Peru, Tunisia	Bolivia (zinc), Namibia (uranium), Senegal (phosphate), Zimbabwe (copper)
Private ownership	revenue collection, regulation, tax monitoring	Afghanistan, Papua New Guinea, Timor-Leste	Chile (lithium), Congo (cobalt), Ghana (gold), Iran (zinc), South Africa (platinum)

I am able, however, to differentiate between major- and minor-producing NOCs based on rough estimates of production activity from the United States Geological Survey (1932–2015), in which the threshold between major and minor is 50 percent. My discussion of operational NOCs (and operational SOEs in general) refers to those with production capacity versus those with no production capacity; for robustness, I also use the stricter definition of major production capacity to differentiate between NOCs with very small roles in production and NOCs that dominate the sector's operations. Historically, the distribution of production share between NOCs and other companies within a given country is for the most part bimodal – most NOCs either produce very little of a country's oil or are nearly monopolists – such that moving the threshold by plus or minus 15 percent does not substantively alter the coding.

These characteristics lend themselves to a typology of state intervention into three categories. These are presented in Table 3.1, with examples in the oil industry as well as in the metals and minerals sector. The first category is private ownership, in which the government has not established an SOE. Here, private firms are regulated and taxed by a ministry or regulatory agency.

The second category is what I refer to as a nonoperational SOE, whereby the company is not involved in the upstream sector beyond trivial levels of shared production alongside other firms. These SOEs are either simply revenue-collection agencies working alongside regulating ministries like the Entreprise Tunisienne d'Activités Pétrolières (ETAP) in Tunisia, or minor co-operators with outside firms in small resource-producing countries like the Ghana National Petroleum Corporation. Some are also remnants of what used to be SOEs with high production capacity in previously petroleum-exporting states like Energie Beheer Nederland (EBN) in the Netherlands.[5] In either case, the company does not physically produce resources on its own, and only does so by shadowing other companies in the upstream sector.

This category also includes nonproducing SOEs that directly regulate private firms operating in the sector. Here an SOE exists solely to manage the sector, award contracts, and collect tax revenue from operating firms. Two classic examples in the oil industry are Nigeria's NNPC and Cameroon's Société Nationale des Hydrocarbures (SNH), both of which manage the bidding process for permits, licenses, concessions, and exploratory blocks, without actually producing or operating any fields (despite being listed in production-sharing agreements).

The third category is the operational SOE. This category includes companies with monopoly production rights like Mexico's Pemex, Iran's NIOC, and Saudi Arabia's Saudi Aramco, but also include nonmonopoly producers like Algeria's Sonatrach, China's combination of Sinopec and the Chinese National Petroleum Company (CNPC), and many NOCs in the former Soviet states like Azerbaijan's SOCAR, Turkmenneft, and Uzbekneftegaz.

States have chosen these three institutional pathways at varying rates over time, as shown in Figure 3.2. Prior to the 1950s, almost all of the world's oil was being produced by private firms in countries without NOCs, with the Soviet Union and Mexico as the primary exceptions. The first wave of NOCs in the 1960s and early 1970s were mostly nonoperational SOEs: two out of every three NOCs in 1970, for example, were not directly engaged in production. This changed in the mid-1970s during the major wave of nationalizations, to the point that operational NOCs oversaw just over 70 percent of global oil production

---

[5] Throughout its oil history, the Dutch hydrocarbons economy has been "privatized," albeit with a twist. The state founded EBN, a fully-state-owned oil and gas company, in 1973 to manage the hydrocarbons sector through joint-ventures and production-sharing. However, EBN has no true production capacity nor does it have any oversight: it is purely a contracting shell whose existence is to manage the Dutch government's national claims to oil and gas production. This is in reference to the government's self-proclaimed right to 40–50 percent of all oil and gas produced within Dutch territories (mostly offshore). The fields themselves were and continue to be operated by IOCs like Amoco, ConocoPhillips, Unocal, and NAM (Royal Dutch Shell's investor-owned subsidiary), and EBN is just there to collect the government's share of revenues (after sale, not at the wellhead). See www.nam.nl/en/about-nam/facts-and-figures.html for more details on both EBN and NAM.

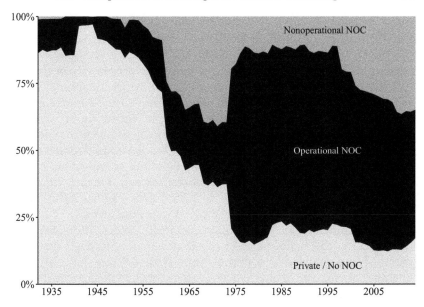

Figure 3.2 State intervention over time: percentage of global oil production, 1932–2015

Note: The share of global oil production (y-axis) is calculated based on the amount of oil produced in countries with each type of state intervention, divided by total world oil production. The starting point of 1932 is based on data availability for oil production by country. (Ross and Mahdavi, 2014)

and 84 percent of total NOC oil production by 1980. By the 1990s there was another wave of NOCs, resulting from the collapse of the Soviet Union. But since 1995, an increasing number of nonoperational NOCs in sub-Saharan Africa and private ownership structures in the emerging producers (in the Caribbean, East Africa, and Southeast Asia) has brought some balance to the mix. In 2014 (the latest year with oil production data), nonoperational NOCs oversaw 35 percent of total oil production and operational NOCs oversaw 48 percent, with the remaining 17 percent produced in countries without an upstream NOC like Canada and the United States.

3.2   Comparisons to Existing Data on State Ownership of Petroleum

The Jones Luong and Weinthal (2010) state-ownership database offers the closest comparison to my measure of national oil companies. At one end of their spectrum is "state ownership with control," which refers to countries with de jure authority over the production of oil. On the other end is "private foreign ownership" and the rarer category of "private domestic ownership," which both refer to countries where legal authority over oil production is vested in private oil companies. In between is the category of "state ownership without control," which refers to instances in which countries may have created a national oil company and nationalized the oil sector, but legal authority over oil production is still vested in private oil companies. Given the focus of Jones Luong and Weinthal (2010)'s theory on dynamics between rulers and the domestic elite (and society), the de jure specification is both appropriate and accurate. For my purposes, however, the de facto ability to produce oil is paramount, since this determines whether the state can earn a greater share of revenues compared to private firms.

This distinction in measurement strategy creates two disparate databases on the nationalization of oil resources. Although there are cases of concurrence – countries with both de jure and de facto operational capacity, or alternatively with de jure and de facto operations vested in private firms – there are roughly 731 country-years out of a total of 2,412 country-years in which our databases differ.[6]

The first category of countries with different coding are those where the state has de jure production control but de facto lacks the capacity to operate the country's petroleum fields. Typically these are instances in which a state may have a national oil company that is legally authorized to control oil production, but in practice the company is unable to handle production; instead, the company plays an oversight role or a revenue-collection role while international oil companies control actual production. The classic case of this mismatch is NNPC, which plays no role in the actual production of Nigeria's petroleum. Instead, NNPC manages the sale of crude oil that is produced by other firms, either through joint ventures with international oil companies whereby NNPC offers an equity stake in return for crude oil produced by the companies, or through production-sharing contracts wherein outside firms pay their taxes to the Nigerian government in the form of crude oil ("tax oil" or "royalty oil") (Sayne et al., 2015). In both cases, NNPC is simply an intermediary: it offers authorization and, in some cases, capital from the Nigerian government in return for the extraction of crude oil from its fields. It then sells that crude oil on the market, or as is more

---

[6] The 2,412 country-years figure is the number of data points in which our two databases overlap, given different starting and ending points and a different set of countries considered oil producers. The Jones Luong and Weinthal (2010) data cover up to 50 countries across 1871–2005 with a total sample size of $n = 2,553$, while my data cover up to 108 countries across 1900–2015 with a total sample size of $n = 5,511$.

often the case, outsources these sales to another firm.[7] For the years of 1969–1990, Jones Luong and Weinthal (2010) code this case as state ownership with control, since NNPC had legal authority over operations, whereas I code this period (and the subsequent 1991–2015 period) as a nonoperational SOE (nationalization without production), since neither the company nor any other state entity actually produced any crude oil.

Another interesting case is Ecuador in the 1972–1982 era, when the national oil company CEPE was authorized to control oil production but in practice farmed this out to Texaco and Gulf Oil. Even though the company had signed production-sharing agreements whereby it would assist in operations, in actuality production was handled entirely by these outside firms.[8] Gulf Oil, for instance, extracted crude oil on behalf of CEPE and paid the government taxes and royalties for its operations, just as it would have absent an NOC existing in the sector. The Ecuadoran government therefore did not have control over the production of oil–a painful lesson it learned in 1977 when Gulf withheld payments from crude oil sales because of a dispute with the Minister of Natural Resources over changes to operating terms in favor of the state.[9] As with the Nigerian case, for these years Jones Luong and Weinthal (2010) code Ecuador as state ownership with control, while I code it as a nonoperational SOE.

The second category of countries with different coding are those with de facto control over production but which lack clear de jure rights over operations. In the Islamic Republic of Iran, for example, the Petroleum Act of 1987 gives authority over production to various subsidiaries and privately owned domestic firms. The law stripped NIOC of its dominion over the industry, replacing it with the Ministry of Petroleum that would oversee all private and semipublic domestic production companies (the law banned foreign investment) (Shahri, 2010). But in practice, this legal framework was largely ignored: NIOC continued its monopoly over production and maintained control over operations throughout the post-1987 period, with only minor operations handled by private domestic firms like PetroPars, Pasargad, and Dana Energy.[10] For the years 1987 onward, the Jones Luong and Weinthal (2010) coding of Iran is state

---

[7] This role naturally lends itself to corruption and graft, to the point that billions of dollars in oil sales routinely "go missing" each year. For more, see Sayne et al. (2015).
[8] "The Mineral Industry of Other Areas of South America: Ecuador." *USGS Minerals Yearbook: 1977.*
[9] Ibid., p. 1375.
[10] After the ban on foreign investment was lifted in the mid 1990s, NIOC also partnered with international oil companies through a variant of the production-sharing contract. See Takin (2009).

ownership without control, while I code the case as an operational SOE given its de facto control over production.

Why do these coding differences matter? Since my focus is on leadership survival and the natural resource revenues that ensure that survival, the de facto control of operations is essential as a measure of nationalization. Without a direct role in the operations of a country's natural resource sector, the state cannot reap the fiscal rewards of its resources. Even with legal rights over operations, if the state does not physically control production, then the combination of information asymmetries and the inability to dictate production levels can reduce the state's take home–resource revenues. Instead, the bulk of these revenues can be captured by outside firms, leaving state leaders with less revenue to bolster their rule and increase their odds of survival in office. Although de jure control over operations is a critical signal to domestic elites and foreign investors, it will only carry a fiscal effect if it is borne out in practice at the wellhead, mine, or extractive site.

3.3   Conclusion

This chapter lays the groundwork for empirical tests of the argument that leaders nationalize natural resource operations to strengthen their rule and increase their time in power. By first defining what operational nationalization is and how it differs from existing concepts of national-ization, the chapter presents a formal typology of three state intervention pathways: private ownership and operations, nonoperational SOEs, and operational SOEs. Although this range restricts the rich variation that exists in SOE formation across countries to just three categories, it allows for a parsimonious evaluation of the causes and consequences of operational nationalization as it is distinguished from other forms of intervention. The chapter draws on the empirical workhorse of the book, the oil industry, to show how this measurement choice is operationalized to create the national oil company database used throughout the book.

The way nationalization is measured here differs from prior work in a number of ways, most notably the focus on de facto state authority over natural resource production. The nationalization of operations as I define it here entails the actual control by the state over the extraction of natural resources, rather than outsourcing this activity to outside firms. This distinction is essential to testing the argument, as private companies that control operations can misreport or withhold information about the true costs and profits of production – thereby depriving the state of natural resource revenues that could be used to strengthen a leader's hold on power.

The oil nationalizations data reveal several patterns about state inter-vention pathways over time. The first is the well-known domination of private ownership in the early era of petroleum, when the Seven Sisters of the oil industry held a monopoly-like control over production across the world. The only fields outside their reach were those of the communist states and the few countries like Mexico that had nationalized operations prior to the 1950s. The first major wave of operational nationalizations occurred in the mid 1970s, when some countries expropriated private assets for the first time and established operational control with a newly formed NOC, as in Qatar and Trinidad, while others used existing NOCs to seize control of production handled by private firms, as in Iran and Malaysia. Operational NOCs would be the dominant choice up until the dissolution of the Soviet Union, after which leaders opted to establish or switch to nonoperational NOCs, or in some cases to privatize their industries all together. The motivating reasons for these patterns of intervention and their consequences for the survival of political leaders are the topics that I turn to in the next three chapters.

4   Why Nationalize?
Evidence from National Oil Companies
around the World

Operational nationalizations have occurred at some point in time in almost every major oil producer in the world and in the majority of minor oil producers. While some states nationalized operations early in the twentieth century, some waited until the early period of the twenty-first century, with the vast majority of nationalizations occurring in the 1970s. The OPEC charter, and indeed one of OPEC's founding philosophies, stresses that its members "take assets from foreign occupiers." Though these kinds of nationalization are rare events – occurring only 61 times since 1900 – their impacts are game-changing in both international markets and the domestic political environment. What accounts for this pattern? Why do leaders choose to nationalize oil operations?

Using both statistical analysis of historical nationalizations and a qualitative case comparison, in this chapter I show that the choice to nationalize natural resource operations is sparked by the diffusion of information about competitors' agreements with outside firms and is ultimately decided by a leader's perceptions of surviving in political power. The diffused information that prompts this choice is knowledge of a better deal to be had over how revenues are shared between host governments and the firms operating and producing their natural resources. Such knowledge spurs leaders to reevaluate their existing agreements with outside firms in an attempt to increase take-home revenues for the government. While these renegotiations can result in a variety of outcomes, two broader choices emerge from the fray: nationalize and reap immediate windfalls at the cost of long-term gains from efficient private operations, or maintain private operating firms but increase their effective tax rates. Faced with this decision, weaker leaders choose nationalization while stronger leaders instead maintain private production and increase taxes on outside operating firms.

This chapter tests these two implications from my argument that the decision to nationalize natural resources affects and is affected by the probability of leader survival. To assess how information diffusion prompts leaders to consider nationalization, I draw on cross-national time-series analysis of the relationship between OPEC membership and the likelihood of operational nationalization, as measured using the database of operational national oil companies described in Chapter 3. In the postwar era of oil production such information was difficult to obtain – outside of the landmark agreements covered occasionally by international media – given the intentional opacity of transactions by the near monopoly of oil companies like Standard Oil, Shell, and British Petroleum. The formation of OPEC in 1960 provided a forum in which leaders could not only try to control oil prices but also meet to exchange information about agreements reached with international oil companies. This entails a variety of terms, namely the agreed-upon levels of extraction and the host government's effective share of petroleum revenues. Leaders of states attending these regularly held meetings were frequently exposed to information about the possibility of obtaining a greater share of oil revenues for their governments, and limiting the amount of oil revenues forfeited to the likes of Standard and BP. With OPEC membership as a proxy for information diffusion, I find that these leaders were more likely to nationalize operations than leaders whose countries were not part of the cartel.

In the same cross-national analysis, I also test an implication from the argument that weaker leaders – those who perceive low odds of future survival – are more likely to nationalize operations than stronger leaders. Here I examine the difference in nationalization likelihood for leaders in younger regimes compared to leaders in older regimes. If it is the case that weaker leaders are more likely to nationalize, then we should also expect that leaders in the early years of a regime will be more likely to nationalize. These regimes have yet to establish firm roots and are more susceptible to failure than regimes in existence for decades when a new leader takes power. Within dynastic dictatorships, for instance, the first ruler will typically face much lower odds of survival than his progeny who will likely rule within a well-established governing body. Using the number of years of uninterrupted regime duration as a measure, I find that nationalization is nearly three times as likely in the first years of a regime than it is after forty years of established rule.

This chapter also provides a methodological contribution to the existing literature on resource nationalization (see Chapter 2 and Victor (2013) for a review). Because the decision to nationalize is tested in the context of longitudinal data with a discrete outcome – a leader either nationalizes or not in a given country in a given year – researchers typically use either ordinary least squares or maximum likelihood regression techniques, including unit-fixed effects to account for country-specific potentially omitted factors. As I discuss in greater detail in the pages that follow, the application of such methods to these data is problematic and can give inconsistent and, in the case of maximum likelihood regression, biased estimates. As such, I operate within a Bayesian estimation framework to mitigate these concerns. As this method necessitates prior distributions for the parameters to be estimated, I combine expert interviews and previous scholarly findings to estimate informative priors for the analysis.

Measuring both information diffusion and perceived leader strength in a cross-national setting can be fraught with imprecision. To bolster support for these two implications of the argument, I consider a qualitative two-case comparison in the pre-OPEC era of oil production in Iran and Saudi Arabia. In both cases, diffused information sparked leaders to renegotiate their agreements with international oil companies. In Saudi Arabia, King Abdul-aziz ibn-Saud opted not to nationalize but instead to maintain private operations, albeit with a higher tax rate. By contrast, the Shah of Iran and his oft-adversarial prime minister Mohammad Mossadegh infamously nationalized operations of the AIOC (which later became British Petroleum) in 1951. Where ibn-Saud perceived strength in the durability of the Saudi monarchy – and thus a high probability of survival – both the Shah and Mossadegh faced uncertainty in the stability of the Iranian government. I argue that perceived strength provided the basis for ibn-Saud to eschew nationalization, whereas perceived doubts of future survival prompted the Shah to accept Mossadegh's plan for nationalization.

Viewing this comparison through the lens of the argument I make in this book helps to understand cases in which prior explanations get the prediction of nationalization wrong (Jones Luong and Weinthal, 2010; Guriev et al., 2011; Hajzler, 2012; Warshaw, 2012; Wilson and Wright, 2017). Iran nationalized in 1951 during a time of low oil prices and during an era with relatively high executive constraints and high political contestation, all three of which are factors predicting a low probability of nationalization. Saudi Arabia, by contrast, opted against nationalization in 1950 despite low constraints on the executive, almost no political contestation, and generally weak political institutions. Instead, the diffusion of information about the viability of greater government take sparks leaders to consider nationalization. This choice is taken by leaders that perceive lower probabilities of surviving power, but is shunned by leaders that instead perceive durability.

4.1 What Factors Determine Oil Nationalization?

A leader's decision to nationalize the oil industry is inherently based on a delicate cost-benefit analysis.[1] A leader must maximize expected utility from nationalization while considering the potential benefits to state ownership and avoiding the potential costs of expropriation.

The primary benefit to nationalization is a short- to medium-term increase in the state's take of revenues from the sale of oil. This is a topic that I revisit in greater detail in Chapters 5 and 6: I show that oil revenues are higher after establishing an operational SOE, even after controlling for prices, production, and other country-specific factors. Other benefits include direct oversight of operations and production decisions, and control over lucrative state-owned enterprise management positions to use as tools of patronage (Nolan and Thurber, 2010).

By expropriating foreign assets, the state not only gains by controlling new hard assets (e.g., rigs, pipelines, and drilling equipment), but more importantly increases the share of profits collected by the treasury from the oil industry (Marcel, 2006; Stevens, 2007). Rather than having to forfeit profits to a foreign company or government, the state *can* collect 100 percent of revenues – not just profits – from the sale of oil. This happens via the operational NOC, and the state can decide how best to reinvest this money back to the company (thus implicitly forcing the NOC to take a negative rate of return). More often than solely relying on the NOC, states like Algeria, Brazil, and the UAE have chosen to employ operators for production alongside the NOC that are facilitated through profit-sharing agreements and joint ventures (McPherson, 2010; Sarbu, 2014). In the realm of oil nationalizations, this framework is adopted by Guriev et al. (2011) to show that leaders nationalize the oil industry when petroleum prices are high as this maximizes the short-term revenues from expropriation and outweighs the potential costs of nationalization.

An additional benefit to nationalization is satisfying domestic sentiments of "resource nationalism," a broad term that captures the concept of perceptions of fairness in revenue-sharing between states and firms. This also refers to the public's perceived "lost profits" from the perspective of the state vis-à-vis private oil operators (Bremmer and Johnston, 2009; Vivoda, 2009; Tordo et al., 2011). Leaders may feel

---

[1] Though I use the term "leader" here referring to an individual political agent, the concept applies equally to consensus-based decisions to nationalize like those by a parliament, junta, oligarchy, etc.

"cheated" by private operators of their fair share of oil profits if they see private companies benefiting more from oil production than entitled. In other words, if the state perceives its share of oil profits to be low relative to the operators' share, the state may see the difference in profits as the opportunity cost of maintaining a private ownership structure.

When private operators are foreign-owned in particular, xenophobic feelings arise that foreigners are "stealing" a country's oil, which leaders and the public feel is the sovereign right of an independent nation. Referring to the period prior to expropriation, scholars use nationalistic quotations from political leaders like "it's our oil," "the oil belongs to the people," and "driving out the foreign devils" (Yergin, 1991; Karl, 1997). If there exists a noticeable gap between what the state treasury collects from oil profits and what foreign operators collect, this could influence the decision to nationalize. Though this is itself a form of revenue maximization, it is a combination of resource nationalism and maximizing state revenues. As Vlado Vivoda has noted, "it is natural that during a period of high prices the phenomenon of resource nationalism comes to the surface, as it is a by-product of high prices" (Vivoda, 2009, 518).

Research by Manzano and Monaldi (2009) similarly finds that high oil prices induce pressure to renegotiate fiscal contracts. Because of the lack of price contingencies in many existing contracts, high oil prices translate to disproportionately higher operator-retained revenues compared to what is allocated to the state. This imbalance, the authors argue, can stoke grievances over revenue sharing that result in contract renegotiation in the form of increasing taxes and royalties to outright nationalization of assets.

Though it has not been tested empirically, this notion of perceptions of fairness has been recognized by existing scholarly work in the framework of resource nationalism. Manzano and Monaldi (2009) recognize resource nationalism as one of the mechanisms behind their explanation for the political left's expropriation of oil and gas in Latin America. Solberg (1979) and Smith (2007) cite resource nationalism as potential factors in the nationalizations of Argentina and Iran, respectively. Singh (1989) and Stevens (2008) note the cyclical patterns of resource nationalism, not just in the oil and gas sector, but also in metals like copper, iron, and steel. Similarly, Kretzschmar et al. (2010) identify resource nationalism as the reason for limited foreign investment after a nationalization due to strong elements of xenophobia and mistrust.

The push for resource nationalism is manifested not only in the ideological preferences of the mass public but also in the ethos of the country's leadership. Prior research on the connection between oil wealth and conflict would suggest that revolutionary leaders in particular are more likely to engage in aggressive behavior. Colgan (2013), for instance, argues that leaders of oil-rich governments that have come to power via domestic revolution – as opposed to gaining control through alternative means like foreign-imposed regime change or regular succession – are more likely to go to war. This stems from both the deterioration of institutional constraints during revolutions and from a selection effect whereby revolutions "tend to select leaders that are systematically more risk-tolerant and ambitious to revise the status quo" (Colgan, 2013, 4). The same mechanisms would also be expected to operate in the decision to nationalize extractive resource operations. Leaders who are more willing to take on risks and who face fewer constraints in doing so should be more likely to nationalize than those who lack either or both characteristics.

The costs of nationalizing the oil sector are more complex. The most straightforward cost is the expected loss of efficiency when switching from a privately run oil company to a state-run firm (Hartley and Medlock, 2008). A more dangerous cost is the loss of oil exports due to international retaliation, as foreign governments may enforce an oil embargo on the nationalizing country. Such was the case after Mexico's nationalization in 1938 and Iran's nationalization in 1951. Lesser sanctions, such as the trade and financial sanctions that were considered by Spain and the EU after the nationalization of Repsol-YPF in Argentina in 2012, may be enacted by the international community following nationalization.

Work in the 1980s by Stephen Kobrin highlighted the "domino effect" of nationalizations in other countries affecting the probability of nationalization in a given country (Kobrin, 1984, 1985). Consider that in December 1936, the Bolivian state nationalized Standard Oil's assets to form Yacimientos Petrolíferos Fiscales Bolivianos (YPFB). Two years later, Brazil's dictator, Getulio Vargas, proposed a new government agency with "extensive powers over all sections of the oil industry." The agency was formally established in 1938 and early 1939 as the country's NOC, the Conselho Nacional do Petróleo (CNP) (Philip, 1982, 230). These two events are not independent of one another: indeed, Vargas' energy commission directly cited the establishment of Bolivia's YPFB and Argentina's YPF (formed in 1911) as examples to be followed (Cohn, 1968). One explanation for this pattern is that the domino effect of nationalizations could simply be a "copycat" effect, whereby countries nationalize the industry to emulate the ownership structure of perceived "pioneer" countries, similar to patterns of "copycat entrepeneurship" among small- to medium-sized enterprises (Philip, 2002).

In minimizing the costs of nationalization, leaders must also take into account the constraints of expropriation given domestic politics and the institutional environment. Jones Luong and Weinthal (2010) consider institutional constraints on expropriation: on the one hand, countries with strong political institutions will find it harder to expropriate without incurring large and possibly disastrous political costs. On the other hand, countries with either weak institutions or institutional settings that favor state control will find it easier to nationalize.

Guriev et al. (2011) similarly characterize strong institutions as impediments to expropriation, and suggest that executive constraints – checks and balances on the executive branch of government – increase the costs of nationalization. In nondemocratic systems in particular, weak or nonexistent parliaments or other veto points may allow a leader to nationalize the oil industry with little political opposition, though this might have long-term costs in the form of diminished foreign investment (Tsebelis, 2002; Henisz, 2004). Indeed, Wilson and Wright (2017) suggest that having a functioning legislative body in a nonpersonalist dictatorship may diminish the risk of expropriation and increase investor confidence, though this pattern does not seem to hold in personalist dictatorships. In general, elites may have the ability to influence dictators and monarchs to press for nationalizations in a way not possible in democracies (Gandhi, 2008).

Executive constraints may also reduce the probability of nationalization by decreasing the leader's share of rents resulting from expropriation (Warshaw, 2012). Compared to a personalist dictatorship or monarchical regime, a leader in a power-sharing position must divide these rents among other high-ranking elites, as in a single-party dominant autocracy like the former USSR or pre-2000 Mexico, or in the case of democracy, among other government branches and bureaucracies.

4.1.1   Implications of the Operational Nationalizations Theory

Taken together, these costs and benefits suggest specific factors at play in a leader's decision whether and when to nationalize the oil industry. I consider two testable hypotheses based on observable implications from the theoretical determinants discussed in the last section. I begin by reframing the question of why leaders nationalize the oil industry into statements that capture the likelihood of oil nationalization based on a given factor or set of factors.

The first is information diffusion. The choice of whether to nationalize operations is sparked when leaders gain knowledge about the revenue-sharing arrangements of their competitors. Yet measuring this diffusion is challenging in a cross-national setting given the difficulties of observing repeated instances of information sharing across borders, particularly in the peak era of nationalizations in the 1970s and 1980s. As such, I consider a proxy for information diffusion in the form of OPEC membership. The observable implication of the argument would be that *states joining OPEC are more likely to nationalize operations.*

But why should OPEC membership matter? This cartel provided a forum in which leaders could periodically meet to exchange information. According to its bylaws, OPEC was founded in September 1960 "to unify petroleum policies among Member Countries to secure fair and stable prices for petroleum producers."[2] While the primary goals of its formal meetings were to coordinate production levels across its members and to prevent price volatility (and later to attempt to control prices directly), these meetings created an institutionalized environment in which oil ministers from different states would discuss terms of the agreements reached between their host governments and the major Western oil companies (Mikdashi, 1972).

One challenge with using OPEC as a measure of information diffusion is confounding. The determinants of joining OPEC are likely endogeneous to other determinants of nationalization, namely autocratic government, a long history of oil production, and increasing levels of oil exports. However, these factors should be considered necessary but not sufficient determinants of OPEC membership, given the absence of major autocratic producers in the 1960s and 1970s like the Soviet Union, Mexico, and Malaysia. In the absence of cross-national data on information diffusion, OPEC membership is a proxy, albeit one with measurement error, for the ability of leaders to share information about the details of their revenue-sharing agreements with IOCs.

The second hypothesis I put to the test in this chapter is that leaders in young regimes are more likely to nationalize operations than leaders in older regimes. Political regimes that have endured for decades are less susceptible to overthrow than those with only limited years of experience (Geddes, 2003). It follows that leaders in more established regimes are less likely to be ousted than leaders in less established regimes (Goemans et al., 2009). However, regime age by itself is neither necessary nor sufficient for a leader's perception of survival odds: one can find leaders with weak odds of survival in old and secure regimes and leaders with strong survival odds in new and unstable regimes.

---

[2] OPEC. (n.d.). "Brief History." Accessed from www.opec.org/opec_web/en/about_us/24.htm.

This hypothesis therefore serves as corroborative support for the larger argument that leaders that perceive lower odds of survival will opt for nationalization, while leaders that feel more secure in power will eschew nationalization and stick with private operating firms for resource extraction. It should be clear that this is not a direct test of the argument – given the limitations of measuring leader-survival perceptions using variables of regime duration – but rather a test of the argument's implications for leaders in regimes of differing strength and experience. But if the argument that weaker leaders nationalize (and thus become stronger) while strong leaders do not (and thus become weaker) is true, then on average it should be the case that *nationalization is more likely in younger rather than older regimes*.

In terms of testing existing theories of nationalization, I consider three implications to test empirically. If leaders are revenue maximizers, then the timing of nationalization should occur in or after moments when the financial return to doing so is at its peak. When global oil prices are high, then oil revenues are high (assuming constant or increasing production). Further, nationalizing when the short-term gains are at high levels outweighs the potential financial costs of nationalization – notably inefficiency and retaliation. If this is true, then I should observe that oil nationalization is more likely when oil prices are high than when prices are low.

Vernon (1971) and Kobrin (1985) suggest that first movers can defray the probability of retaliation for followers. Here the notion of first-movers is relaxed somewhat to refer to the sum of nationalizers occurring in a previous period with respect to a given country that has not yet nationalized. This probability decreases with the number of countries that nationalize in this prior period. For instance, if six countries nationalize in a given year (t), this reduces the retaliation probability in the following year ($t + 1$) more than if only two countries nationalize. In general, the domino effect would imply that oil nationalization is more likely when others nationalize than when there are no nationalizations in prior years.

Jones Luong and Weinthal (2010) and Guriev et al. (2011) show that leaders with more executive constraints find it harder to expropriate private assets for fear of domestic backlash. With increasing numbers of institutional veto points, a leader will find it difficult to push nationalization through the requisite legislative and judicial channels (Henisz, 2000; Wilson and Wright, 2017). Alternatively, Warshaw (2012) contends that executive constraints can limit a leader's consumption of rents by virtue of having to share rents from expropriation with power-sharing elites. By contrast, leaders with few constraints can nationalize without overcoming institutional roadblocks. Thus, one should expect national-ization to be more likely in authoritarian states than in democratic states. However, the empirical tests conducted here do not discern between which mechanisms drive the resulting relationship between institutional quality and nationalization.

4.2 Data, Methods, and Research Design

4.2.1 Data

The outcome of interest is the probability of operational nationalization in a given country in a given year. Following my discussion in Chapters 1 and 3, I measure operational nationalization as a binary variable according to whether a state establishes a majority-state-owned SOE that de facto operates the country's oil fields – whether as a monopoly producer or alongside other operating firms. All years prior to SOE establishment are coded 0; the year of nationalization is coded 1. For all years after nationalization, the country is removed from the data, given that nationalization as defined here cannot occur twice in the same country, unless a state privatizes a previously nationalized oil industry or removes operational authority from the SOE. This is similar in structure to data involving regime "spells" or leader survival, such that any period prior to nationalization could be characterized as a "non-nationalized spell."

Consider again the example of Canada, which nationalized oil operations in 1976 upon the establishment of Petro-Canada, based on existing assets held by the private companies Panarctic and Syncrude. In 1995, under the premiership of Brian Mulroney, Petro-Canada was privatized, with the government holding only a 19 percent share in the company (Grayson, 1981). Thus, Canada "exits" the data set after nationalization in 1976 but "re-enters" in 1996 upon privatization. After 1996, since it becomes logically possible for Canada to renationalize the oil industry, Canada remains in the data set with the nationalization measure set to 0.

In the statistical models that follow, I include covariates to capture the theoretical implications of different factors determining nationalization. To test the information-diffusion hypothesis, I use two approaches. First, in the statistical analysis of nationalization I use an OPEC dummy indicator for whether a country is a member of the cartel in a given year; as a robustness check I also use a dummy indicator for whether a country is a member of the Nonaligned Movement (NAM). Second, in the two-country case comparison I directly assess how information about an oil revenue-sharing agreement reached in one context (Saudi Arabia) spread to another (Iran). To test whether leaders in young regimes are more likely to nationalize, I employ the regime-age indicator from Cheibub et al. (2010). This measures the duration of the existing governing regime in years, and resets to 1 at every regime change. The latter is defined as any discrete transition within a six-fold regime classification that includes parliamentary democracy, mixed or semipresidential democracy, presidential democracy, civilian dictatorship, military dictatorship, and royal dictatorship (Cheibub et al., 2009, 9–10).

To control for geological factors in the decision to nationalize, two proxies for the oil-production cycle are included in the empirical analysis. The first is a measure of a country's "oil history," or more specifically, a measure of how long a country has been producing oil. This is measured simply as the number of years since first oil production. The second measure is one that captures growth in the production cycle. This is measured as the year-to-year growth in oil production, calculated using the reported oil-production figures published cross-nationally by the United States Geological Survey (USGS). Nolan and Thurber (2010) argue that both measures should be positively correlated with increased probabilities of nationalization. Countries must deal with higher risks early in the production cycle or when production begins declining. Both reflect the inherent risks of exploration and risks associated with aging oil fields.

The measure of oil price is a detrended, residual price of oil, used to proxy for oil price shocks to observe long-term oil price cycles. A detrended price is used for ease of interpretation and to reduce year-to-year noise in price changes.[3] Aside from oil prices, the relationship between the international oil market and nationalization might be affected by the importance of a country's oil sector in global terms. For example, a country with modest oil production like Bahrain or Bolivia will not be as likely to face international retaliation when choosing to nationalize operations. By contrast, the chances of retaliatory actions are much higher if operations are nationalized in a major producer like Saudi Arabia or Mexico. It could be the case, then, that a country's importance to the global oil market influences the decision to nationalize

---

[3] Calculated first by Pindyck (1999) and adapted by Guriev et al. (2011), the formula for creating this residual is $\ln p_t = \alpha * \ln p_{t-1} + \beta_1 + \beta_2 * t + \beta_3 * t^2 + \epsilon_t$ where p_t is the price of oil at time t and p_{t-1} is the lagged price of oil, for each year $t \in [1945, 2015]$. The deviation from this price trend is the corresponding price shock, so we can estimate the shock by computing yearly residuals, ϵ_t. As a robustness check, the nominal oil price is used based on data from the British Petroleum *Statistical Review of Energy*.

oil operations. To control for this possibility, I use country share of global production as calculated using the USGS oil production measure.

To control for the domino effect, I use a count measure of nationalizations occurring in each year and then lag it by one year. For example, if in 1995 there were no nationalizations and in 1996 there were two nationalizations, the count measure in 1996 would simply be 0 and in 1997 would be 2. To control for broad economic factors covered in the earlier theoretical discussion, I add to the analysis a measure of economic development. This entails the GDP per capita indicator, collected from the Maddison project on global incomes, as well as annual GDP growth. To measure political constraints and institutional strength, I employ the *Polity* index of democratic governance (Marshall et al., 2011). In alternative model specifications, I include a measure of relative political capacity – specifically, *relative political reach* – that "gauges the capacity of governments to mobilize populations under their control" (Kugler and Tammen, 2012, 11). This effectively proxies for the state's infrastructural capacity, the relative strength of the state's bureaucracies, and the state's ability to develop social capital through educational institutions and social safety nets. I also include indicators for autocratic regime type, ranging from military and personal dictatorships to single-party regimes and monarchies (Geddes et al., 2014). In terms of leader ideologies, I test a subset of models using an indicator for revolutionary leadership from Colgan (2013).

The sample includes 70 oil-producing countries across the period 1945–2015. Though the nationalization measure is coded beginning in 1900, the lack of data on covariates reduces the time frame of the multivariate analysis. However, this is not an egregious loss of data, given there were so few nationalizations prior to 1945 (only six occurred in the period 1900–1944). The selection of cases is determined by the universe of oil producers among all 175 sovereign states in the period with populations above 200,000. Defining "oil producer" as a state that at any point in time produces more than 100 tonnes of oil per year (or about two barrels per day), 79 of these 175 states qualify as oil producers.[4] Three states drop out due to missingness in covariates[5] and

---

[4] For comparison, the median production level among producers is 1.2 *million* tonnes per year. Changing the threshold to any state producing more than 10,000 tonnes/year drops the total to seventy-one. Within this group of seventy-nine, there are eight countries included that have yet to produce oil but have discovered it and are actively discussing nationalization: Botswana, Kenya, Liberia, Mozambique, Namibia, Tanzania, Uganda, and Uruguay.

[5] The three countries with missing data on covariates are Poland (nationalized in 1945), Albania (nationalized in 1945), and Suriname (nationalized in 1982).

a further six states leave the sample because they nationalized prior to 1945 to give a sample size of seventy states.[6]

4.2.2   Empirical Methods

I use longitudinal statistical analysis of cross-sectional time-series data on oil nationalizations to test the hypotheses described in the previous section. The decision to nationalize in a given country in a given year is treated as a dichotomous variable that is a function of country-level and time-specific covariates. The two hypotheses of interest are both temporal and spatial in nature; inference is made via between-country and within-country analysis over time. Though I am unable to make strong causal inferences with this research design, the identification strategy for each hypothesis relies on capturing within-country variation over time augmented with techniques for statistical control.[7] Here, I employ Bayesian methods with Markov Chain Monte Carlo estimation of the logistic regression model with country-random effects. To account for country-specific factors, instead of adding country dummy variables I estimate country-specific intercepts in the form of a random variable with a standard normal distribution. I estimate a Bayesian hierarchical logistic regression model, though I also provide results from non-Bayesian (frequentist) hierarchical logistic regression and the linear probability model with and without country fixed effects. The full

---

[6] Refer to Table 1.1 in Chapter 1 for a list of the timing and location of these NOCs.

[7] It is unrealistic to control for all possible determinants of nationalization, particularly country-specific factors. One such factor is the economic ideology of political leaders, given that left-leaning governments are more likely than right-leaning governments to expropriate assets (Boix, 1997; Manzano and Monaldi, 2009). However, such a factor is difficult to include in statistical analysis given the lack of reliable cross-national data on government ideology over time (especially in nondemocratic governments and developing democracies). The typical solution to this problem in political economy studies is to add country dummy variables or, as they are better known, country-fixed effects. This chapter takes a different approach to the MLE unit-fixed effects problem. Adding country-fixed effects to longitudinal analysis with a dichotomous variable is subject to inconsistent estimates due to poor convergence of maximum-likelihood methods (Weiss, 2005). Further, Greene has shown that even the commonly held belief that probit regression is robust to unit-fixed effects is incorrect in finite samples. One solution to this problem is to apply linear ordinary least squares (OLS) models to these fundamentally nonlinear data, given that the OLS estimator is unbiased and consistent in finite samples (Heckman and Snyder, 1977). This is the approach taken by Guriev et al. (2011) in analyzing the determinants of acts of expropriation in the oil sector, and robustness checks using nonlinear methods show similar substantive results. Yet the linear probability model, as the OLS estimator with a dichotomous outcome is known, suffers from improper bounding on the 0–1 interval of probabilities and heteroskedasticity of the residuals, a problem made all the more challenging with rare-events data (Horrace and Oaxaca, 2006).

model specification and information on priors used for the analysis are presented in the chapter Appendix (Section 4.5).

4.3   Modeling Nationalizations in the Oil Industry

4.3.1   Statistical Findings

Results from empirical analysis lend strong support for hypotheses that nationalization is more likely in states that are OPEC members and in states with leaders in young regimes. To aide in interpretation of model output, I present visual results in the form of added-variable plots and modeled probability plots. A full table of statistical results from the Bayesian analysis is presented in Table 4.1, along with Table 4.4 that shows results from non-Bayesian regressions (see also Tables 4.2–4.5).

Predicted probability plots are shown in Figure 4.1 for the two variables of interest – the OPEC dummy and regime age – along with control variables that account for existing explanations of nationalization (oil price shocks) and geological determinants (number of years producing oil). Each plot shows the predictor of interest on the x-axis with the model-predicted probability of nationalization, conditional on the full

Table 4.1. *Determinants of operational nationalization: model results from Bayesian hierarchical logistic regression*

	Mean	SD	2.5%	97.5%	"p"
Intercept	−4.931	0.251	−5.423	−4.460	0.000
Years producing	0.688	0.208	0.273	1.092	0.001
Oil price shock	0.798	0.383	0.070	1.530	0.019
Regime age (yrs)	−0.665	0.244	−1.167	−0.217	0.002
Regime (Polity)	−0.365	0.193	−0.755	0.004	0.027
OPEC dummy	0.846	0.463	−0.048	1.755	0.038
GDP/capita (log)	0.295	0.149	−0.004	0.580	0.026
Change in oil production	0.261	0.082	0.090	0.411	0.002
Nationalizations count ($t-1$)	0.099	0.156	−0.215	0.388	0.259
Growth	−0.188	0.138	−0.439	0.079	0.091
Production share	0.005	0.166	−0.408	0.273	0.428

Posterior estimates for model coefficients from Bayesian hierarchical logistic regression with informative priors. Coefficient estimates are on the logistic scale. Column 2 (Mean) is akin to the $\hat{\beta}$ coefficient estimates from non-Bayesian models; Column 3 (SD) is like the standard error of $\hat{\beta}$, and columns 3 and 4 (2.5% and 97.5%, respectively) give the 95 percent credible interval. Column 5 ("p") is the Bayesian version of the frequentist p-value: the integral of the posterior distribution greater than zero for negative posterior median estimates (less than zero for positive posterior median estimates) of the model coefficients. Sample size: $N = 2,325$.

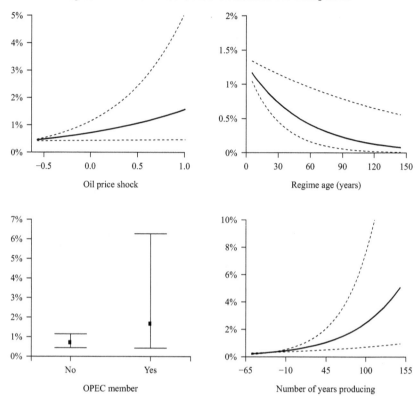

Figure 4.1 Determinants of operational nationalization: model results from Bayesian analysis

Note: Predicted probabilities of nationalization (y-axis, in percent) for logistic regression coefficients with 95 percent credible intervals for selected variables (x-axis), holding other variables fixed at their means (0 since the variables are standardized). Based on posterior estimates from the Bayesian hierarchical logistic model with informative priors. See results in Table 4.1 for coefficient estimates.

set of controls, on the *y*-axis. The top right plot shows the negative correlation between regime age and nationalization probability.[8] In the first years of a political regime, leaders are predicted to nationalize

---

[8] To test whether there are nonlinearities in the effects of regime age, I use an alternative model specification that includes third-order polynomials for the regime age variable. There is no substantive difference in the results: younger regimes are the most likely to nationalize, with the probability of nationalization declining monotonically as regime age increases. The lack of support here for this hypothesis could be driven by how the sample is defined. Since regimes "exit" the sample once they nationalize, and since oil privatization is a rare event (among nondemodemocratic regimes in particular), there are few cases of nationalization at the upper boundaries of regime age. Two notable exceptions are Gabon and Denmark.

operations with a probability of 1.3 percent. By the 40th year under the same regime, this predicted probability drops to 0.5 percent and attenuates thereafter. Substantively, these model results would predict that a leader in an advanced-age regime like King Mohammed VI of Morocco – entering power in the forty-fourth year of the regime – is two-and-a-half times less likely to nationalize than his father King Hassan II, whose rule began in only the seventh year of the Alawite dynastic regime.

As the OPEC dummy is a discrete predictor, the visualization of the "OPEC effect" is clear and easily interpreted: joining OPEC doubles the nationalization probability from 0.7 percent to 1.6 percent. While the credible intervals clearly overlap, note that the difference between the two predictions is positive in 96 percent of all MCMC simulations (akin to a p-value of 0.04). The top left plot shows the nationalization probability for a given country in a given year that is predicted by the model corresponding to changes in the oil price shock variable (measured in standard deviation units). With an oil shock increase from the mean shock across time (0) to a shock 1 standard deviation above the mean, the predicted probability of nationalization increases from roughly 0.5 percent to 1.5 percent, but with much higher uncertainty for larger price shocks. The last plot shows the expected relationship between production years and nationalization: a near zero probability of nationalizing prior to oil production and increasing probabilities as countries gain more experience with oil production.

To better place the magnitude of these effects in context, I show scatterplots in Figure 4.2 of country-specific, within-sample predicted probabilities for two periods of interest. The first is the change in predicted nationalization probability from 1959 to 1960, reflective of the formation of OPEC in 1960. If there had been no change in predicted probabilities, then all countries would lie along the dotted line. This is generally the case, except for four countries – Iran, Iraq, Saudi Arabia, and Venezuela – that are four of the five founding members of OPEC.[9] For these four states, the act of joining OPEC had an increased predicted effect on the probability of nationalization. For Venezuela, the pre-OPEC nationalization probability is predicted to be 3.4 percent, which jumps to just above 6.3 percent the year Venezuela joins OPEC. Indeed, Venezuela nationalized its oil operations in 1960 with the formation of Corporación Venezolana del Petróleo (CVP), the

---

[9] There are only twenty-nine cases plotted here instead of the full seventy due to the fact that thirty-three countries were not yet sovereign (independent) and eight countries had already nationalized and are thus removed from the sample postnationalization. Kuwait, the other founding member of OPEC, was not yet technically independent (Kuwait gained sovereignty from the UK in 1961).

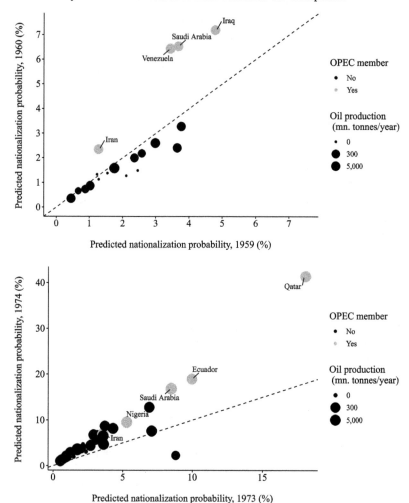

Figure 4.2 Year-to-year changes in predicted probability of operational nationalization, 1959–1960 and 1973–1974

Note: Year-to-year changes in predicted nationalization probability, based on posterior estimates from the Bayesian hierarchical logistic model including all control variables identified in the text. Countries on the 45-degree dotted line reflect no year-to-year changes; countries above (below) the line reflect increased (decreased) predicted probability of nationalization. Size of points represents oil production (in millions of metric tons per year). Dark grey points are OPEC member countries; black points are all others.

predecessor of the modern PdVSA. Saudi Arabia, by contrast, despite nearly doubling in probability to nationalize after joining OPEC from 3.6 percent to 6.5 percent, did not nationalize until much later, in 1974, with nationalization not complete until 1980.

The second two-year period of interest is 1973–1974, shown in the bottom plot of predicted probabilities. This year-to-year change highlights the 1973 Arab oil embargo, when prices increased by 4.5 standard deviations, the highest one-year increase in the sample. The modeled nationalization probability increased for all but one of the 41 countries in the sample in that year, as indicated by the representation of all countries being above the dotted line.[10] Saudi Arabia's predicted nationalization probability increases from 8 percent in 1973 to 17 percent in 1974, while Qatar's probability increases from 18 percent to 45 percent (both nationalized in 1974). The highest predicted probabilities of the sample are estimated for the year 1974, indicative of substantively large coefficient estimates for the oil shock variable and the OPEC dummy.

To assess the model's predicted values, I look at within-sample modeled outcomes compared to actual outcomes. This is accomplished by comparing the model's predictions over time for each country to its actual year of nationalization. Instead of plotting all seventy countries, I present six cases illustrative of the model's predictive strengths and weaknesses in Figure 4.3. For Saudi Arabia, Trinidad, and South Africa, the predicted probability of nationalization is indeed highest during the year of or before actual nationalization, which is represented in the plots by the dotted vertical line. (Note that for all cases, predictions are absent during the years of a nationalized industry.) These cases represent instances of model predictions with relative accuracy of predicted versus actual nationalization. Note, however, that the magnitude of predictions (typically peaking at 15 to 20 percent) is relatively low due to the rare-event nature of nationalizations as discussed earlier.

For the United States, Sudan, and Ecuador, however, the model's predictions are noticeably weak. Sudan, for instance, is predicted to nationalize in 1991, when the model's predictions are at their highest levels (around 17 percent). Yet, Sudan did not nationalize until 1996, when the government established Sudapet on the 15 percent expropriated stake of the Greater Nile Operating Company international consortium (Hansohm, 2007). Interestingly, Sudan's government pursued broad

---

[10] Bangladesh is the exception. Despite establishing a national oil company in 1972 (Petrobangla), the government never nationalized production, opting instead to vest operations in companies like Occidental and Total, as well as smaller independents like Cairn Energy of the UK and Holland Sea Search of the Netherlands (USGS, 1993).

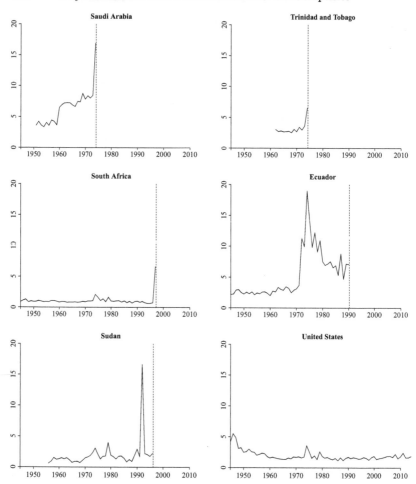

Figure 4.3 Predicted probabilities of operational nationalization for selected countries over time
Note: Predicted probabilities of nationalization (y-axis, in percent) over time (x-axis, in years) for selected countries based on posterior estimates from the Bayesian hierarchical logit model with informative priors. The dashed vertical line indicates actual year of oil nationalization.

nationalizations in 1970s, expropriating assets in the agricultural, manufacturing, and financial sectors, yet did not nationalize the nascent oil industry. The United States never nationalized (see Chapter 7), though the modeled probability of nationalization peaks at 5 percent in 1947.

To assess the impacts of revolutionary ideology on the decision to nationalize, I run the same models as above with the addition of a binary

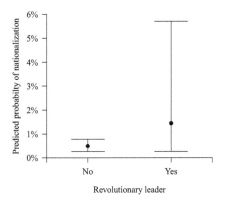

Figure 4.4 Determinants of operational nationalization: revolutionary leadership

Note: Predicted probability plot for nationalization likelihood and revolutionary leadership, holding other variables fixed at their means (0 since the variables are standardized). Based on posterior estimates from the Bayesian hierarchical logistic model with informative priors. See results in Table 4.6 for coefficient estimates. Note that while the credible intervals overlap, the likelihood that the coefficient is greater than zero is 97.4 percent (akin to a frequentist "p" value of 0.026).

indicator for revolutionary leadership. The results support the idea that revolutionary leaders are more likely to nationalize operations. Looking at the predicted probabilities of nationalization in Figure 4.4, the likelihood of seizing operations increases from 0.5 percent to 1.4 percent when comparing countries with and without revolutionary leaders but with the same average characteristics on all other covariates. To put these numbers in a more concrete perspective, consider again Chapter 1's opening vignette describing the Libyan revolution. Plugging in Libya's political and economic characteristics, the model would predict that the shift from a nonrevolutionary leader in King Idris to a revolutionary leader in Qaddafi would increase the probability of nationalization eightfold, from 2 percent in 1968 to 16 percent in 1969. Although Qaddafi did not complete operational nationalization of the oil industry until 1973, both the argument and the empirical support suggest that it was *very* unlikely for his predecessor Idris to nationalize operations given his perceived (albeit incorrect) strength in power.

As for the other variables of interest – notably regime age and the OPEC dummy – the results remain substantively similar (see Table 4.6). One noticeable change is the estimate for democratic regimes as captured by the Polity variable. In the baseline model this result is negative and statistically distinguishable from zero, suggesting that leaders in regimes with stronger and more constraining political institutions are less likely to nationalize. In the revolutionary leaders model, this effect shrinks by roughly 75 percent and is no longer statistically distinguishable from zero. This could suggest that the constraining effects of political institutions are less relevant in the decision to nationalize once leader ideology is accounted for. This should be interpreted with some caution, however, since this model is estimated using only a subset of the sample. The sample size drops from 2,325 observations to 1,979 observations, given the lack of complete data on revolutionary leaders for all observations.[11]

One implication from the argument is that within the realm of autocratic regimes, leaders in some types of dictatorships are more likely to nationalize than in other types. Specifically, personalist dictatorships and military dictatorships should have the lowest perceived odds of future survival when compared to monarchies. It should be the case that leaders in these regimes will be the most likely to nationalize operations, while those in monarchies will be the least likely to nationalize (with single-party regimes somewhere in between). The results offer mixed support for this conjecture: Figure 4.7 shows that while personalist dictators are indeed more likely to nationalize, leaders in military regimes are the *least* likely to nationalize. Interestingly, leaders in single-party regimes are just as likely to nationalize as personalist dictators, but both are discernibly more likely to nationalize when compared to monarchies and to military dictatorships.[12] Why are military dictators less likely to nationalize when they have such short time horizons? It could be that this result is driven by the fact that very few major oil producing countries have been in the hands of military dictatorship (prior to nationalization, that is). Indeed, only three such cases stand out in the data: Ecuador (1973–1979), Nigeria (1967–1979, 1984–1999), and Venezuela (1949–1958). Two of the three eventually nationalized but a key concern for each was the ability to handle production if the state were to seize operations; this is what I referred to in Chapters 1 and 2 as the "technical preconditions" for nationalization.

---

[11] Most of these missing observations stem from the different time range used in both datasets; the last year of data in the Colgan revolutionary leaders database is 2004, while the last year in the NOC database is 2015. Some notable nationalizations not covered in the revolutionary leaders sample: Bolivia (2007), Equatorial Guinea (2008), Congo (2010), Tunisia (2010), Argentina (2012), Cameroon (2013), and Gabon (2013). Although none would be classified as having revolutionary leaders, the loss of seven cases out of fifty total nationalizations in the post-1945 period is significant.

[12] See Figure 4.8 for paired comparisons of effect sizes, which are calculated using the differences in posterior distributions for the coefficients of each indicator variable. The baseline category (i.e., the omitted indicator) is monarchy.

Consider the case of Ecuador. When the military overthrew the incumbent regime in 1972, it quickly set up a state-owned petroleum enterprise: on June 23 of that year, the government created the Corporación Estatal Petrolera Ecuatoriana (CEPE). The new Minister of Natural Resources following the coup, Captain Gustavo Jarrin Ampudia, pressed for full nationalization of the industry during his tenure (1972–1974), but his demands were neglected by the elite and the ruling Junta (Philip, 1982). However, the creation of CEPE marked a new era in Ecuador in which the military "had hoped to take the initiative in using the oil wealth to transform the Ecuadorian economy and modernize its society" (Philip, 1982, 276). But operational nationalization did not occur in the early 1970s because the state knew it lacked the technical expertise to explore and develop new fields (Martz, 1987). As such, the state would not gain control over operations until much later, when in 1990 Petroecuador (which subsumed CEPE in 1989) took on production after gaining sufficient technical expertise over fifteen years of working alongside foreign partners and service companies. The desire to nationalize operations was certainly present, but the technical inability to do so hindered the military dictatorship.

Returning to the robustness of the main findings, how do the baseline results compare to those obtained using other model specifications? Does conducting a Bayesian analysis provide noticeably different point estimates? To answer these questions, I analyze the data using numerous model specifications and techniques,[13] the results from three of which are presented in Table 4.4. In terms of direction, all models provide consistent coefficient estimates: negative estimates for regime age; positive estimates for the OPEC dummy, oil price shock, and annual production changes variables; and null results for the domino effect. There is some variation in statistical significance for the GDP per capita measure, regime type, and years producing, particularly in a model controlling for country-fixed effects, while all three approaches yield statistically significant results for regime age, the OPEC dummy (but not in model 3; see table notes for discussion of poor convergence), and oil prices, as well as for the control variable for annual changes in oil production. In terms of magnitude, the Bayesian estimates are more conservative in that the coefficient estimates for the variables of interest (regime age in particular) are closer to zero than the estimates obtained via

---

[13] Other models analyzed: pooled linear probability model (OLS), linear probability model with country-fixed effects, MLE logistic model with country-fixed effects, MLE probit model with and without country-fixed effects, Bayesian mixture model clustering by country and region, and a survival (Cox Proportional Hazards) model.

maximum-likelihood hierarchical logit (which does not include priors). In other words, results from non-Bayesian models could be potentially overestimating the relationship between nationalization and the variables of interest by solely using information from the data, without considering information from prior studies and interviews.

As for alternative specifications, running a model with polynomial terms for regime age provides roughly the same estimates as the baseline model. Figure 4.9 shows that even with third-order polynomials for regime age, the probability of nationalization is still highest in the early stages of the regime and declines monotonically thereafter.

Replacing the OPEC variable with an indicator for whether a country is a member of the NAM similarly shows the same results across all coefficients in the model (Table 4.5). This allows for an expanded scope of testing the diffusion hypothesis as there are far more NAM members than OPEC members (note that all OPEC states are also NAM members). The estimated relationship is slightly smaller when compared to the OPEC dummy, but still shows that nationalization is more likely for leaders in countries that are connected through a forum in which information about production contracts can be shared.

Interestingly, replacing the Polity regime variable with a measure of a regime's relative political capacity shows no discernible relationship between nationalization and political capacity (Table 4.7). While the regime age and OPEC estimates remain roughly the same in substantive and statistical terms, there is no evidence that leaders in states with limited political capacity are any more or less likely to nationalize operations than leaders in states with strong political capacity.

Nonetheless, the key message from these results is that neither model specification nor prior selection substantively alters the findings of the study that the likelihood of nationalization increases when states join OPEC and in the early years of the governing regime, when leaders perceive lower relative odds of survival.

4.3.2 Information Diffusion and Perceptions of Survival: Iran versus Saudi Arabia

In both Iran and Saudi Arabia oil production began before 1940 and initial operations were conducted by foreign-owned oil companies. The production profiles shown in Figure 4.5 illustrate the near convergence of production levels by the late 1940s. Yet the leaders of each country – King Abdul-aziz ibn-Saud and Shah Mohammad Reza Pahlavi – took separate paths in natural resource ownership. Iran's government infamously nationalized the AIOC's operations in 1951. Saudi Arabia, on

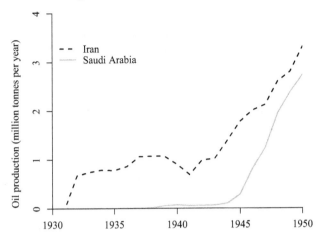

Figure 4.5 Oil production in the 1930–1950 period, Iran compared to Saudi Arabia
Note: Data collected from Mu'assasat al-Naqd al-Arabi al-Saudi, Saudi Arabian Monetary Agency (1960), Noori (1965), and Mikdashi (1966).

the other hand, waited until 1974 to nationalize the Arabian-American Oil Company (Aramco) and did so only gradually, with Saudi Arabia taking full ownership by 1980. Why did Iran nationalize operations in the early 1950s while the Saudi leadership waited another quarter-century to follow suit?

I explore the differences in both oil-producing countries during their early years of production to show evidence in support of the information diffusion and leader survival perceptions hypotheses. In Saudi Arabia, knowledge of underpayments by Western oil firms to the Saudi government coupled with the passage of an equitable fifty–fifty arrangement in 1948 in Venezuela prompted King ibn-Saud to renegotiate in search of a better deal. But the king opted to maintain outside operating firms and continue with the existing tax-and-royalty system, albeit at higher rates, in what became the 1950 Agreement. In choosing not to nationalize operations in 1950, the king would forgo short-term windfalls but would reap the long-term gains of international oil company operations. This choice, I argue, reflected the longer time horizons of the kingdom – given the high level of consolidation of the Saud regime by the late 1940s – and thus the favorable perceptions of political survival. In Iran, the 1950 Saudi deal sparked renewed debate within the Iranian government about its own terms of agreement with the AIOC. But in contrast to the Saudi case, the Shah of Iran and his oft-adversarial prime minister, Mohammad Mossadegh, both had reasons to doubt a long, stable grip on power. This perceived weakness in survival odds, I argue, led to nationalization of the AIOC's operations and the formation of an operational national oil company.

Saudi Arabia

The first successful oil concession in the Kingdom was the 1933 drilling agreement between King ibn-Saud and the Standard Oil Company of California (SOCAL). After the discovery in 1938 of what SOCAL called a "veritable oil bonanza" the company joined forces with Texaco in setting up Aramco.[14] Aramco soon discovered that it enjoyed a substantial market advantage over Western oil companies because of the relative ease in extracting Saudi oil: compared to the unit costs of producing American oil at $1.01 per barrel (or in Venezuela, $0.50/barrel), oil could be produced in Saudi Arabia for only $0.23 per barrel (Mikdashi, 1966, 94). On December 30, 1950, the company signed a new agreement whereby the Saudi government taxed the net operating revenue of Aramco to the point of creating a fifty–fifty split of revenues. This would be the first equal partnership in the Middle East between host government and operating company. By 1952, Aramco revised the 1950 agreement and provided for a complete split of the profits *before* any payments were sent to the United States in the form of income taxes, effectively giving the Saudi government a greater share in operating revenues and profits than Aramco itself.

Two events sparked the renegotiations that led to the 1950 agreement. The first was the increasing awareness that Aramco was paying more to the US government in income taxes than it was to the Saudi government in royalties. This paved the way for demands to renegotiate the 1933 agreement and served as the foundation on which the Saudis would pressure Aramco, and later the US government, to come to a more fair and just arrangement. In 1948, Aramco's chairman testified before the US Congress that the company acquiesced to the king's demands to divert the money owed to the IRS to the king's treasury instead:

[The Saudi government] wanted more. They asked as early as 1948, "Isn't there some way where we can get a greater take?" and a little later than that they said, "Isn't there some way in which the income tax you pay to the United States can be diverted to us in whole or in part?"[15]

The second, and more pivotal, event was Venezuela's 1948 revisions to the 1943 Petroleum Law toward a "true" fifty–fifty agreement with Standard Oil of New Jersey (later Exxon) and Shell. This reform gave

---

[14] Standard Oil Company of California (1946), *Autumn Bulletin*, 33 (7): 1–2.
[15] United States Congress, *Emergency Oil Lift Program and Related Oil Problems, Hearings* (Washington, DC: 1957, 1429).

the Venezuelan government a dramatic increase in total revenues, which by 1948 amounted to six times greater than its total government income in 1942 (Yergin, 1991, 436). The Saudis, of course, took notice of this windfall, "compelling [Standard Oil] to initiate concrete negotiations ... on the pattern of the arrangement adopted by Venezuela two years earlier" (Hurwitz, 1956, 315).

King ibn-Saud's desire to maximize oil revenue did not result in nationalization. Instead, the government pushed Aramco for both higher taxes and higher levels of production – since the state lacked the ability to achieve its production goals on its own. "To keep King ibn-Saud satisfied with the operation of the concession," Texaco's president later remarked to the Federal Trade Commission, "it is important that production be increased substantially so that the King would receive greater royalties."[16] This corroborates the argument that leaders that perceive strength in their survival odds will eschew operational nationalization given its long-term costs and its potential for short-term retaliation. For ibn-Saud, nationalization was simply not worth the gamble. Even if maintaining private operating firms for oil production led to lower immediate returns – given asymmetries of information about true operating costs and profits between the government and Standard Oil – the king chose long-term gains at the cost of short-term windfalls.

Iran

As with Saudi Arabia, the Iranian government was compelled to improve the terms of revenue sharing with the international oil companies. The perception of an unfair split in oil revenues between Britain and Iran began to be disputed politically with the passage of Iran's own 1933 Agreement. Immediately after 1933 there existed a small but noticeable gap between host and foreign state; from 1940 onward Iran's absolute oil revenues did increase but clearly did so at a much slower rate than that of Britain (Noori, 1965; Mikdashi, 1966). Fourteen years after the 1933 agreement, on October 22, 1947, Iranian members of parliament passed an amendment to the 1933 oil concession law requiring government officials to be present in AIOC policy decisions when they pertained to Iran's oil royalties. The motivation for this amendment originated in parliament's perceptions that "the rights of the nation were impaired" when it came to AIOC royalty receipts (Noori, 1965) and the 1933 Agreement was invalid as it "had been forced upon Iran" (Makki, 1950).

---

[16] Subcommittee on Monopoly of the Select Committee on Small Business, US Senate, *The International Petroleum Cartel: Staff Report to the Federal Trade Commission* (Washington, DC: 1952, 124). Note that to expand production, the Aramco consortium grew from a joint venture of two companies to a group of four companies: SOCAL, Texaco, Jersey, and Socony.

Two years later, the AIOC and the government negotiated the 1949 Supplemental Agreement, which provided for a modest increase in Iran's royalty payments. But noticeably absent from the new terms was any discussion of an even fifty–fifty split between the two countries. Hossein Makki, a member of the parliamentary opposition and Mossadegh's right-hand man, charged before parliament that the 1949 agreement was still unfair to the Iranian people, especially when compared to the terms given to other oil producers at the time:

The new agreement deprived Iran of her share in the reserves of subsidiary and allied companies. ... While the Supplemental Agreement gave Iran seven shillings a ton, *the government of Iraq was negotiating for a new agreement that would bring that country eighteen shillings per ton. In Venezuela, the government was receiving approximately thirty shillings per ton.*[17]

With this speech, and several others by prominent opposition members, members of parliament rejected the agreement. The British, upon seeing the failure of the negotiated agreement to make it through Iran's parliament, told then-premier Saed that Iran should either take the 1949 agreement or leave it; but in no way was Britain to agree to a fifty–fifty sharing agreement (Noori, 1965).

After an attempted assassination of the Shah in February 1949, coupled with a disputed parliamentary election, the Shah tried to placate nationalistic demands with a new election in 1950. With campaign promises of a new oil settlement, Mossadegh and his National Front Party secured only 8 of the 143 seats in parliament. The new prime minister, Ali Razmara, was a conservative ex-soldier who sought to ease tensions between Iran and Britain with new negotiations between the government and the AIOC. Upon Britain's rejection to open a new round of negotiations, Razmara was forced to take the unpopular 1949 Supplemental Agreement before parliament again in 1951, when it was rejected for a second time. In the face of growing public opposition to the AIOC and Britain's involvement in Iran – accompanied by street demonstrations throughout the winter of 1950–1951 – Razmara publicly rejected nationalization in March 1951, calling it "imperialistic and unwise" (Lenczowski, 1949, 17). This was to be his last speech, as the prime minister was assassinated on March 7 by the extremist xenophobic group *Fedayan-e Islam*. Thirteen days after Razmara's death, both the parliament and the unelected senate passed Mossadegh's nationalization bill, on March 20, 1951, and soon thereafter established the National Iranian Oil Company.

---

[17] Makki (1950, 332–340). Emphasis added.

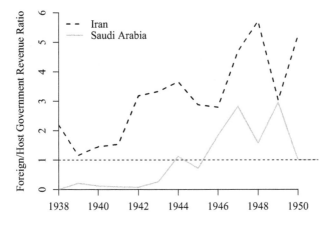

Figure 4.6 Ratio of collected oil revenues between foreign and host state, Iran versus Saudi Arabia, 1938–1951

Note: The benchmark for this metric is 1; values at or below the benchmark are more fair from the perspective of the host state. Higher values indicate more revenue for the foreign operator and state relative to the host state. The starting point of 1938 is the first year of oil production for Saudi Arabia.

Comparing Kingdoms

The Iranian nationalization of the AIOC was a complex and drawn-out endeavor. There were grievances based on fair treatment of Iranian workers, demands for substituting foreign managers by Iranian nationals, adequate transparency of the AIOC's accounting books, and the company's unwillingness to renegotiate terms of payment to the state. Yet the general message of the Iranian government's decision to nationalize was that the 1933 concession and 1949 agreement were fiscally unfair to Iran relative to what the government learned that the Saudis, Iraqis, and Venezuelans were receiving. Compared to Saudi Arabia's 1950 agreement in particular, the amount of revenues collected by the international oil companies and their Western governments was substantially higher than the payments sent to the Iranian government (see Figure 4.6). Failure to renegotiate a payment plan or even consider a fifty–fifty profit-sharing agreement ultimately led to outright nationalization of the AIOC in 1951.

Information about the agreements reached in Saudi Arabia, in addition to the earlier wave of renegotiations in Iraq and Venezuela, provided the spark for the Iranian government to reconsider its position vis-à-vis Britain and the AIOC. The diffusion of this information did not directly cause nationalization; rather, it caused the Shah and his government to update their chances of survival in deciding whether to pursue nationalization. By contrast to the stability and security of ibn

Saud in 1950 – operating in an environment of low political contestation and few internal threats to his rule – the Shah had not only survived an assassination attempt in 1949, but was facing the erosion of monarchic rule due to the rising prominence of parliament led by Mossadegh. Mossadegh's own nationalist party similarly faced uncertainty over their duration in power, given the precarious situation posed by the Shah's parliamentary loyalists. Indeed, neither man felt the same level of security in their future as did the Saudi monarch. This perception ultimately diminished the value of long-term returns from continuing to tax the AIOC – and instead bolstered the necessity of seizing oil operations for the state despite its future costs.[18]

4.4   Conclusion

The list of oil-exporting states has been consistently growing, with new producers emerging as of 2019 along the Gulf of Guinea (Ghana, Ivory Coast), East Africa (Uganda, Tanzania, Kenya), Central America (Belize), Central Asia (Afghanistan), South America (Suriname, Guyana), and the Eastern Mediterranean (Israel, Lebanon, Cyprus). Governments in these states have yet to decide on ownership structures of their nascent petroleum industries, with several states in the midst of implementing new petroleum regulation at the time of writing. Indeed, many have already established NOCs, like Staatsolie in Suriname, GNPC in Ghana, or the National Oil Corporation in Kenya. And some, such as Lebanon, are actively considering an operational NOC even before oil discoveries are confirmed to yield viable commercial production (see Chapter 7). What political factors drive these decisions?

This chapter provides two empirical assessments of the argument that leaders nationalize to increase their duration in power. The cross-national statistical analysis shows that oil nationalization is more likely in states with access to diffused information, as proxied by membership in OPEC, and in states whose leaders rule within the early years of a governing regime. The two-case comparison of Iran and Saudi Arabia in the pre-OPEC period illustrates the diffusing nature of new agreements

---

[18] Though the consequences of nationalization are outside the scope of this vignette, the immediate response by the British was to send the Royal Navy to Iranian waters to threaten an occupation of the oil city of Abadan to protect British interests overseas. The British never occupied Abadan, but the royal navy was used to enforce an embargo of Iranian oil exports. After two years of back-and-forth negotiations and subsequent sanctions, Mossadegh was ousted as premier by the CIA and MI6 in what was then termed "Operation Ajax." The Shah was reinstated in full, and in 1954 reversed the nationalization bill to establish a joint consortium of NIOC with American, British, and French oil companies. For more on the AIOC nationalization, see Mahdavi (2012).

signed by other oil-producing governments as a spur to renegotiate contracts and reconsider nationalization. Both findings corroborate the implication that nationalization is sparked by information that prompts leaders to update their odds of survival, and that nationalization is ultimately chosen by leaders who perceive their time in office as limited. Faced with the same choice, leaders that perceive higher survival probabilities opt instead to keep private firms in charge of operations and tax these companies at higher rates as necessary.

At the heart of this choice is the knowledge that nationalization brings with it an immediate infusion of revenues at the cost of long-term gains. Hence, leaders who perceive a long rule will opt for the choice that provides future benefits, while leaders facing low odds of survival will opt for the choice that provides sorely needed short-run windfalls, with less concern over how this choice might impact future rewards. Next, in Chapter 5, I examine how nationalization increases the government's actual take of resource revenues and how these windfalls foster stronger and more durable leaders.

4.5   Appendix: Model Specification and Additional Results

The outcome variable $\pi_{i,j}$ is the country-specific probability of nationalization in country i at time j; $\mathbf{x}_{i,j}$ is a matrix of mean-centered and standardized predictors; α is a vector of the intercept and fixed effects; β_i is the country-random effect; and $\epsilon_{i,j}$ is the over-dispersion parameter. The inverse-Wishart prior for the random effects variance τ is chosen for mathematical convenience (Box and Tiao, 1973). The model is given by:

$$y_{i,j}|\pi_{i,j} \sim \text{Bernoulli}(\pi_{i,j}) \tag{4.1}$$

$$\text{logit}(\pi_{i,j}) = \mathbf{x}'_{i,j}\alpha + \mathbf{z}'_i\beta_i + \epsilon_{i,j} \tag{4.2}$$

$$\alpha \sim \text{N}(m, v) \tag{4.3}$$

$$\beta_i|\tau^2 \sim \text{N}(0, \tau^2) \tag{4.4}$$

$$\tau^2 \sim \text{InvWishart}(r, R) \tag{4.5}$$

$$\epsilon_{i,j} \sim \text{N}(0, D) \quad \text{where } D = 1 \tag{4.6}$$

Prior information for m, v is a combination of three sources: an elicited prior, estimates from previous work, and the quasi-informative range method for parameters that have not yet been estimated in the literature.[19] The elicited prior is used for the intercept (α_0), and is drawn

---

[19] The prior for the inverse-Wishart degrees of freedom parameter r is set at k number of countries ($k = 70$). The prior for the hyperparameter $\mathbf{R}_{1\times1}$ is estimated using a variation of the range method. In this case, $\mathbf{R}_{1\times1}$ is set to $\left(\frac{\text{logit}(.95)-\text{logit}(.05)}{9}\right) = 0.654$.

Table 4.2. *Interview questions used in eliciting priors for Bayesian analysis*

(1)	What is your guess for how many oil nationalizations will occur in the coming decade?
(2)	What is your guess for the maximum number of oil nationalizations in the next decade?
(3)	In a given country, what is your guess for the probability of oil nationalization next year, all other factors equal? What is the maximum probability? The minimum probability?
(4)	What information are you using to make these guesses? Experience, data, risk models?
(5)	Have you ever used or heard about the Kobrin expropriation dataset?

Questions used for prior elicitation for the intercept term α_0. Question #3 in particular is used for m_0 and v_0, mean and variance of α_0.

Table 4.3. *Model results from Guriev et al. (2011) analysis of oil expropriations*

	Odds ratio	2.5%	97.5%
Oil price	1.038	1.0125	1.0635
Executive constraints	0.994	0.9920	0.9956
Log GDP per capita	1.000	0.9902	1.0098

Regression estimates from Guriev et al. (2011: 316; table 3, column 7) as Odds Ratios with 95 percent CI. Sample size is 1718. Executive constraints is one measure included in the Polity index of regime type used in this study. These estimates – which the authors transformed from the logit coefficients to odds ratios – are transformed back into the logit scale for prior estimates.

from interviews in October 2012, with oil experts working at petroleum consulting firms in Dubai, UAE (set of questions listed in Table 4.2). The experts noted a 0.5 percent chance of nationalization in a given country in a given year, all other factors equal, with a minimum estimate of 0.1 percent and maximum of 1 percent.[20] Priors for some predictors – oil price, regime index, and GDP – are collected from previous work by Guriev et al. (2011), who employ a different dataset (adapted and updated from Kobrin (1985)), replicated in Table 4.3.[21] Priors for

---

[20] This is transformed to the Logit scale to a mean of -5.29 with a variance of $\left(\frac{\text{logit}(.01)-\text{logit}(.001)}{2}\right)^2 = 1.34$.

[21] Guriev et al. (2011) also estimate a logistic model, the values for m and v are the coefficient estimates and inflated standard errors (obtained from reported 95 percent CIs, and downweighted to represent 1 percent as many observations as the data; this specification is relaxed in sensitivity analysis).

Table 4.4. *Determinants of operational nationalization: model results from OLS and logistic regression*

	Dependent variable: Operational nationalization		
	(1)	(2)	(3)
Intercept	0.02***	0.23**	−4.53***
	(0.00)	(0.07)	(0.26)
Years producing	0.01*	0.03˙	0.66**
	(0.00)	(0.01)	(0.24)
Oil price shock	0.04***	0.04***	1.36**
	(0.01)	(0.01)	(0.46)
Regime age (yrs)	−0.02***	−0.02*	−0.81**
	(0.00)	(0.01)	(0.25)
Regime (Polity)	−0.01*	0.00	−0.33˙
	(0.00)	(0.01)	(0.20)
OPEC dummy	0.03**	0.04*	0.60
	(0.01)	(0.02)	(0.50)
GDP/capita (log)	0.02***	0.02	0.55**
	(0.00)	(0.01)	(0.20)
Change in oil production	0.01***	0.01***	0.27***
	(0.00)	(0.00)	(0.07)
Nationalizations count ($t − 1$)	0.00	0.00	0.13
	(0.00)	(0.00)	(0.15)
Growth	−0.01˙	−0.00	−0.21
	(0.00)	(0.00)	(0.15)
Production share	0.00	0.00	0.07
	(0.00)	(0.00)	(0.15)
Num. obs.	2325	2325	2325
Num. groups			70

***$p < 0.001$, **$p < 0.01$, *$p < 0.05$.
Model specifications: Column 1 – Linear probability model; Column 2 – Linear probability model with country-fixed effects; Column 3 – Hierarchical logit model with country random intercepts. Note that the variance-covariance matrix for the latter model does not properly converge using either penalized quasi-likelihood or maximum-likelihood methods; as such the standard errors should be interpreted with caution. This is one reason, among others, for the use of Bayesian models to estimate these parameters.

the remaining predictors – the OPEC indicator, diffusion effect, GDP growth, years since first production, and offshore dummy – are estimated using the range method.[22]

[22] This assumes a normal distribution with mean zero and variance $\left(\frac{1}{2} \frac{\text{logit}(.95) - \text{logit}(.05)}{x_H - x_L} \right)^2$.

Table 4.5. *Determinants of operational nationalization: nonaligned movement membership*

	Mean	SD	2.5%	97.5%	"p"
Intercept	−5.156	0.316	−5.777	−4.556	0.000
Years producing	0.746	0.200	0.366	1.163	0.000
Oil price shock	0.768	0.377	0.072	1.440	0.020
Regime age (yrs)	−0.709	0.244	−1.216	−0.259	0.001
Regime (Polity)	−0.368	0.195	−0.778	0.010	0.028
Non-Aligned Movement member	0.564	0.365	−0.160	1.322	0.061
GDP/capita (log)	0.394	0.141	0.112	0.656	0.006
Change in oil production	0.259	0.077	0.094	0.409	0.001
Nationalizations count ($t − 1$)	0.093	0.152	−0.248	0.373	0.251
Growth	−0.172	0.139	−0.445	0.105	0.116
Production share	0.075	0.143	−0.244	0.312	0.276

Table 4.6. *Determinants of operational nationalization: revolutionary leadership*

	Mean	SD	2.5%	97.5%	"p"
Intercept	−5.334	0.276	−5.930	−4.837	0.000
Years producing	0.657	0.218	0.197	1.064	0.000
Oil price shock	0.797	0.403	−0.007	1.522	0.029
Regime age (yrs)	−0.587	0.269	−1.094	−0.063	0.010
Regime (Polity)	−0.098	0.225	−0.537	0.346	0.319
OPEC dummy	1.157	0.479	0.238	2.094	0.007
GDP/capita (log)	0.333	0.156	0.042	0.651	0.009
Change in oil production	0.298	0.080	0.132	0.447	0.002
Nationalizations count ($t − 1$)	0.249	0.160	−0.048	0.557	0.060
Growth	−0.277	0.155	−0.585	0.019	0.033
Production share	−0.005	0.171	−0.421	0.265	0.536
Revolutionary leader	1.073	0.510	−0.016	2.031	0.026

Table 4.7. *Determinants of operational nationalization: relative political capacity*

	Mean	SD	2.5%	97.5%	"p"
Intercept	−4.589	0.607	−5.798	−3.370	0.000
Years producing	0.457	0.205	0.058	0.852	0.012
Oil price shock	0.927	0.395	0.128	1.683	0.016
Regime age (yrs)	−0.842	0.239	−1.305	−0.374	0.000
Relative political reach	−0.414	0.576	−1.594	0.733	0.235
OPEC member	0.806	0.460	−0.074	1.680	0.037
GDP/capita (log)	0.387	0.154	0.085	0.687	0.007
Change in oil production	0.240	0.099	0.031	0.415	0.014
Nationalizations count ($t-1$)	0.131	0.166	−0.218	0.437	0.202
Growth	−0.228	0.159	−0.526	0.084	0.081
Production share	0.435	0.243	−0.082	0.898	0.045

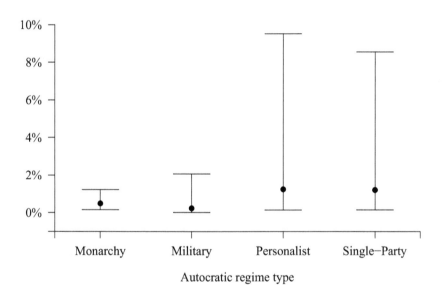

Figure 4.7 Predicted probability of nationalization by autocratic regime type

Note: Predicted probability of nationalization (y-axis, percent) with 90 percent credible intervals for autocratic regime type dummy variables (x-axis), holding other variables fixed at their means (0 since the variables are standardized). Based on posterior estimates from the Bayesian hierarchical logistic model with informative priors with dummy variables for autocratic regime type using the Geddes–Wright–Frantz framework (monarchy is the omitted baseline category). Note that the sample excludes nondemocracies (N = 1,218).

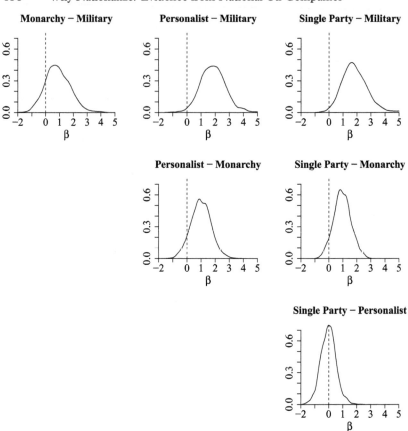

Figure 4.8 Paired comparison of autocratic regime types and nationalization

Note: Each plot shows the posterior density (y-axis) of the coefficients for each paired comparison (x-axis). These are calculated using the differences in posterior distributions for the coefficients of each indicator variable (see Figure 4.7). For example, the top-right panel shows the posterior density of the difference between the Single-party indicator and Military coefficients; that nearly all of the distribution is greater than zero suggests that single-party regimes are more likely to nationalize than military regimes. By contrast, there appears to be no difference in the probability of nationalization when comparing single-party regimes to personalist regimes (bottom-right panel).

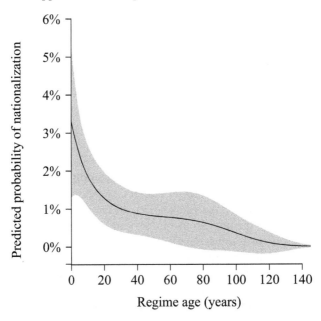

Figure 4.9 Predicted probability of nationalization by age of the regime
Note: Predicted probability of nationalization (y-axis, percent) by regime age (x-axis, years) using third-order polynomial transformation. Because informative priors for regime age squared and regime age cubed are not well-established, the predicted probabilities are based on model results from a hierarchical logistic model with noninformative priors.

5   NOCs, Oil Revenues, and Leadership Survival

The previous chapter assessed the empirical implications for how the diffusion of information prompts leaders to reevaluate their survival probabilities and opt for nationalization under certain conditions. But the key reason *why* leaders choose to nationalize operations is rooted in its consequences for fiscal strength. By nationalizing operations, leaders increase take-home revenues from the sale of natural resources that otherwise flow to private firms. These increased resource revenues can be life-saving: they allow leaders to buy political support and to deter potential challengers to increase their own duration in power.

Using cross-national statistical analysis, this chapter tests the two pillars of this claim. First, operational nationalization leads to greater government revenues from the sale of oil; second, the combination of nationalization and increased revenues fosters stronger and more durable leaders.

While the second finding of this chapter will seem intuitive to the reader – higher government revenues translate to more stability – the first finding will seem paradoxical, particularly to readers familiar with the classical economics literature on the consequences of state intervention (Stigler, 1971; Buchanan et al., 1980; Hartley and Medlock, 2008). That is, nationalization should lead to lower revenues given the operational inefficiencies of SOEs and the costs of potential retaliation by expropriated firms and their backing governments. The counterargument, in other words, is that even if the share of revenue captured by the state should increase upon nationalization, the overall amount of revenues collected should decline.

This is not the case for countries rich in natural resources that have established operational SOEs. These entities have operational capacities that enable them to produce crude oil without relying solely on other companies, be they foreign or domestic. States with these institutions, as I show in this chapter, increase both the share and overall levels of oil revenues (and slightly increase production levels as well) when compared to the period prior to nationalization.

To assess the validity of this argument, I continue the methodological approach taken in Chapter 4 by using evidence in the form of cross-national statistical analysis of observational data. Here I again apply the NOC dataset developed in Chapter 3, combined with data on government collection of oil revenue that is assembled from existing data on government revenues and oil income per capita. To show that governments are more durable after nationalizing oil assets, I then analyze data on leader survival as well as the stability of political regimes. The results are corroborative: operational nationalization leads to increased revenues and increased probabilities of political survival.

5.1 Reexamining Theories of Government Revenue and Leader Survival

Broadly speaking, one view that scholars provide for why revenues are linked to leader stability is the "spending mechanism." Proponents of this framework argue that leaders survive through direct spending of government revenues on dissatisfied groups in society, such as members of the opposition and citizens living in poverty, or through general spending of revenues on public goods like infrastructure, education, and healthcare. Yet the source of this spending matters: if spending were to increase simply by raising income taxes – which typically will be met with stern public opposition – then the net effects on stability will be null or perhaps even negative. What matters for stability is balancing the precarious ratio between income taxes and spending. So how then to increase spending without increasing demands on the citizen public? The argument I present throughout this book posits that leaders survive by increasing government revenue through state intervention in the natural resource economy.

5.1.1 Stability through Spending

The canonical work of Lipset (1959) set the stage for studies trying to explain political stability, and perhaps "has generated the largest body of research on any topic of comparative politics" (Przeworski, 2000, 78–79). Lipset's view is that economic development leads to regime survival, particularly within democracies. Stronger economies – in the form of increasing income growth and levels – should lead to stronger and thus more stable regimes.[1] Conversely, economic crisis

---

[1] This holds unless the initial regime is one of autocratic rule, such that increasing growth will shift a country from relatively poor to rich, sparking modernization pressures for

threatens the survival of the leader because of the state's failure to satisfy popular demands (Diamond et al., 1989; Przeworski, 2000). Yet the evidence remains mixed: some studies show that economic growth increases leader duration (Haggard and Kaufman, 1995; Feng, 1997), while others find no such relationship in the data (Kohli, 1986), or one that diminishes in the long run (Treisman, 2015). But how does development translate into stability for the state?

The answer with the most consensus is spending – more economic growth leads to more income tax revenues that in turn lead to stability. Levi (1989, 2) provides one of the foundational studies establishing the second part of this link:

> The greater the revenue of the state, the more possible it is to extend rule. Revenue enhances the ability of rulers to elaborate the institutions of the state, to bring more people within the domain of those institutions, and to increase the number and variety of the collective goods provided through the state.

Indeed, in theories of leader stability based on clientelism (Stokes, 2005; Magaloni, 2006; Arriola, 2009; Stokes et al., 2013), selectorate satisfaction (Bueno de Mesquita et al., 2003; Bueno de Mesquita and Smith, 2010), and rentierism (Ross, 2001), one method for survival is direct spending on disgruntled groups of society, be they elites in general, members of the opposition, or poor voters. Leaders that spend on these constituents – winning-coalition elites in autocracies and voters in democracies – with public goods and patronage are rewarded with political support and thus decrease their chances of ouster.

Within this view is the theory that state spending increases the odds of survival by alleviating income inequality. Acemoglu and Robinson (2005) and Boix (2003) argue that income inequity within a country can prompt citizen demands for regime transition – especially from autocracy to democracy – but elites can ward off revolutions by redistributing government revenue to the lower and middle classes dissatisfied with the regime. Naturally, any increase in the government's coffers will help leaders alleviate demands through redistribution of newfound revenues.

Morrison (2009, 2015) applies this theory in the context of nontax revenue – primarily generated by either natural resources or foreign aid – to find that indeed, "higher levels of nontax revenue are associated with less regime transition and less leadership turnover" (Morrison,

---

a transition to democracy (see Przeworski (2000) for a review of these studies). At higher levels of income, strong economic performance will increase regime survival, regardless of being in a democratic or authoritarian state. Treisman (2015) shows that rapid economic growth in particular helps dictators survive, though this stabilizing effect wears off in the long run (after 20 years).

2015, 56). In the case of Mexico's single-party dictatorship, increases in government revenues from the oil boom of the late 1970s and early 1980s allowed the ruling PRI to placate redistributional demands enough to remain in power. This lasted until the collapse of nontax revenue in the late 1980s and 1990s led to democratic transition in 2000 (Greene, 2008).[2]

In the political economy literature on natural resources, Ross (2001, 2012), Smith (2004), and Ulfelder (2007) show that natural resource wealth prolongs leaders' time in office in part due to increased government spending allowed by the collection of resource rents. This "allocative strategy" of resource wealth spending is in many ways the theoretical foundation of the political economy of natural resources (Luciani, 1990). In democracies, Robinson et al. (2006) find that resource-derived government revenue is spent on providing jobs to persuade voters to reelect the incumbent government. Wright et al. (2015) argue that oil wealth similarly increases the survival of autocracies by reducing pressures to democratize and by decreasing the probability of coups through military spending. Cuaresma et al. (2011) corroborate these arguments to show that revenue from oil production increases the duration of autocratic regimes through increasing payments to elites and "kingmakers." In general, we should expect that any increase in government revenues should positively affect the survival chances of leaders, be they democratic or otherwise.

5.1.2   *Politics in the Economy: State Intervention*

Yet some scholars have challenged this claim, particularly when these revenues come from the sale of natural resources. Recall from earlier chapters that Haber and Menaldo (2011) find increasing revenues from oil have little effect on survival (and even a small positive effect on regime change in the form of democratization). Andersen and Ross (2013) point out this "null effect" finding is present only in the pre-1980 period. Andersen and Ross (2013) show evidence of a positive relationship between oil revenues and survival after 1980, using both the data and model specification from Haber and Menaldo (2011) (see also Liou and Musgrave (2014)). In Chapter 2, I discussed how the "post-1980 resource curse" is in part due to the timing of state intervention in the petroleum industry, drawing on the work of Jones Luong and Weinthal (2010), Ross (2012), Andersen and Ross (2013), and Menaldo (2016).

---

[2] See, however, Garrido de Sierra (2012) and Magaloni (2006) for alternative accounts for the collapse of the PRI.

Here, I expand on this discussion and restate my argument that state intervention – in particular, natural resource nationalization – increases leader survival through its impact on government revenue.

The argument is as follows. A shift from private ownership of natural resources to state ownership generates an increase in government revenues from the sale of these resources; this increased revenue is used by the leader to remain in power. During the period of private ownership, the host government – that is, the government of a country with natural resource production within its borders – relies on various tax and royalty mechanisms to collect resource revenues. These are collected from operating companies unaffiliated with the host state, including major MNCs like ExxonMobil and BP, independent contractors like Baker Hughes and Halliburton, smaller domestic operators like Cairn in India or Sinclair Oil in the US, and even international SOEs like Norway's Equinor and China's CNOOC.[3] The rate of taxation is set by an initial contract between the host government and operating company, typically prior to resource exploration. I define the "effective tax rate" as the net percentage of all oil revenues collected by the state, inclusive of corporate income taxes (that is, taxes on the net incomes of private firms), royalties, dividends, and "special taxes." I define "net income" as gross income minus costs, and "net profits" as gross income minus costs and taxes.

After oil is discovered and companies begin producing at commercial quantities, the government may decide the initial effective tax rate is too low. As I argue in Chapters 1 and 2, this change of heart is in part due to how leaders perceive their own odds of survival after the diffusion of information: weaker leaders will want to seize greater net profits to bolster their rule, while stronger leaders will eschew nationalization, given its potential long-term costs for survival. The initial tax rate can either be renegotiated while maintaining a market structure of private ownership, or renegotiated forcibly through nationalization of operations. Recall from Chapter 4 that the Saudi government of the 1940s opted for the former option and renegotiated a higher tax rate with Standard Oil of California (Socal), while the Iranian government pursued nationalization of AIOC and increased its effective tax rate from 27 percent to nearly 100 percent (of net income, not gross income).

But the civil renegotiation of tax rates typically does not last for long. The conventional wisdom is that nationalization is in many ways inevitable as a means to increase government revenues (Vernon, 1971).

---

[3] On the internationalization of NOCs, see Jones Luong and Sierra (2015) and Cheon (2015).

Even in Saudi Arabia, the state eventually nationalized all assets during the 1974–1980 period. Consider again the case of the Libyan nationalization from the opening pages of the book. In January 1970, newly minted Libyan dictator Muammar Qaddafi pressured Italian, British, French, and American oil companies to increase the posted price[4] of Libyan oil by $0.43 a barrel, along with an increase in the state's take from 50 percent to 55 percent. Qaddafi knew he had leverage over the firms' home countries – by 1970, Libyan oil provided 30 percent of Europe's total crude imports – and used this bargaining position to bully the twenty-one oil companies operating in the country to accept his terms or else be forced to shutdown all production. Qaddafi's message to the Western oil firms was to give the state a bigger share of oil revenues or risk losing the entire pie: "People who have lived without oil for 5,000 years can live without it for a few years to attain their legitimate rights" (Yergin, 1991, 578). The companies initially resisted but by November 1970, faced with the threat of nationalization, acquiesced and increased the posted price by $0.30 a barrel and gave the Libyan state a 5 percent increase of the profits, bringing the total to a 55 percent stake in the consortium (i.e., the twenty-one operating companies) profits from the sale of Libyan oil. But this did not quench Qaddafi's thirst for a greater share in oil rents. Three years later, on September 1, 1973 – the fourth anniversary of the military coup – Qaddafi nationalized 51 percent of all foreign-owned oil operations (Waddams, 1980). The motive was clear: by taking a controlling interest in operations and by increasing the overall state percentage take of oil profits, Qaddafi's government could increase state revenues in a way that was not possible by simply raising the tax rate on the consortium companies or maintaining a nonoperational SOE.

The increase in net profits from private operators to state operators is the result of two factors, all undergirded by the existence of an operational NOC under state ownership. In some ways, operational nationalization can be thought of as what economist James Meade has termed a "second-best option" in which Pareto optimality, wherein it is impossible to make one party better off without making another worse off, is unattainable (Meade, 1955). When the government cannot credibly commit to an expropriation-free marketplace – that is, the state cannot commit not to expropriate private firms – private firms will not invest in the country's oil sector at an optimal rate. The sector will

---

[4] Before the advent of the spot market for oil sales, the posted price was the agreed-upon price of a barrel of a producing country's oil. This price was the primary factor in determining how much revenue would be collected by the producing government versus how much would be collected by the operator(s).

suffer from underinvestment and tax revenue will either be zero (in the event of no firms entering the market) or some suboptimal level. But by nationalizing the oil sector and setting up an NOC, private firms will enter the market, given that there is already high certainty surrounding expropriation risks. With this added investment where little to none had existed prior to NOC establishment, government revenues from oil will be higher, even if the effective tax rate on firms remains unchanged.

The first mechanism driving this effect is that a shift from private to state ownership decreases the information asymmetry between government and producer regarding the true level of revenues and operating costs. During the period of private ownership, the government must rely on proper reporting of revenues by the operating companies, which have strong incentives to underreport production and sales as the effective tax rate increases. This is particularly problematic since taxes on operating companies are on net income and not on gross revenues, making it relatively easy for a firm to inflate costs to recover a greater share of pretax revenues. As such, the government must choose an optimal tax rate that reduces the likelihood of misreporting. After nationalization, the knowledge gap between government and NOC is substantially smaller,[5] so the government is able to tax directly on revenues instead of having to tax on reported income.

Second, nationalizing operations provides production elasticity: the ability to change production levels in response to changing prices. This allows leaders to capitalize on high international prices and in the case of dominant producers, to drive up prices by withholding production in the context of low prices. Nationalizing production by setting up an operational SOE allows resource-rich governments to control their fiscal destinies, particularly if private firms are producing at politically or economically suboptimal levels.

Note that an underlying assumption is that a government can set the optimal effective tax rate on an NOC at 100 percent without concern for market flight. Specifically, the state can force the NOC to take a negative rate of return (ROR) if the state takes revenues before allowing for the NOC to repay its operational costs. Under private ownership, no firm will enter the market for a negative ROR, meaning zero production and revenues for the host government. The optimal ROR under private ownership must be nonnegative (or greater than some value ϵ) for the government to earn any revenues. Indeed, the optimal tax rate on gross

---

[5] In theory there is no knowledge gap, but in practice some gaps still exist. See Heller (2012) for a discussion of the information asymmetry regarding revenues between the Angolan government and its NOC, Sonangol. See also Section 2.2.2.

revenues is much closer to 5 to 30 percent in practice (Johnston, 2001). In the UK, for example, the effective tax rate is 31 percent since the 1999 amendment to the Finance Act, and in the US, the effective tax rate is 16.7 percent for shallow-water oil fields in the Gulf of Mexico. These are taxes on net income (gross income minus costs but not taxes) and thus are much lower in gross income terms.

In principle, these factors will work to increase the effective tax rate upon nationalization. A higher, acceptable optimal tax rate combined with lower information asymmetry should enable the government to extract as much revenue as desired from its NOC, with the only constraint being the amount to consider reinvesting in the NOC for future exploration and production. Within the range of different degrees of state intervention I discuss in the previous chapters, information asymmetry between government and operators (including the NOC) should be lowest when an NOC has production capacity and is actively involved in on-the-ground operations. States establishing these operational SOEs should thus have the highest levels of revenue after nationalization compared to the period when private firms control production.

5.2   Data, Methods, and Research Design

This increased level of resource revenues will enable leaders in states with NOCs to endure, based on the redistribution and spending mechanisms linking revenues to leader stability. To assess the validity of this argument, I consider three observable implications that serve as testable hypotheses in the context of oil nationalizations:

H_{1a} *States with operational NOCs will have higher resource revenues than states without operational NOCs.*

H_{1b} *State revenues from oil – both in terms of total resource revenues collected and in terms of revenues captured by the government – will be higher postnationalization than in the years preceding operational nationalization.*

H_2 *With higher revenues, leaders in states with nationalized operations are more likely to survive than in states without nationalized operations.*

H_3 *More revenue from oil in operationally nationalized states corresponds to increased regime stability.*

I now turn to a discussion of how I test these hypotheses using the data on NOCs used throughout this book, combined with cross-national data on natural resource revenues collected by the government, leader survival, and regime stability. I begin by describing these data and continue by discussing the statistical techniques used to analyze each of the three hypotheses.

5.2.1   Data

To measure government revenues from oil, I focus on two related measurement concepts. The first is the overall level of oil revenues collected by the state, measured as percentage of GDP for comparability across countries of differing size.[6] By "collected by the state," I mean that these revenues are actually processed by a treasury department or similar agency such that oil revenues are included in any government accounts. In some extreme cases, such as Kuwait, these revenues are then returned to the oil company (in this case, Kuwait Petroleum), which is responsible for production in the form of reinvestment for future exploration and production. Still, since this money is at some point held in the government's coffers, it is counted as collected by the state.[7]

The second concept for measuring revenue is what is referred to as "state capture" of oil revenues. This refers to the percentage of revenues collected by the state compared with the total amount of oil revenues. A state collecting the entire share of oil revenues would have 100 percent capture – akin to having a 100 percent effective tax rate on revenues – while a state getting absolutely no oil revenue from production within its borders would have 0 percent capture.[8] As I describe in the previous section, states with NOCs should have higher capture almost by definition given that nationalization of oil companies can be seen as simply a higher tax on oil revenues. However, recall from Chapters 2 and 3 that NOCs have different institutional characteristics across countries. It should come as no surprise that NOCs are also taxed differently across countries, ranging from a low of a 1 percent effective tax rate on gross revenues of Trinidad's Petrotin, to a middling effective tax rate of 60 percent on Algeria's Sonatrach, all the way up to a 99 percent effective tax rate on Chad's SHT (Heller et al., 2019). This variance accounts for why my argument that *states with NOCs also have*

---

[6] I also use the same measure in per capita terms to ensure that the results are not driven by any endogeneity introduced by having GDP in the denominator. Results using this measure are presented in the Appendix (Section 5.5).

[7] In terms of what is counted as costs, I do not consider the issue of fuel subsidies that are provided directly by an NOC. In some countries' central bank reports, these subsidies are included as nonoperating costs while in others they are excluded and considered instead as state expenditures. For more on subsidies and NOCs, see Cheon et al. (2015).

[8] States without any oil production are thus excluded from this measure since the calculation of capture would be mathematically undefined.

higher rates of capture is not tautological, thus allowing for the empirical exercise below to verify or reject this claim.

I calculate both measures of oil revenue collected by the state using data from the International Centre for Tax and Development (ICTD) *Government Revenue Dataset* (GRD) (Prichard et al., 2014). This dataset was developed to build upon the quality of existing IMF data by identifying consistent government sources of revenues and the various tax and nontax components of state revenues. This team of researchers, led by Wilson Prichard, has greatly improved the quantitative measure of government revenues, which for some time have been prone to temporal inconsistencies, reporting errors, and other measurement errors. The focus of my analysis is on one variable in particular, that is, the amount of government revenues collected from the sale of natural resources either through taxes or nontax tools, in percentage of GDP to allow for comparability across states. I refer to this measure as "total resource revenues" or sometimes simply "resource revenues." The temporal coverage of the ICTD data spans from 1980 to 2010.

Measures of state capture, as I discuss more in the results section below, are unfortunately scarce. Out of a possible 3,348 country-years for states with any oil and gas production in the 1980–2010 period (108 states, 31 years), data on state capture of resource revenues is only available for 512 country-years or roughly 15 percent of the sample. As such, while this is a more accurate measure for the concept of state collection of resource revenues, I rely more heavily in the analysis on the other two measures – oil and gas income per capita (data for nearly 100 percent of the sample) and total resource revenues as a percentage of GDP (data for 30 percent of the sample).

Although the oil income data are more complete, I use resource revenues data as an additional measure. Nearly all analyses of the relationship between resources and stability have employed measures of government revenue from the IMF, which problematically do not allow the researcher to distinguish between tax and nontax revenue that is derived from the sale of natural resources (see Prichard et al. (2014) for a thorough review of these studies). As such, scholars like Morrison (2009) and Wright et al. (2015) have equated nontax revenue with natural resource revenue, without accounting for the fact that much of a country's resource revenues can come from direct taxation of oil companies. Further, nontax revenue may include other forms of revenue aside from resource revenue, such as foreign aid, interest earned on loans, and revenue from nonresource SOEs (Morrison (2015) accounts for these distinctions). By using the ICTD GRD, I avoid this pitfall and can measure the full amount of government revenue from natural

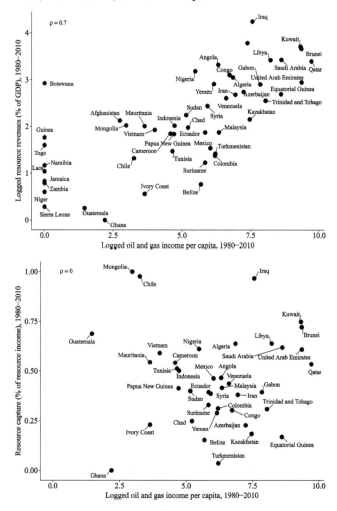

Figure 5.1 Petroleum income per capita, resource revenues, and state capture.

Country averages over the 1980–2010 period are plotted for 51 oil-producing countries, defined as having greater than $100 of oil and gas income per capita on average during the entire period. Pearson correlations are included in the top left corner of each plot.

resources, both taxed and not taxed – not accounting for missingness or misreporting, of course.

In Figure 5.1, I visualize the distribution of these measures and how they relate to a more conventional measure of resource wealth – oil income per capita (production times price divided by population) – used in previous analysis by Ross (2012) and Prichard et al. (2014). In the top panel, I plot countries' oil incomes against their total resource revenues as a percentage of GDP, averaged across the 1980–2010 period. Both are in log units to account for the skewed distribution of these measures, given that the majority of countries has little by way of natural resource wealth. Overall, there is a strong relationship between oil income and resource revenues, as expected. The fact that the relationship is not perfect is simply a reflection of differing importance of natural resources within a country's economy (as measured by GDP) as well as natural resource income earned not due to oil and gas – the block of countries with almost no petroleum wealth but some resource revenues is made up mostly of sub-Saharan African states with mineral wealth, such as Botswana.

The plot in the bottom panel shows almost no relationship between petroleum wealth and state capture of natural resource wealth. Consider Chile and Côte d'Ivoire, for example: two countries with similar petroleum income per capita, but different resource revenue and capture. Côte d'Ivoire, despite having slightly more petroleum income and higher resource revenues as a percentage of GDP, has a much lower rate of state capture than Chile. Indeed, state capture of natural resource revenue in Côte d'Ivoire is among the lowest in the sample, averaging 23 percent for the period, whereas state capture in Chile averages above 90 percent.[9] One notable difference between these two countries that Empresa Nacional del Petroleo (ENAP), Chile's NOC, is practically the only producer in the country with a near 100 percent share of production. The Ivorian state, on the other hand, has no de facto role in the production of petroleum fields in the country; its NOC, Petroci, plays only an oversight role in operations.[10]

This simple comparison offers a glimpse at testing the first part of my argument that operational nationalization affects resource revenues. In Figure 5.2, I make this same comparison across all countries in the sample with data on total resource revenues, adjusted using an oil price index (2011 = 100) to look at changes in revenues not due to price increases. What this plot shows – again, absent any multivariate statistical analysis – is the average levels of resource revenues for countries before and after establishing an operational NOC. As such, years are relative to when a given country sets up an operational NOC (for each country, this is marked year zero). Note that the plot is not balanced: because of data limitations, countries that established operational NOCs prior to 1980 (the first year of resource revenue data) are only counted in

---

[9] This is higher than the estimated mid-range government take on ENAP's production, which stands at a 83 percent tax on gross revenues (Johnston, 2001, 74).
[10] "The Mineral Industry of Côte D'Ivoire." *USGS Minerals Yearbooks: 2012.*

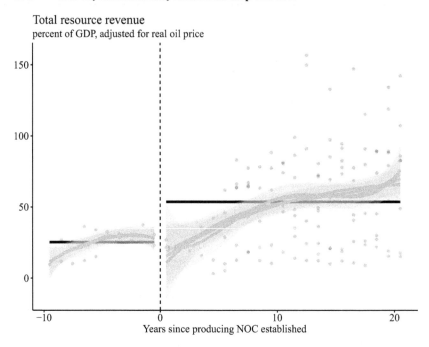

Figure 5.2 Resource revenues (adjusted for real oil price) before and after establishing an operational NOC.

Average resource revenues before and after an operational NOC is established are shown by the solid horizontal lines. I overlay four additional metrics to capture temporal changes in revenues, with 95 percent confidence bands: (1) loess smoother, (2) quadratic smoother, (3) cubic smoother, and (4) a fourth-order polynomial smoother. Total number of countries in the sample is 36. Note: "operational NOC" refers here to an NOC that de facto produces the country's oil and gas. Revenues/GDP are adjusted for a constant oil price index (price in 2011 = 100), hence values above 100 percent. Refer to Figure 5.8 for the same plot without price adjustment.

the "after" stage. I also plot various ways to show the pre- and post-NOC levels of revenues, including a simple average represented by the solid horizontal black line and multiple local regression and polynomial smoothers represented by the gray lines with 95 percent confidence bands. Recall that I construct a similar plot in Figure 2.1 in Chapter 2 for changes in oil production levels, in which the data show that production levels are higher after establishing an operational NOC.

The pattern that emerges from the data is that there is a marked increase in collected revenues after the shift to an operational NOC. Note that the initial dip in resource revenue in the two years after nationalization is not representative of the sample. Due to lack of data on revenues in the pre-1980 period – a key reason I use oil income as an additional measure – Algeria is the only state with data in the one-year pre- and postnationalization window. Revenues slightly declined with the country's deliberate decision to cut output as part of OPEC's effort to revive prices amidst the 1986 oil glut. Data availability is greater in the two years beyond postnationalization, where the increasing revenue is initial evidence in support of H_{1a}.

Measuring Survival: Leader Duration and Turnover

The second outcome variable of interest is leader survival, which is captured using a binary measure of leader failure. Using this framework, leaders "survive" for the duration of their rule, from entry in office up until their exit. Leaders can exit, or lose office, in a number of ways. I employ the Archigos measure of leader exit, which is split into four categories (Goemans et al., 2009). Leaders can step down in a "regular manner" that follows from defeats in elections, term limits, and voluntary retirements (including naming a successor); they can be removed by a foreign occupying power; they can leave office as a result of natural death; or they can be ousted in an irregular manner. The latter category includes removals from office via coups d'etat (or the threat of coup), popular revolution, and assassinations. The overthrow of King Idris of Libya by Qaddafi in 1969, the fall of the Shah of Iran in 1979, and the military-assisted coup of Robert Mugabe of Zimbabwe in 2017 are all examples of irregular removal of leaders from power.

This "irregular exit" is precisely that which I predict can be avoided by nationalizing resource operations: with greater resource revenues, a leader can prevent ouster by buying off would-be revolutionaries, co-opting opposition elites, and/or repressing popular movements to remove the leader from power. I therefore use the measure of irregular exit as the outcome of interest in the empirical analysis, coding a given leader-year as 1 if he or she suffers an irregular exit, and 0 if otherwise. Survival, then, can be modeled in one of two ways: predicting the duration of a leader's tenure (as measured in the time between entry and irregular exit) or predicting the probability of irregular exit in any given year. As a check on the argument's broader implications about survival, I also consider "any exit" as a measure of leader failure, which includes regular exit, irregular exit, and foreign removal (but does not include natural death).

I use regime change as an additional outcome variable, defined as a change in the formal rules and structure of government. The most prominent example among these changes is a shift from autocratic government to democracy, or vice versa. Two canonical measures of regime change are the Geddes et al. (2014) database of political regimes (GWF) and the Marshall et al. (2011) Polity IV project on regime characteristics and transitions. I focus both on transitions to and from democracy and on transitions to and from different nondemocratic regimes. For the GWF database, the definition of regimes "emphasizes the rules that identify the group from which leaders can come and determine who influences leadership choice and policy," meaning that a transition from one ruling group to another counts as a regime change. Such is the case, for example, when the Pahlavi monarchy in Iran was replaced by an Islamic theocracy ruled by clerics. The Polity measure would not necessarily count such a shift as regime change if the level of electoral competition, executive constraints, and openness of executive recruitment all remained the same. On the other hand, this measure would record a regime change of having occurred if these levels changed without changes in the general rules of the regime. Going back to the example of Iran, there were slight changes in electoral competition in 1997 when President Khatami was first elected, but the Islamic theocracy remained unchanged, with Supreme Leader Khamenei still in power as head of government. The GWF measure would not count this as regime change, while the Polity measure would (indeed, Polity records three regime changes since the 1979 revolution).[11]

How does leader survival vary under operational nationalization? Before turning to the modeling and statistical analysis of my argument, in Figure 5.3 I plot the survival rates of leaders with and without operational NOCs during the period of data analysis discussed below (1932–2014) using the Archigos data. These survival rates can be thought of in terms of how likely it is in a given year of power that the average leader will endure; plotting these rates shows the proportion of leaders in the sample that did not fail as time goes on. The figure plots the survival odds for leaders in each category as separate lines: the black line for leaders in states without operational NOCs and the grey line for leaders in states with operational NOCs. For instance, in the tenth year of power, the survival rate for leaders with operational NOCs was roughly 80 percent, meaning that the other 20 percent was either ousted (irregular exit) or intentionally stepped down from power (regular exit). The numbers below the table provide more specifics at

---

[11] These measurement variations account for the differences between both the GWF and Polity measures of regime change. Despite the moderate correlation of 0.6 between both measures, clearly the Polity measure perceives regimes as changing much more often than the GWF score. Nonetheless, I use both measures given the prevalence of Polity in particular in prior studies of natural resources and regime change (Ross, 2001; Ulfelder, 2007; Morrison, 2009; Haber and Menaldo, 2011).

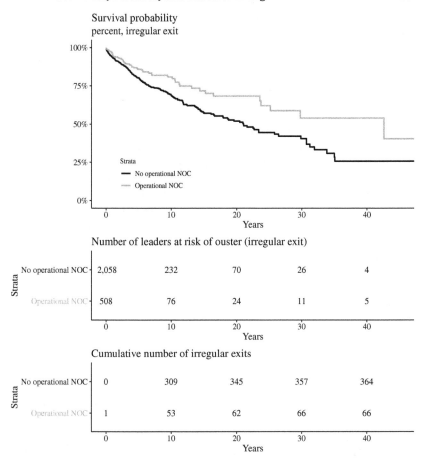

Figure 5.3 Leader survival and operational nationalization.

each ten-year mark: by year ten, for instance, 53 leaders in states with operational NOCs were ousted out of a starting point of 515. By year ten, 76 leaders survived in office while the remaining leaders either exited regularly ($n = 333$) or were still in office as of 2014 ($n = 29$).[12]

That the grey line is higher throughout indicates that leaders in states with nationalized operations are more durable (they fail less often). Of course, these plots offer just a first glimpse at the data, without

_____

[12] In addition, two leaders were deposed by foreign intervention and twenty-one died in office or stepped down due to ill health. The starting point is 515 instead of 508 listed in the table because seven leaders left office within the first year of power.

adding any other variables or modeling assumptions.[13] Nonetheless, this visualization provides initial support for the general argument that nationalization prolongs leader survival.

5.2.2   Testing and Modeling: Operational NOCs Increase Survival

I test two components of the argument that NOCs increase stability through increased government revenue. The first is to directly model the revenue-increasing effects of operational nationalization without consideration of leader survival. Here the outcome is natural resource revenues and the predictor of interest is whether a country has an operational NOC. Specifically, this model tests whether a country's establishment of an operational NOC corresponds with changes in resource revenues as measured by oil income per capita and the state resource revenue measure from ICTD. Both dependent variables are additive functions of several factors (revenues are purely functions of prices, production, institutions, and noise) and so can be modeled using standard OLS assumptions. A simple model of state resource revenues is then a linear function of institutional type (NOC or not), petroleum prices, petroleum production, and other country-specific characteristics captured using country-fixed effects. The same is the case for oil income per capita.

The next set of models consider the two mechanisms – NOCs increase revenues and revenues increase stability – together using interactions between nationalization and resource revenues with political survival as the outcome. Here I only use the general oil and gas income per capita variable to measure resource revenues. I make this choice because interacting the NOC variable and income is itself a proxy for resource revenues, while interacting the NOC variable with capture or collected revenues is conceptually redundant. My argument is that NOCs increase revenues and capture directly so that an interaction between the two tells nothing more than each variable by itself (if there is an NOC then there should be higher revenues). Conversely, if there is an NOC there will not necessarily be higher oil income – and indeed could very well result in lower income due to inefficiencies – but if my argument is correct, then states with NOCs and higher oil income will also have higher rates of

---

[13] Because this sample includes leaders that exited regularly (and are thus not coded as "failing" when they exit from power) the survival probability does not converge to 0. For example, the survival probability for leaders in states without operational NOCs is roughly 25 percent by their 35th year in power; this implies that their odds of surviving an irregular exit are 25 percent (but the odds of surviving any exit would be close to 0 percent).

leader survival because leaders will be able to capture a larger portion of resource income.

Model specification for this second approach is subject to greater debate, as there are numerous approaches to modeling leader survival as it is affected by government revenue. Prichard et al. (2014) provides a thorough review of different econometric techniques (using regime survival as an outcome instead of leader survival), including the following: pooled OLS regression, fixed-effects OLS regression, random-effects logistic regression, General Method of Moments (GMM), Difference-GMM, Sys-GMM, Mean Group-Common Correlated Effects (CCE-MG), and panel Error-Correction Models (ECM). The relationship between stability and government revenues – in particular, nontax revenues – is consistently positive (more nontax revenue, less likelihood of change) across all specifications except fixed-effects OLS and Diff-GMM models. The authors attribute these exceptions to the poor fit of these models to large-N and large-T dynamic panel data, a concern also shared by Andersen and Ross (2013).

Given the stability of model specification, I choose to analyze the revenue and stability hypothesis using a simple, interpretable approach in logistic regression.[14] To account for country-level heterogeneity, I use a mixed-effects logit model with country random intercepts (sometimes referred to as "random-effects logit"). Due to the difficulty in computing mixed-effects logit models using maximum likelihood methods, particularly for data in which the count of 0s is much higher than 1s (as is the case for leader and regime failures), I employ Bayesian methods for computation (Weiss, 2012; Gelman et al., 2013). Nonetheless, alternative specifications are tried, with results presented alongside the Bayesian models.

In modeling leader survival as a function of resource revenues and nationalized operations, I add a limited set of covariates to prevent overfitting. These include the following: regime type to account for heterogeneity in irregular exits across democratic and nondemocratic regimes (Miller, 2012); GDP per capita and year-to-year growth in total GDP, to account for the effects of economic crises on instability (Haggard and Kaufman, 1995; Przeworski, 2000); logged population, to account for theories of state size and stability (Herbst, 2000; Fearon and Laitin, 2003); presence of civil war to account for the increasing

---

[14] Regarding proportional hazard models, which are not included in the Prichard et al. (2014) analysis: Wright et al. (2015) find that results are consistent between conditional logit models and Cox Proportional Hazard Models, and further, find that the hazard assumption is not violated following a stratified (by country) test of nonproportional hazards in a Cox model.

likelihood of ouster during periods of conflict (Debs and Goemans, 2010); leader characteristics including age at entry, type of entry, and number of previous times in office (Goemans et al., 2009); and a continuous polynomial time trend to account for various temporal effects like "waves of democracy" (Huntington, 1991).

Given that I am using observational data, there is the ever-present and thorny issue of endogeneity. As I discuss at length in Chapter 4, regimes matter in the establishment of NOCs: states with strong executive constraints, independent judiciaries, and robust rule of law are less likely to nationalize and form an NOC, whereas states with weak executive constraints have higher nationalization probabilities. Controlling for regime type helps allay this problem, but there are still other potential lurking variables that can confound the relationship between nationalization and survival.

These concerns cannot be definitively ruled out and thus hinder my ability to make causal claims using this research design. Nonetheless, I am able to make strong claims about the validity of my argument by showing empirical support for three observable implications: resource revenues are higher in states with operational NOCs, leader survival is more likely as resource revenues increase, and thus, the probability of survival increases with resource revenues conditional on nationalization.

5.3   Statistical Analysis of Nationalization, Revenues, and Survival

5.3.1   Nationalization Increases Natural Resource Revenue and Government Capture

In Table 5.1, I present the results of five regressions in which the outcome is total resource revenue collected by the government, in percentage of GDP.[15] The first regression, in column 1, shows a trivial but necessary baseline result that indeed total resource revenues are predicted by petroleum production levels and prices. This result provides some support for the assumption that the omission of metals and other nonoil minerals, while not ideal, is not detrimental to the analysis.

The second and third columns of Table 5.1 include the "general NOC" measure that captures the presence of an NOC – regardless of production and operational capacities – both on its own and interacted with production. Specifically, the presence of an NOC increases total resource revenues by 3.21 percentage points (0.23 standard deviations).

---

[15] Results using total resource revenues per capita are presented in Table 5.4 and show similar results both in terms of statistical significance and magnitude.

Table 5.1. *Nationalization increases resource revenues collected by the government*

	Model 1	Model 2	Model 3	Model 4	Model 5
Petroleum production	0.467***	0.453***	0.386***	0.457***	0.424***
(tonnes/year) (logged)	(0.061)	(0.062)	(0.060)	(0.061)	(0.060)
Oil price (US$)	0.186***	0.184***	0.179***	0.194***	0.189***
	(0.019)	(0.019)	(0.018)	(0.019)	(0.019)
NOC indicator		0.233**	−1.168***		
		(0.111)	(0.223)		
NOC × production			2.901***		
			(0.405)		
Operational				0.306***	−1.581***
NOC indicator				(0.116)	(0.343)
Operational					2.841***
NOC × production					(0.487)
R^2	0.792	0.794	0.806	0.794	0.802
Adj. R^2	0.779	0.780	0.793	0.781	0.789
Num. observations	871	871	871	871	871
Num. countries	51	51	51	51	51

***$p < 0.01$, **$p < 0.05$, *$p < 0.1$
All variables are lagged one year and, except for the NOC variables, all variables are standardized with mean zero and variance one. All models include country-fixed effects, the estimates of which are omitted from this table.

The interaction with production levels – which proxies in some ways for having an operational NOC – indicates that a state with an NOC and production levels 0.5 standard deviations above the mean (13,000,000 metric tonnes per year, roughly what Equatorial Guinea produced in 2008) has higher resource revenues than a state with an NOC and production levels at the mean (350,000 metric tonnes per year, roughly what Ghana produced in 2008), with a difference in revenues of 22.6 percentage points (1.64 standard deviations) of GDP.[16]

---

[16] This is calculated by multiplying the sum of the coefficients for production and the interaction term by the difference in production levels, all in standard deviation terms given that these variables are demeaned and standardized: $(0.5 - 0) \times (0.386 + 2.901) = 1.644$. Then I back-convert to percentage points of resource revenues by multiplying 1.644 by the standard deviation of the total resources revenue, 13.776, to get 22.643 percentage points.

Table 5.2. *Nationalization increases state capture of natural resource revenues*

	Model 1	Model 2	Model 3	Model 4	Model 5
Petroleum production (tonnes/year) (logged)	0.106** (0.045)	0.105** (0.045)	0.065 (0.046)	0.101** (0.045)	0.084* (0.045)
Oil price (US$)	0.147*** (0.027)	0.147*** (0.027)	0.143*** (0.027)	0.154*** (0.027)	0.151*** (0.027)
NOC indicator		0.023 (0.141)	0.108 (0.143)		
NOC × production			0.519*** (0.170)		
Operational NOC indicator				0.210 (0.147)	0.038 (0.169)
Operational NOC × production					0.406** (0.198)
R^2	0.674	0.674	0.679	0.675	0.678
Adj. R^2	0.652	0.652	0.656	0.653	0.655
Num. observations	662	662	662	662	662
Num. countries	40	40	40	40	40

***$p < 0.01$, **$p < 0.05$, *$p < 0.1$
All variables are lagged one year and, except for the NOC variables, all variables are standardized with mean zero and variance one. All models include country-fixed effects, the estimates of which are omitted from this table.

The model results from columns four and five show similar results. Bear in mind that the interaction between operational NOC and production is interpreted differently than the general NOC and production interaction. Here the interaction term results show that high-production (0.5 standard deviations above the mean) states with operational NOCs have higher resource revenues than average-production states with operational NOCs, with a difference in revenues of 21.07 percentage points (1.53 standard deviations).

When it comes to state capture, the substantive results are similar but with higher uncertainty given the smaller sample size (662 country-years and forty countries compared to 871 country-years and fifty-one countries). The results in Table 5.2 show that having an NOC means higher revenue capture, though the only results that cross the threshold of statistical significance are the models with NOC-production interaction terms. For a sense of the magnitude of these results, a 1 standard deviation increase in production from the mean corresponds to a 11.48 percentage point increase in state capture for a state with an operational NOC, but only a 1.96 percentage point increase for a state without an operational NOC.[17]

Both sets of regressions show results that are consistent with the first hypothesis that states with operational NOCs have higher resource revenues collected by the government.

5.3.2   Nationalization Increases Leader Survival

To test H_2, I analyze predictors of leader survival using a mixed-effects Bayesian logistic regression model. The model is run with the binary outcome of suffering an irregular exit from power in a given year. The two mechanisms that I argue will increase survival – operational nationalization increases revenues and revenues prolong leader tenure – are modeled together using interactions between nationalization and resource revenues (using the general oil and gas–income per capita variable to measure resource revenues). Controls for these models include the Polity regime index, logged GDP per capita, annual GDP growth, logged population, incidence of civil war, and polynomial time trends, along with leader-level baseline characteristics (age at entry, number of previous times in office, and whether the leader entered via regular means). These represent the standard battery of predictors for the duration of leader tenure (Goemans et al., 2009). Country-level random intercepts are also included in the models.

In Figure 5.4, I plot the posterior medians and 95 percent credible intervals of the posterior distributions of the coefficients for oil revenues, operational nationalization, and the interaction term from a model that includes the complete set of controls, time trends, and country-random effects. The median of these distributions are roughly interpreted as the $\hat{\beta}$ from non-Bayesian models. The results indicate that at higher levels of oil revenues, leaders with nationalized operations are less likely to fail compared to leaders without nationalized operations: the posterior median for the interaction term is -0.168 with a standard deviation of 0.076. The probability of a negative correlation (akin to a p value in the non-Bayesian context) is given by the integral of the distribution less than zero; in this case, the interaction term has a 99.4 percent probability of being negative (or a "pseudo p-value" = 0.006). In countries without nationalized operations, the correlation between oil revenues and survival is slightly positive, with a posterior median of 0.047 and standard deviation of 0.048 (pseudo p-value = 0.161).

---

[17] Note that these analyses do not include the oil and gas–income variable, given that this measure is deterministic: it is simply a product of price and production.

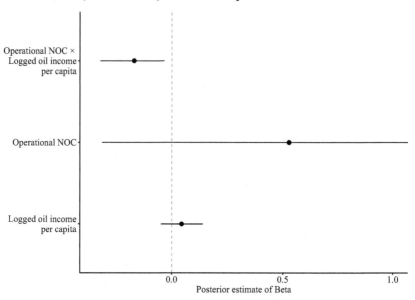

Figure 5.4 Bayesian model results for leadership survival: posterior estimates.

Posterior medians and 95 percent credible intervals for the operational NOC and oil income interaction from a Bayesian hierarchical logit model of leader failure. Controls include democracy levels (Polity), GDP per capita, GDP growth, leader age at entry, mode of entry (irregular versus regular), incidence of civil war, number of previous times in office, cubic time trends, and country-random effects. Estimates from a Gibbs sampler with 100,000 iterations and a thinning interval of 100, with uninformative priors for coefficients (mean zero, variance 10,000).

To help interpret the results, Figure 5.5 depicts the predicted probability of leader failure for an autocratic country (Polity = −10), with and without an operational NOC over different values of logged oil income, holding all control variables at their means. The plot in the bottom panel shows the conditional effect of having an operational NOC on the probability of leadership failure across different values of logged oil income. Note that while the posterior credible intervals overlap considerably in the predicted probability plot, the conditional effects plot in the bottom panel shows that the difference in predicted probabilities is different from zero for countries with oil incomes per capita above six logged units, or roughly $400.

Similar models are run using more conventional approaches in OLS (i.e., the linear probability model), logistic regression, and a Cox Proportional Hazard Model, with results shown in Table 5.3. The interpretation

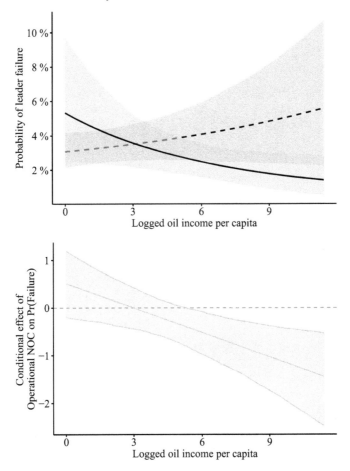

Figure 5.5 Bayesian model results for leadership survival: predicted probabilities.

Top panel: Predicted probability of leader failure for autocratic countries (Polity set to −10) with operational NOCs (solid line) and without operational NOCs (dashed line) across supported values of logged oil income per capita. Based on model results from the Bayesian hierarchical logit regression with all other control variables set to their mean values.

Bottom panel: The conditional effect of operational NOC on leader failure across supported values of logged oil income per capita.

of these models will be more straightforward for readers less familiar with the Bayesian approach depicted in Figure 5.4. Model 1 in Table 5.3 presents the results from a logistic regression on irregular leader failure, including as covariates only oil revenues, the operational NOC indicator,

Table 5.3. Leader failure, oil revenues, and operational nationalization around the world, 1932–2014

Dependent variable:	Irregular failure					Time to failure	Any failure
Estimator	Logistic				OLS	Cox PH	Logistic
	(1)	(2)	(3)	(4)	(5)	(6)	(7)
Log oil income	-0.030 (0.029)	0.049 (0.038)	0.032 (0.045)	-0.011 (0.073)	0.001 (0.001)	0.037 (0.036)	-0.045** (0.018)
Operational NOC	0.410 (0.296)	0.795** (0.321)	0.579* (0.347)	1.438** (0.601)	0.016* (0.010)	1.021*** (0.305)	0.404** (0.162)
Log oil income × Op. NOC	-0.155** (0.065)	-0.188*** (0.069)	-0.155** (0.075)	-0.322*** (0.111)	-0.004** (0.002)	-0.231*** (0.065)	-0.057* (0.033)
Regime index		-0.083*** (0.013)	-0.093*** (0.016)	-0.114*** (0.026)	-0.002*** (0.0003)	-0.021* (0.012)	0.064*** (0.006)
Log GDP per capita		-0.345*** (0.089)	-0.413*** (0.119)	-0.143 (0.201)	-0.007*** (0.002)	-0.367*** (0.087)	0.053 (0.036)
GDP growth		-3.723*** (0.671)	-4.171*** (0.883)	-5.100*** (1.157)	-0.145*** (0.022)	-3.602*** (0.559)	-5.310*** (0.442)
Log population		-0.140*** (0.051)	-0.114* (0.061)	0.019 (0.085)	-0.005*** (0.001)	-0.188*** (0.049)	0.038 (0.024)
Age at entry		-0.0003 (0.001)	-0.0005 (0.001)	-0.001 (0.003)	-0.00002 (0.00003)	0.001 (0.001)	0.001** (0.0005)
Regular entry		-0.215 (0.141)	-0.011 (0.187)	-0.437 (0.268)	-0.013*** (0.005)	-0.220 (0.134)	-0.432*** (0.094)
Civil war		0.774*** (0.149)	0.630*** (0.188)	0.417 (0.295)	0.033*** (0.005)	0.988*** (0.145)	0.229*** (0.084)
Previous times in office		0.307*** (0.109)	0.401*** (0.154)	0.416* (0.236)	0.011*** (0.004)	0.341*** (0.099)	0.090 (0.061)
Observations	10,278	8,899	5,663	2,723	8,899	8,899	8,899

Note: $^{*}p < 0.1$; $^{**}p < 0.05$; $^{***}p < 0.01$

Coefficient estimates for the intercept and time trends are not shown. Model 1 shows a regression on only oil income, operational NOC, and the interaction. Model 2 shows the full regression with all controls. Models 3 and 4 restrict the sample to oil producers and major oil producers, respectively. Model 5 is the full regression using a linear probability model instead of logit. Model 6 is the Cox Proportional Hazard (PH) model. Model 7 shows the results for predicting leadership failure of any kind.

and the interaction between the two variables. Without controlling for other factors, the coefficient for the interaction term is negative and statistically significantly different from zero at conventional levels, while the coefficient for the NOC indicator is positive and statistically insignificant. This suggests that in countries with no oil production, leaders who nationalize operations are less likely to survive than those who maintain private operations. Of course, this is an unlikely scenario: rarely do leaders nationalize without seeing evidence of viable resource revenue streams, but if they choose to do so, the political costs of nationalization clearly outweigh the (nonexistent) fiscal benefits.

Perhaps a more interesting comparison is found in a sample restricted to countries with nontrivial levels of oil production.[18] Model 4 shows the results of a model using this restricted sample, along with a battery of controls for leader survival (regime type, economic development, conflict, demographics, and leader characteristics). To better interpret the interaction between nationalization and oil revenues, I plot the conditional effects of operational nationalization at different levels of oil wealth in Figure 5.6. The results again indicate that for countries with 6 logged units or roughly $400 of oil income per capita or more – just over half of the sample (visualized in the histogram at the bottom of the plot) – operational nationalization is associated with a lower likelihood of leader failure. In other words, leaders who seize control over the production of a highly lucrative oil industry (as opposed to more modest levels of oil wealth) are more likely to survive than those who vest operations in the hands of private firms.

But here again there is a *positive* correlation between operational nationalization and leader failure at low levels of oil revenues: the segment of the line above zero is statistically significant for countries with oil revenues up to roughly $20 per capita. At these low levels of resource wealth, it is apparent that the costs of operational nationalization still outweigh the benefits. Note that in this sample, there are countries with years of little to no oil production, which could be the case at either the beginning or the end of the country's resource production cycle. For example, Suriname's military dictator Desi Bouterse nationalized oil production in 1982 – twenty years after the first major oil discoveries by Shell, but two years prior to commercial production onset. The gamble did not pay off entirely as expected in strengthening

---

[18] This is defined as a country with greater than $100 of oil income per capita at any point in its production cycle; this leaves 51 countries in the sample. Note that a country could still have zero oil production in a given year, as I am not dropping country-years prior to the onset of production.

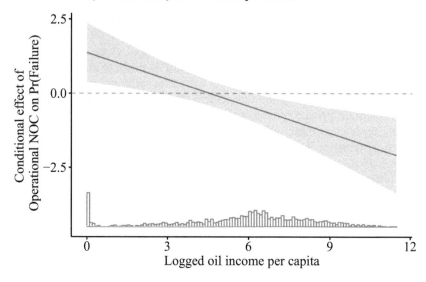

Figure 5.6 Conventional model results for leadership survival: conditional effects

The conditional effect of operational NOC on leader failure across supported values of logged oil income per capita for conventional (non-Bayesian) logit model, with all controls fixed at their means. See column 4 in Table 5.3 for coefficient estimates.

his rule: Bouterse was forced to cede power after free elections were held in 1987, but ultimately returned to rule through various puppets of his military regime starting in 1990 (Goemans et al., 2009, 239).

These results are robust to different model specifications and samples, notably the use of OLS regression (column 5), survival models (column 6), and when using an outcome variable capturing any type of leader exit (column 7). This last specification considers an operationalization of leader failure that, in addition to irregular exit, includes foreign invasion, retirement due to ill health, unnatural death (suicide), and regular exits like the transition from power after a lost election or leader replacement by the ruling party or family. It is interesting to find that operational nationalization still substantively corresponds (albeit at weaker magnitudes and higher statistical uncertainty) to more durable leaders using this measure. One interpretation, implied from the main argument in this book, is that leaders with greater fiscal strength as a result of nationalization are less likely to accept outcomes that see them removed from power – even if such a refusal to step down violates existing norms and rules of the regime.

As the argument implies that the effect of nationalization on survival is mediated by its effect on resource revenues, I also try models that estimate the average indirect and direct effects of nationalization. One such approach is causal mediation analysis (Imai et al., 2010). This method estimates the average causal mediated effect (ACME), the average direct effect (ADE), and the total effect of a treatment variable, which in this case would be the presence of an operational national oil company. Results using this method, plotted in Figure 5.10 and shown in Table 5.5, suggest that the effects of nationalization on survival operate primarily through the effect of nationalization on increased resource revenues. There is little evidence of a direct effect of nationalization on the probability of leader failure. That is, there is nothing to suggest that nationalization directly prolongs leader duration; rather, it is through indirect channels, such as increasing government capture of resource revenues, that nationalization impacts the survival of leaders in power. While this corroborates the argument's key mechanism – that leaders choose to nationalize operations because it will increase their odds of survival by increasing their take of resource revenues – results from this approach should be interpreted with caution, given its strong assumptions.[19]

5.3.3 Regime Stability through Resource Revenues and Nationalization

The concepts of leader survival and regime stability are naturally intertwined but do not perfectly overlap. A regime can endure the irregular exit of its leaders over time; leaders can forcibly change the regime while staying in power. The Saudi monarchical regime, for instance, survived the assassination of King Faisal in 1975 by his nephew Faisal bin Musaid, with the royal family coalescing to appoint his younger brother Khalid immediately after Faisal's assassination (Herb, 1999).

---

[19] Specifically, the accuracy of the estimates of the ACME and ADE depend on the assumption of "sequential ignorability" that there is no omitted variable that would account for both increased resource revenues and leader survival. This is a tough assumption to satisfy in the context of historical observational data: it could be the case that countries endowed with natural resources just happen to have the conditions necessary for durable leaders. Although there is a host of observable variables that could account for this relationship – notably the quality of political institutions and the strength of political opposition prior to the discovery of oil (Smith, 2006; Menaldo, 2016) – it is difficult to definitively rule out the existence of any other such factors. A sensitivity analysis plotted in Figure 5.11 shows that even in the presence of modest unmeasured confounders, the ACME becomes statistically indistinguishable from zero.

By contrast, Venezuela's Hugo Chávez forcibly reshaped the existing democratic regime into a personalist dictatorship in 2005, thereby surviving (and initiating) a regime change in the form of democratic failure. But in general, a stable regime often reflects stable leadership, with the only exits coming via the regular means of elections, term limits, and voluntary retirements, or death from natural causes. If nationalizing operations will increase government revenues, as my argument suggests, then regimes should similarly be able to leverage this increased wealth to bolster their durability.

The data offer convincing support for this claim. In Figure 5.7, I plot the results from logit models of regime survival with an interaction between NOCs and oil income per capita, controlling for growth in GDP per capita, logged population, logged GDP per capita, and polynomial temporal trends (following Wright et al., 2015).[20] Results from a model in which the outcome is autocratic failure of any kind, including regime change from one autocracy to another, are plotted in the top graph, while results from a model in which the outcome is a transition to democracy are plotted in the bottom graph. In both cases, more oil income corresponds to lower regime failure but only in states with operational NOCs. Indeed, among the nonoperationally nationalized states, regimes with high levels of oil income per capita have higher chances of failure than those with lower levels of oil income. Though not plotted here, the same is true for autocratic failure using the Polity measure of regime change.[21]

5.4   Conclusion

This chapter presents statistical evidence to corroborate the argument that not only does nationalization increase revenues (and capture) but these revenues also increase leader survival and, among autocrats, regime survival. These results are consistent when leader survival is measured either in terms of the probability of irregular exit or the duration of uninterrupted rule, as well as when survival is measured using any kind of leader exit, including regular, irregular, and foreign-imposed. All of these results suggest that the correlations between nationalization, revenues, and stability are robust to different modeling specifications and approaches and using multiple measures of resource revenues, leader

---

[20] Full model results are presented in the chapter's Appendix (Section 5.5).
[21] See Figure 5.5.

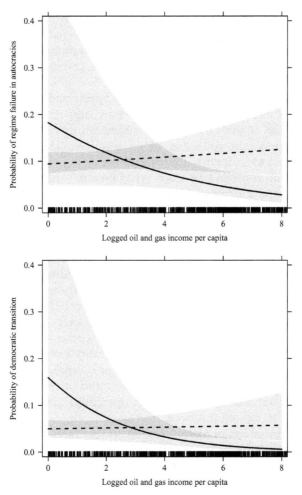

Figure 5.7 Predicted probability of autocratic failure and transitions to democracy.

Probabilites (y-axis, percent where 1 = 100%) obtained from logistic regression controlling for GDP per capita growth, logged GDP per capita levels, logged population, and polynomial temporal trends. The dotted curve in each graph shows the predicted probability of regime failure for states without operational NOCs, while the solid curve shows the same for states with operational NOCs.

survival, and regime change. Even absent any multivariate modeling, as in Figures 5.2 and 5.3, the general patterns predicted by my argument are reflected in the data. Nationalization of resources helps to increase resource revenues that are collected by the state, and these increases help leaders survive.

In addition to the data and results I have presented up to this point, the next set of evidence that would offer more support for the argument is a within-case analysis of how nationalization precisely and causally increases government collection of oil revenues. This necessitates a framework that can identify the revenue-increasing effects of nationalization without confounding from other factors – namely, those that influence the decision to nationalize – as well as identifying effects against a proper counterfactual.

In a given country, how does nationalization increase revenues relative to the change in revenues had the leader not nationalized? In other words, would revenues have increased after nationalization even if a leader had not nationalized operations? This is entirely possible since nationalization tends to occur when prices are rising and production levels are increasing. Existing theories on expropriation posit that this is when a government gains greater leverage over private operating firms, as the costs of nationalization decline relative to the early years of the production cycle or when potential profits are hampered by low international oil prices. So, if nationalization is indeed *not* the cause of these revenue increases, then leaders looking to increase their odds of survival in power will not gamble with operational nationalization as I have argued throughout this book.

To isolate the effects of nationalization on revenues, ideally, one could randomize the assignment of nationalization and track how revenues change compared to countries that did not receive the "treatment" of nationalization. Of course, this is neither feasible nor practical given the wide-reaching consequences of nationalization for leaders, elites, and civil society, let alone the costs for undertaking such a research program. Instead, I attempt to identify the revenue-increasing effects of nationalization by constructing a viable counterfactual based on projected oil revenues constructed prior to nationalization. Such projections can be found in the case of Iran in the 1970s, when the Shah seized control of oil operations from the consortium of Western oil firms led by BP. It is to this fascinating point in history that I now turn.

5.5   Appendix: Additional Figures and Tables

Total resource revenue

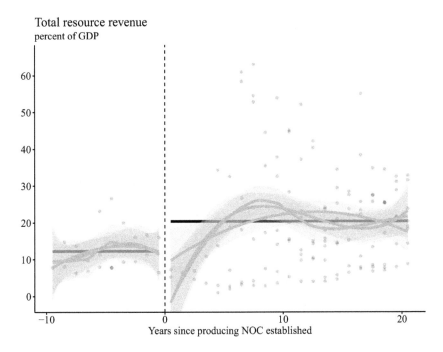

Figure 5.8 Resource revenues before and after establishing an operational NOC.

Average resource revenues before and after an operational NOC is established are shown by the solid horizontal lines. I overlay four additional metrics to capture temporal changes in revenues, with 95 percent confidence bands: (1) loess smoother, (2) quadratic smoother, (3) cubic smoother, and (4) a fourth-order polynomial smoother. Total number of countries in the sample is 36.

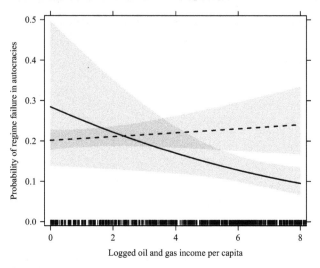

Figure 5.9 Predicted probability of autocratic failure using the Polity measure.
Probabilites (y-axis, percent where 1 = 100%) obtained from logistic regression of autocratic failure using the Polity measure of regime failure in autocracies, controlling for GDP per capita growth, logged GDP per capita levels, logged population, and polynomial temporal trends. The dotted curve in each graph shows the predicted probability of regime failure for states without operational NOCs, while the solid curve shows the same for states with operational NOCs.

Table 5.4. *Nationalization increases resource revenues (per capita) collected by the government*

	Model 1	Model 2	Model 3	Model 4	Model 5
Petroleum production	0.505***	0.480***	0.411***	0.501***	0.471***
(tonnes/year) (logged)	(0.040)	(0.039)	(0.037)	(0.040)	(0.038)
Oil price (US$)	0.205***	0.201***	0.196***	0.209***	0.204***
	(0.012)	(0.011)	(0.011)	(0.012)	(0.011)
NOC indicator		0.382***	−0.879***		
		(0.067)	(0.126)		
NOC × production			2.675***		
			(0.232)		
Operational				0.142**	−1.329***
NOC indicator				(0.071)	(0.204)
Operational					2.247***
NOC × production					(0.293)
R^2	0.922	0.925	0.935	0.922	0.927
Adj. R^2	0.917	0.920	0.931	0.917	0.923
Num. observations	857	857	857	857	857
Num. countries	49	49	49	49	49

***$p < 0.01$, **$p < 0.05$, *$p < 0.1$

All variables are lagged one year and, except for the NOC variables, all variables are standardized with mean zero and variance one. All models include country-fixed effects, the estimates of which are omitted from this table.

Table 5.5. *Mediation analysis of operational nationalization and resource revenues*

A. *Without interaction term*

	Estimate	95% CI lower	95% CI upper	p-value
ACME (control)	−0.00979***	−0.01495	0.00	0.001
ACME (treated)	−0.01066***	−0.01974	0.00	0.001
ADE (control)	0.00338	−0.00834	0.02	0.596
ADE (treated)	0.00251	−0.00689	0.01	0.596
Total Effect	−0.00728*	−0.01503	0.00	0.063
Prop. Mediated (control)	1.34522*	−4.05422	9.22	0.064
Prop. Mediated (treated)	1.46523*	−5.60599	12.65	0.064
ACME (average)	−0.01022***	−0.01712	0.00	0.001
ADE (average)	0.00295	−0.00757	0.01	0.596
Prop. Mediated (average)	1.40523*	−4.80696	10.97	0.064

B. *With interaction term*

	Estimate	95% CI lower	95% CI upper	p-value
ACME (control)	−6.69e−03*	−1.31e−02	0.00	0.0694
ACME (treated)	−2.45e−02***	−4.48e−02	−0.01	0.0002
ADE (control)	1.75e−02*	−7.45e−04	0.04	0.0628
ADE (treated)	−3.68e−04	−1.07e−02	0.01	0.9502
Total Effect	−7.06e−03*	−1.45e−02	0.00	0.0854
Prop. Mediated (control)	8.98e−01	−3.07e+00	6.84	0.1496
Prop. Mediated (treated)	3.03e+00*	−1.46e+01	28.98	0.0852
ACME (average)	−1.56e−02***	−2.62e−02	−0.01	<0.0001
ADE (average)	8.54e−03	−3.50e−03	0.02	0.1960
Prop. Mediated (average)	1.96e+00*	−8.94e+00	17.80	0.0854

Sample Size Used: 8899 (Simulations: 10000)
***$p < 0.01$, **$p < 0.05$, *$p < 0.1$
Summary of model results from causal mediation analysis. ACME: average causal mediation effects; ADE: average direct effects; Total effect: average treatment effects (ACME + ADE). The top table shows results from a model without an interaction between operational NOC and oil income per capita; the bottom table shows results from a model with this interaction. No other covariates are included in the models given the likelihood of post-treatment bias introduced by controlling for postnationalization factors like economic development, regime type, civil war incidence, and irregular leader entry. A test of the difference between the ACME(0) and the ACME(1) for the model with the interaction term yields a difference of −0.0178 with an estimated p-value of 0.0358.

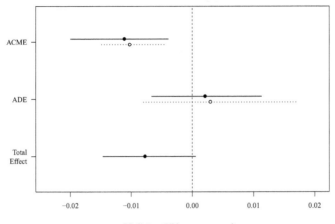

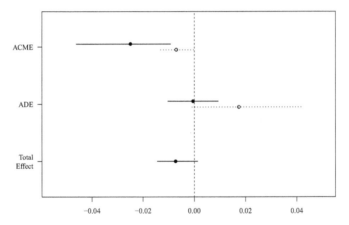

Figure 5.10 Model results from mediation analysis of operational nationalization and resource revenues.

Graphical summary of model results from causal mediation analysis. ACME: average causal mediation effects; ADE: average direct effects; Total effect: average treatment effects (ACME + ADE). The top panel shows results from a model without an interaction between operational NOC and oil income per capita; the bottom panel shows results from a model with this interaction. The solid lines for the ACME and ADE show the effects for the treated (i.e., countries with operational NOCs) while the dashed lines show the ACME and ADE of the control (i.e., countries without operational NOCs).

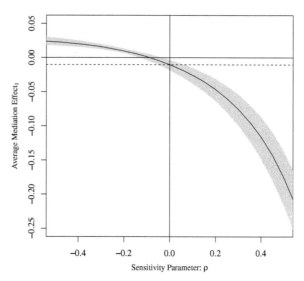

Figure 5.11 Sensitivity of mediation analysis to unmeasured confounders.

Sensitivity analysis to assess effects of unmeasured confounders on estimates of the ACME for the treated group of countries with operational NOCs. The x-axis shows the range of the sensitivity parameter ρ, which represents the correlation between the error terms of the first-stage (mediator) and second-stage (outcome) models. Note that the ACME is no longer negative and statistically distinguishable from zero if ρ is less than roughly −0.05. This suggests the results are highly sensitive to the presence of even a modest confounding variable that positively influences resource revenues and negatively influences leader survival (or vice versa).

6   The Dynamics of Nationalization in Pahlavi Iran

On January 23, 1973, the Shah of Iran announced that control over oil operations would thereafter be vested in the state-owned (but heretofore operationally incapacitated) NIOC. In response to a barrage of inquiries by BP, Shell, and Standard Oil of New Jersey as to why he was seizing their operations, the Shah was curt but unrelenting in his reply via emissary nine days later. "The Iranian government has the right," the Shah proclaimed, "To make any rules and regulations concerning the exploitation of its oil resources for the best interest of its people, and cannot allow that the exercise of such a fundamental right to be left to the whims of the Companies."[1] This dramatic turn of events exemplified a global trend among oil producers, ranging from operational nationalizations in Syria in 1968 and Algeria in 1969, to Peru in 1973 and Angola in 1978. In total, over one-quarter (seventeen) of all major oil-producing countries nationalized their petroleum sectors between 1968 and 1978.

Scholars point to this wave of nationalizations, coupled with the 1973 oil price shock, as the pivotal moment several producing countries transformed into resource-reliant petro-states (Gelb, 1988; Karl, 1997; Jones Luong and Weinthal, 2010; Liou and Musgrave, 2014). This period turned the industry "downside up" and resulted in an enormous transfer of future wealth from the energy-importing developed world to the energy-exporting developing states (Pratt, 2013). Proponents of the political resource curse argue that leaders used this newfound wealth to ensure their survival, through the many avenues espoused by rentier-state theorists, such as reducing taxes, increasing patronage, co-opting rivals, and investing in praetorianism (Skocpol, 1982; Beblawi and Luciani, 1987; Chaudhry, 1997; Ross, 2001).

In Chapters 1 and 2, I argue that this transfer of wealth was not distributed equitably: some governments opted for maintaining

---

[1] Quoted from BP 113478. "Teheran Negotiations." Attachment to Letter no. 313 dated February 1, 1973. Accessed June 14, 2016 at the British Petroleum Archives, Coventry, UK. © BP plc.

private ownership, while others nationalized operations. Governments that designed NOCs with de facto control over petroleum operations benefited far more in short-run fiscal terms than those that did not. Recall that a key but heretofore missing component of the political resource–curse argument – as it is validated and invalidated across different historical periods (Smith, 2004; Dunning, 2008; Haber and Menaldo, 2011; Ross, 2012; Menaldo, 2016) – is whether the state can actually capture its resource wealth or whether it relinquishes these foregone rents to outsiders. The differences across operational control thus play a profound role in understanding why some governments reap the gains of this wealth while others founder.

This chapter revisits the argument from Chapter 2 and the empirics from Chapter 4 on why leaders choose SOEs with de facto control over operations while some leaders opt to keep production in the hands of nonstate firms. I dive into a single country case to make stronger causal inferences that this institutional choice leads to increased capture of oil revenues. These results corroborate Chapter 5's cross-national statistical analysis of oil nationalizations across the world. In addition, I posit that this choice should be theorized separately from the oil price shock in 1973 – a turning point many scholars point to as the key moment when oil wealth shifted from a blessing to a curse for governance – that often confounds the relationship between nationalization and survival.

I provide evidence for these claims with an in-depth case analysis of the Shah of Iran's decision in 1973 to take back control of production from the BP-led consortium and to place these decisions in the hands of NIOC. That this operational nationalization was announced in January 1973 and implemented in July 1973 – three months before the breakout of war between Israel and the Arab nations and the subsequent oil embargo that rocked the modern world – allows me to distinguish the revenue effect of nationalization from the effect of changing international prices. I support the argument using documented conversations between the Western oil companies and the Shah and his court using declassified materials from the British Petroleum Archives in Coventry, United Kingdom.[2]

In addressing these points, this chapter offers a new approach for data collection to estimate causal effects in the context of an observational study. The fundamental challenge to causal inference is the inability to observe counterfactual outcomes: we can never see what *would*

---

[2] These materials were accessed in June 2016 at the Modern Records Centre of the University of Warwick, with permission granted from BP plc. I provide citations to documents from the archives using the archive reference number (e.g., BP 4779), the title of the document, and the date of the document if applicable.

have happened absent some treatment or intervention. In our case, it is impossible to know what Iran's oil revenues would have been after July 1973 had the Shah not nationalized operations. Although other techniques exist to estimate this counterfactual using a mix of comparable country cases, like matching or synthetic control, I propose to formulate counterfactuals from corporate financial projections from the intervention case itself. Here I utilize BP's internal projections of Iran's oil revenue stream for the months before and after nationalization. The viability of this counterfactual rests on the assumption that BP made these projections without prior knowledge of or exposure to the Shah's decision to nationalize. I assess this assumption by drawing on archival records of the Shah's conversations with BP, coupled with the company's own internal communications. This approach thus combines within-case counterfactuals with qualitative techniques for probing the validity of assumptions needed to estimate causal effects.

This chapter therefore shows that establishing state control of oil operations in Iran led to higher revenue capture than would have been the case absent the Shah's nationalization of BP's operations. I begin by revisiting the book's central theory on why leaders nationalize operations. This is followed by a discussion of how the case of 1970s Iran provides an ideal testing ground for the theory. I then explore the causes of operational nationalization in 1973 by drawing on the archival record to assess empirical support for the explanatory influence of information diffusion and leader perceptions of future survival. This is followed by the second empirical section of the chapter, which begins with an explanation of the proposed methodology and ends with a quantitative analysis that finds that nationalization increased oil revenues. Before concluding with a summary of findings, I briefly examine why the increase in oil revenues was not sustained in the long run – ultimately leading to the shocking collapse of one of the period's strongest monarchs.

6.1 Revisiting the Operational Nationalization Theory in the Context of Prerevolutionary Iran

What drives the decision to nationalize operations, and how does this choice impact fiscal strength? Let us briefly revisit the argument I advance in Chapter 2 on how state intervention is a strategy through which leaders strengthen their hold on power.

Recall that the first component of this question – why leaders nationalize operations – finds an answer in the standard expected-utility framework. Leaders want to maximize their time in office. The key conduit that helps them do so is the maximization of state revenues.

With more money in the treasury, leaders can finance a wider range of expenditures to ward off challengers and to buy political support, either directly via patronage and cooptation or indirectly via financing broad economic development (Levi, 1989; Geddes, 2003; Acemoglu and Robinson, 2005). In the context of natural resource wealth, the degree of state intervention is one factor that affects how much revenue accrues to the state versus how much accrues to outside private firms (Jones Luong and Weinthal, 2010; Hughes, 2014). What I argue thus far is that specifics matter when it comes to nationalization: SOEs with operational roles will provide the state with more revenues in the short run compared to alternatives. Leaders who perceive that their survival odds are low will choose to nationalize operations to seize these short-term gains, despite knowing that nationalization bears negative long-term consequences. By contrast, leaders who perceive higher odds of survival will eschew these short-term gains and instead will continue to rely on nonstate firms for operations of natural resource extraction.

The case of 1970s Iran provides a testing ground for two mechanisms that underpin these claims. The first is that the decision to nationalize is sparked by the international diffusion of information. The preconditions for this choice rest on technical skills and levels of operational experience, coupled with the desire to capture short-term rewards at the expense of long-term losses. The second is that operational nationalization affects revenues, and thus fiscal strength, through its effects on reducing information asymmetries and allowing the state to adjust production at will (what I referred to earlier as production elasticity).

The preceding chapters raise an interesting empirical question: if operational SOEs maximize revenues, why wouldn't all leaders adopt them? The answer is based on a combination of short-term and long-term costs. In the short run, taking operational roles away from private firms and giving them to the SOE increases the chances of retaliation by the affected firms. This can range from punitive damages from international court cases, such as the 1974 settlement between BP and the Libyan government, to outright embargoes by consumers and distributors. The US boycott of Mexican oil in 1938 and the British boycott of Iranian exports in 1951 serve as the most extreme examples of such international retaliation for expropriation.

In the long run, operations managed by SOEs are less efficient when compared to private firms. In 1970s Iran, the Shah knew this to be true – and the foreign consortium led by BP made sure that he did. In a letter to be delivered to the Shah at court, BP's managing director to Iran wrote to the company's CEO that only the consortium – and not NIOC – could provide "vital functions," including

the provision of integrated expertise at all stages, from the fruits of research in every aspect of the Exploration and Production business; through the application of latest techniques in the difficult fields of reservoir engineering, drilling and production; the design and supervision of construction of large scale and complicated facilities; to the development and maintenance of balanced shipping programmes together with training services in all these fields.[3]

Put together, these arguments suggest a trade-off for leaders of resource-rich countries. Although an operational SOE will immediately provide a larger portion of the revenue pie for the government, the overall size of the pie will eventually shrink. This is either due to production inefficiencies or to interruptions like embargoes and other retaliatory actions, or the technical inability to successfully implement nationalization (see Chapter 2).

So when might the benefits of an operational SOE outweigh the costs from the perspective of a leader aiming to maximize revenues? A spark for the decision to nationalize that we learn from the preceding chapters is the diffusion of information over how revenues are shared between producers and host governments. Specifically, when a leader knows that his competitors – leaders of countries with similar geological endowments and similar roles in the international market – are receiving better deals than he is, the leader will want to renegotiate the terms of his own arrangements with producing firms. In extreme cases, these renegotiations will result in complete takeover by the state: there is no better deal in the eyes of a leader than not sharing revenues at all, instead of dealing with arrangements like fifty–fifty contracts.

So what does all of this imply? What kinds of patterns would we expect to see if these arguments held true? Looking at the oil sector in 1970s Iran in particular, there are two implications for which we should find supportive evidence.

H_1 Operational nationalization of oil in Iran is more likely after the diffusion of information about the revenue-sharing agreements of Iran's oil competitors.

The choice of adopting the operational SOE framework is more likely when a leader observes his peers (that is, leaders in other oil-producing countries) getting better deals in terms of how revenues are shared with producing firms. This diffusion effect should be most observable when

---

[3] Quoted from BP 4780. "Iran: Major Problems Facing the Oil Industry." Letter from J.A. Cole to D.E.C. Steele, dated May 21, 1975. © BP plc.

the same foreign firms (e.g., Standard Oil, BP) are operating in multiple markets, but offering different terms in different countries.

H_2 Oil revenues accruing directly to the Iranian government will be higher when NIOC has an operational role.

Compared to the alternative, the operational SOE will reduce information asymmetries between host government and producer when it comes to reporting accurate figures on extraction costs and quantities. In comparison to nonoperational NOCs in particular, NOCs with operational roles gain valuable financial and managerial experience that helps to increase government return on investment per barrel produced. If these two mechanisms accurately describe the effects of NOC choices, then we should observe greater oil revenues for the state when NIOC controls operations.

6.2   Case Selection, Data, and Design

I test these hypotheses using a mixed methods approach. To trace the process through which the Shah decided to reform NIOC into an operational NOC, I utilize declassified archival documents on the dynamics of negotiations between the Shah of Iran, his advisors, and the group of international oil companies led by BP. These documents are held in the British Petroleum Archives in Coventry, United Kingdom, and consist of confidential letters sent between BP, members of the consortium, and the British government; transcriptions of conversations with the Shah and his ministers; and financial documents regarding transactions and agreements between the consortium and the Iranian government. To increase confidence in the evidence found in BP-held documents, I also draw on documents contained in the Foreign Relations of the United States (FRUS) series, volumes XXVII and XXXVI, and the Foreign and Commonwealth Office (FCO) letters at the British National Archives and online at the National Archives of the United States. In addition, I complement these materials with secondary accounts, namely BP's historical volumes (Bamberg, 2000) and the published diary of the Shah's court minister (Alam, 1991), as well as diplomatic histories like Cooper (2012) and Dietrich (2017). To determine the validity of hypothesis 1, I examine these materials to evaluate whether and to what extent the diffusion of information about revenue-sharing agreements of the Shah's international competitors influenced operational nationalization.

To test hypothesis 2, I statistically assess whether operational nationalization increased government revenues from oil more than it would have compared to a counterfactual world in which operations were not nationalized. The challenge of comparing outcomes to viable counterfactuals besets nearly all observational studies of politics, and the analysis of NOCs is no different. When assessing the effects of NOCs, and operational nationalization in particular, it is difficult to make definitive claims by simply comparing each case to other countries that did not consider these choices. Instead, what is needed are justifiable counterfactuals, which are hard to come by in the absence of experimental conditions. I address this challenge by leveraging corporate projections of outcomes of interest, in this case oil revenues, and compare these to actual outcomes after operational nationalization. The viability of the counterfactual rests on the assumption that these projections were made without prior knowledge of or exposure to the decision to nationalize.

I test this assumption and collect data for this analysis by again drawing on archival records. Here I collect information from the BP Archives on *actual* and *projected* amounts of revenue transferred between the consortium oil companies and the Shah's government in the 1970s. Importantly, these records indicate that while preparing projections of oil revenues to be paid to the Shah, BP had no knowledge of the Shah's decision to nationalize operations in 1973. I provide more details on these data and the models used to analyze the data in Section 6.4.

6.2.1 The Case of Iran in Comparative Context

Nearly all of the world's oil producers have established NOCs of one kind or another, so what makes the study of Iran both crucial and generalizable? My case selection depends on two factors. The first is Iran's role in global oil politics for over a century. Since the first well was spud in 1908, Iran's oil history has experienced the full range of positive and negative political effects of resource wealth. An internationally sponsored coup in 1954 was the direct result of oil nationalization. Massive societal and economic modernization in the post-1954 period could not have been financed without the rapid increase in oil wealth. A popular revolution could not be thwarted in part because of an unexpected decline in oil wealth. A costly eight-year war with Iraq, starting in 1980, resulted in the targeting and destruction of the oil-producing regions of each side. And the oil-fueled theocratic regime continues to survive despite facing some of the strongest bilateral and international sanctions in modern history. Indeed, there is a slice of Iran's tumultuous oil history that is representative of each oil-producing country's own political experiences, whether they involve war, revolution, stability, or development.

The second factor is the specific timing of its operational nationalization in 1973. As I describe in more detail in the following sections, the Shah's decision to nationalize the oil industry offers a window into understanding the effects of nationalization that are distinct from international oil market conditions. Since nationalization was implemented three months prior to the Arab oil embargo of October 1973 and the subsequent quadrupling of oil prices, I can identify nationalization itself as a shock to Iran's oil revenues that occurred exogenously to the price increase. Further, I can examine how nationalization's effect on revenues was amplified by the price effect. For these reasons, 1973 Iran is a great case to put the theoretical framework outlined above to test.

6.3   Why Did the Shah Opt for an Operational NOC?

6.3.1   The 1973 Agreement

On January 23, 1973, in a special National Congress to commemorate the tenth anniversary of the White Revolution, the Shah outlined his vision for the oil industry. After months of negotiations, nationalization of operations was formalized in an agreement signed with the consortium on July 16, 1973, and implemented six months later by parliament. The agreement established that "full and complete ownership, operation and control in respect of all hydrocarbon reserves, assets and administration of the petroleum industry shall be exercised by NIOC."[4] In addition to production control, NIOC was also granted the ability to set prices for oil sold and delivered to the market.

The agreement completely restructed the oil industry. NIOC had previously existed as a fully state-owned enterprise but lacked a commercial role in production, which was completely controlled by the BP-led consortium. NIOC had de jure control of the oil industry prior to 1973, but the company had no de facto ability to determine the volume of production or exports (Bamberg, 2000). The 1973 agreement was quickly followed by the Petroleum Act of 1974, which formally heralded the culmination of operational nationalization. NIOC was given complete ownership, production rights, and control over exports and prices.[5] The consortium were to be reduced to contractors paid for their services as assistants to NIOC's operations. With one fell swoop, nationalization implied maximum state control over operations and maximum government take from oil revenues.

---

[4] Quoted from BP 14381. "Iran: Sale and Purchase Agreement and Related Arrangements, 1973." Preamble, p. 4. © BP plc.
[5] Petroleum Law, National Iranian Parliament, Iran Senate, 1974. Article 3, paragraph 1.

6.3.2 Preconditions for Operational Nationalization

Before assessing the validity of hypothesis 1, it is important to examine the preconditions for operational nationalization. In other words, did the Shah have both the desire and the capability to reform NIOC into an operational NOC? The archival record is unequivocal in affirming both preconditions.

The desire for operational nationalization encompassed two primary grievances against the consortium: past production levels and the adjustment of prices. By late 1971, the Shah grew concerned about Iran's "stalled capacity" of crude oil production. In closed meetings with the consortium, he demanded that production should reach 8 million barrels per day by October 1976, up from 4.5 million barrels per day in 1971.[6] This would have made Iran the largest oil producer in the Middle East and the third largest in the world, behind only the US and the USSR. To appease the Shah, the consortium agreed to the 8 million barrel per day target by 1976.[7] But in private, the members indicated that 7.1 million barrels per day would be the maximum capacity physically possible, and certainly not sustainable without drastically draining reserves.[8] By January 1973, it was clear to the Shah that the consortium was making no progress toward the 8 million barrel per day target, and declared as such not only in his National Congress speech, but also in a sixteen-point "list of grievances" delivered by Minister of Finance Jahangir Amouzegar to the consortium.[9]

There was also frustration over the asymmetry of information regarding the true price that Iran's oil fetched on the international market. At a time when a spot market did not exist in full, the difference between the price of a barrel negotiated between companies and host governments (the "posted price") and the price garnered in selling to refiners in consuming countries (the "market price") represented a substantial profit opportunity for the IOCs. All taxes, fees, and royalties paid to the host government were made on the basis of the posted price, not the market price. The latter was largely hidden from the host government, and this became a key grievance between Iran and the consortium during negotiations in January 1973.[10]

---

[6] BP 4779. Letters from Roger Bexon, dating from February 16, 1972 to June 27, 1972.
[7] BP 4923. "Audience with H.I.M. on Kish Island on Monday, 27th March (1972) at 10 a.m." Attachment #1 to Letter no. 143.
[8] BP 4779. "Brief for Sir David Barran." Letter dated December 8, 1971.
[9] BP 113478. "Teheran Negotiations." Attachment to Letter no. 313 dated February 1, 1973.
[10] BP 113502. "Meeting with Dr. Fallah at 12:30 p.m. on Saturday, 13th January." Attachment #1 to Letter No. 298. See also: BP 113478. "Teheran Negotiations." Attachment to Letter no. 313 dated February 1, 1973.

In terms of the technical capability for operational nationalization, the Shah himself knew Iran was ready. Conversations with the consortium in January 1973, days before the Shah publicly announced his intentions for reform, offer evidence that the Shah believed Iran was capable of sustaining an operational NOC. In one instance, the CEO of Standard Oil of New Jersey (Exxon), J. Kenneth Jamieson, urged the Shah that giving operational management to NIOC would be not only be a grave error but also technically infeasible. "Iran should not underestimate the difficulties of running the operation and obtaining the necessary people," warned Jamieson. "So far as management is concerned," the Shah quipped back, "we can hire experts and firms to advise us what should be done ... although this would require the re-organisation of NIOC." Jamieson pressed on anyway, concerned that even if that were true, the idea of 100 percent control over operations would "certainly spread elsewhere" to oil producers around the world. "Why should it spread?," the Shah responded, "The other countries are not in a position to manage their oil industry." And asked why he hadn't negotiated for this in the past, especially during the first 1954 agreement and the 1971 revisions, the Shah explained that back then "Iran was not qualified to run the operation. The situation was now completely changed."[11]

In short, the preconditions for giving operational control to NIOC were met both in the Shah's strong desire for change and in the perceived technical capability of undertaking operational nationalization. During their meeting, Jamieson at one point asked the Shah why he even wanted 100 percent control in the first place. "The point is," the Shah replied, "we own the oil, we can produce it, and you are our customers."[12]

6.3.3   International Diffusion of Revenue-Sharing Agreements

The issue of how oil revenues are shared with producing governments has perennially been at the forefront of contract negotiations. The Shah's demands for receiving fair income – i.e., relative to what others were receiving – from the companies operating his oil fields is in line with nearly all such negotiations and renegotiations preceding him. This "leapfrogging effect" was a key fear of the companies in conducting individual negotiations with host governments, as they knew that each

---

[11] Quoted from BP 113502. "Audience with H.I.M. at 3:30 p.m. on Sunday, 14th January." Attachment #2 to Letter No. 298. © BP plc. The Shah's confidence in being able to manage the oil sector was unwavering even in private meetings with his court minister, Asadollah Alam. In a discussion on January 21st, the Shah stressed to Alam that whatever Iran lacked in qualified personnel to manage the oil sector could be made up by expatriates with the proper technical qualifications (Alam, 1991, 279).

[12] Ibid.

agreement would set off a new chain reaction across the producer governments (Yergin, 1991; Dietrich, 2017).

The issue of revenue sharing compared to other host governments came up in prior negotiations during the 1971 Tehran Agreement to adjust terms of the 1954–1957 agreements. The Shah agreed to engage in the 1971 negotiations with BP and Shell only on the condition that "there is no discrimination, no favoritism, and no dirty tricks on the part of the company negotiators."[13] This was a common complaint. Indeed, the Shah felt spurned year in and year out with how foreign companies were not giving him the best deal – an especially egregious fault given the Shah's image of himself as a friend to the West.[14]

If these renegotiations and grievances were such a regular occurrence, what made 1973 different enough to trigger all-out operational nationalization? The diffusion effect would prove to be quite strong here. In his desire to "keep up with the Joneses," the Shah was adamant during negotiations in 1971 that any new agreement reached would have to be "at least as good – though not necessarily identical – with those agreed with other countries."[15] But fresh off of what he saw as successful negotiations in 1971, an agreement between three Arab states and the West in 1972 would break that trust. The new 1972 participation agreement reached between the oil companies and Saudi Arabia, along with Iraq and the UAE, ensured that they would have a better deal than Iran. In a meeting with the consortium negotiating team on January 14, 1973, the Shah declared that the fact of giving 51 percent participation to the Arabs was unacceptable – and effectively gave the Arab governments control over oil operations.[16]

This deal was the tipping point of the Shah's relationship with the West. Upon hearing Saudi Arabia's oil minister Sheikh Yamani brag on

---

[13] FRUS 1969–1976, Volume XXXVI: "Telegram from the under Secretary of State (Irwin) to the Department of State, Tehran, January 18, 1971, 1632Z."

[14] "The Shah sincerely feels that his record of cooperation with the West entitles Iran to increased production and revenues that outstrip those accorded to other oil exporting nations." FRUS 1969–1976, Volume XXXVI: "Memorandum Prepared in the Central Intelligence Agency, January 18, 1971, 1632Z." See section 25.

[15] Quoted from BP 4779. "Brief for Sir David Barran." Letter dated December 8, 1971. © BP plc. Note that this pattern of the Shah proclaiming that he needed to "follow suit" with the Arab oil producers is consistent across different archival sources. Dietrich (2017), for example, finds evidence for a similarly strong domino effect using materials from the British National Archives and documents from the US National Security Council Files.

[16] In their own internal correspondences the consortium heads agreed as much to be true: "[The Shah] feels his image is badly dented by the fact that 51 percent was given to the Arabs and by the assumption (at least in his mind) that Iraq will 'get away with it'." Quoted from BP 113502. "Audience with H.I.M. at 3:30 p.m. on Sunday, 14th January." Attachment #2 to Letter No. 298.

the radio that his new deal was "four times better than the Shah's," he was so incensed that he sent emissaries to the US in November and December 1972 to garner support for a new arrangement of his own (Bamberg, 2000). The result of these visits was a personal letter from President Nixon to the Shah on January 19, 1973, urging him to show restraint in oil negotiations and maintain a stable course "in light of our long friendship . . . and the whole course of our mutual relationship" (Alam, 1991, 278). But what the American side viewed as well-crafted statesmanship on Nixon's part – a rare feat amidst a tumultuous postelection period, to put it lightly – the Shah perceived as a major sleight to him personally and to Iran's sovereignty over its internal affairs when dealing with the oil companies.[17] "Nixon," the Shah announced at a court dinner the next day, "has the audacity to tell me to do nothing in the interest of my country until he dictates where that interest lies . . . I say to hell with such special relations" (Alam, 1991, 278).

Three days later, the Shah would prove true to his word of breaking this "long friendship" in his January 23rd address to the National Congress. The next step in the game of leapfrog with the oil companies thus became not a better deal in terms of revenue sharing, but outright control over operations and setting prices. Scoffing at the idea of the traditional tax and royalty arrangement, the Shah proclaimed a new era in which NIOC would control everything and the consortium would simply become customers for Iran's crude oil.[18] And the price these customers would have to pay to NIOC "shall be no less favourable than those applicable at present or in the future to other countries in the Persian Gulf."[19]

6.3.4   Did the Shah Think That His Clock Was Running Out?

An alternative dynamic at play in the decision to nationalize was the Shah's potentially shifting time horizons for personal medical reasons. In 1980, the Shah passed away from histiocytic leukemia, a rare form of lymphoma that spreads slowly throughout the body.[20] There is much uncertainty in pinpointing the earliest moment that the Shah knew of the

---

[17] FRUS 1969–1976, Volume XXXVI: "Memorandum from Harold H. Saunders of the National Security Council Staff to the President's Assistant for National Security Affairs (Kissinger), Washington, January 30, 1973." See also Bamberg (2000, 472).

[18] Transcription of the speech is contained in BP 113502, "Telegram from van Reeven to Manson," PT 0112 dated January 23, 1973.

[19] Quoted from BP 14381. "Iran: Sale and Purchase Agreement and Related Arrangements, 1973." Article 6.A.(3), p. 14. © BP plc.

[20] For details, see "The Shah's health: A political gamble." *The New York Times Magazine.* May 17, 1981.

cancer that would ultimately take his life, but there is some speculation that he knew was terminally ill and knew of his formal diagnosis as early as 1973 (see Afkhami, 2003, 340). With the agreement for NIOC to take control of operations made in July 1973, it is possible – though not definitive – that the Shah's illness played a role in the timing of his decision.

If the Shah were aware of his lymphoma in 1973, then the desire to increase Iran's revenues via NOC reform would effectively outweigh its known long-term costs. The historical record is clear that the Shah was indeed cognizant of these costs, especially the loss of foreign investment and technical human capital needed to run the fields efficiently.[21] But with his diagnosis, the window of opportunity for fulfilling his legacy of transforming Iran into the "Great Civilization" (tamadon-e bozorg) was now closing much faster than expected. This plan, intended to advance Iranian society to the levels of the developed world, was first put forth in 1971. To secure the means to achieve this goal before his death, the Shah would have highly discounted the future and amassed as much revenue as possible, and as quickly as possible.

The decision to reform NIOC in 1973–1974 instead of doing so earlier or later – for example, when the lavish modernization program was unveiled in 1971 – could therefore have been motivated by the Shah's recalculation of time horizons. Indeed, there are some accounts that as early as 1973, "the Shah was fighting for his life as he was fighting for his political survival" (Post and Robins, 1995, 6). This would fit in with my broader argument that leaders engage in opportunistic behavior when they face low odds of enduring in power.

But there are several aspects of the historical speculation of when the Shah knew he was fatally ill that simply do not conform with this timeline. For example, if he knew he was dying in 1973, why did he keep it hidden from his close allies within the United States government who could have provided him discreet access to state-of-the-art treatment?[22] How did he keep his chemotherapy a secret from his wife, who reportedly did not know he was ill until 1977 (see Zonis, 1991)? A more likely possibility is that the Shah's knowledge of a nonfatal malady was not known until January 1974 when French doctors

---

[21] Diary entry by Alam, Sunday January 21, 1973, p. 279.
[22] One of the leading treatments for the disease at the time was plasma exchange, a procedure that was advanced by medical researchers at the University of Chicago, the University of California System, and the National Cancer Institute. See, for example, P.J. Schwab and JL Fahey, 1960, "Treatment of Waldenstrom's macroglobulinemia by plasmapheresis," New England Journal of Medicine 263: 574–579, and M.R. MacKenzie and H.H. Fudenberg, 1972, "Macroglobulinemia: An analysis for forty patients," Blood 39(6): 874–889.

diagnosed him with an early-stage treatable form of lymphoma (Zonis, 1991; Cooper, 2012).[23] He may not have learned of the fatality of his illness until the Spring of 1975, at which point he "began to refer to his own death in speeches" (McDermott, 2008, 250).[24] Perhaps the strongest evidence of when he knew he had cancer came from the death of his close confidante and court minister, Asadollah Alam, who passed away from leukemia in 1977 – and who was treated by the same team of French doctors as the Shah (Alam, 1991; McDermott, 2008). All of this is to say that even if the Shah knew he was dying, there is no strong evidence that he knew of his illness – let alone its severity – as early as January 1973, when he first announced the decision to nationalize oil operations.

Instead, the Shah's calculations of his survival in power were more likely to be affected by fiscal pressures and perceived threats to his rule from his foreign and domestic adversaries. Of particular concern to the Shah was the completed withdrawal of British armed forces in the Persian Gulf by 1970 and the fear that agents loyal to the Soviet Union in Ba'athist Iraq and in the smaller Gulf states would "stir up mischief" in the region.[25] He was publicly outraged, for instance, when Sheikh Zayed of the UAE cozied up to the USSR in May 1972 by allowing the establishment of a Soviet Embassy in Abu Dhabi.[26] And the disintegration of Pakistan in December 1971 stoked fears of rising instability in Iranian Baluchestan (a southeastern province bordering West Pakistan) given its history of separatism and secessionist desires. Of course, much of this posturing may have been a calculated exaggeration of outside threats to persuade the US government to continue selling him advanced armaments (Kurzman, 2004; Cooper, 2012). But it is clear

---

[23] This diagnosis turned out to be incorrect because the Shah would only let his physicians perform minor tests without the use of proper equipment in a hospital setting. Some accounts suggest that the Shah refused a thorough diagnosis – which could have revealed the true extent of his illness – because he did not want to be seen as weak and requiring medical attention (see Shawcross, 1988). This refusal extended to his postdiagnosis treatment as well: McDermott (2008, 250), for instance, notes that "the Shah was unwilling to undergo any treatment that might expose his illness or which would impose long absences from his country or other inconveniences that he believed might hamper the speed of his While Revolution political program."

[24] See also Zonis (1991).

[25] FRUS Volume E–4, Documents on Iran and Iraq, 1969–1972: "Memorandum from the President's Assistant for National Security Affairs (Kissinger) to President Nixon, Washington, May 13, 1970."

[26] This is noted in both Alam (1991) and the FRUS archival record of a meeting between the Shah and Kermit Roosevelt, the CIA operative who aided in the deposition of Mossadegh in 1953. FRUS Volume E–4, Documents on Iran and Iraq, 1969–1972: "Memorandum from the Director of Central Intelligence (Helms) to the President's Assistant for National Security Affairs (Kissinger), Washington, May 8, 1972."

from conversations among US officials that, ever since Mossadegh was deposed, the Shah held an "ever present fear of Iran's being encircled by hostile or potentially disruptive neighbors."[27] Indeed, the growing pact between the USSR and Iraq, the continued tactical support for the Arab states by the British government, and mounting instability in Pakistan and Afghanistan all in part drove the Shah to pursue more weaponry than his military could even handle.

The threat of his ouster by what he saw as radical clerical influences supported by the Iraqi government burgeoned in June 1970, upon the death of the Shi'ite spiritual leader Ayatollah Seyed Mohsen Hakim. Hakim's death opened the door for a new spiritual head; to counter Iran's growing regional prowess, political forces in Iraq and Soviet Azerbaijan favored the selection of Ayatollah Ruhollah Khomeini. Although he was not an Iraqi Marja, Khomeini held widely known and well-documented sentiments against the Shah, beliefs that led to his exile from Iran in 1964. After Hakim's death, clandestine radio programs broadcast into Iran began to praise Khomeini's "struggles ... in support of freedom, democracy, and anti-imperialism," and Iraqi-backed smugglers began to distribute leaflets supporting Khomeini's selection.[28] On the eve of the nationalization announcement in January 1973, the position was still unfilled (and would remain so until the 1979 revolution), adding further pressure on the Shah amidst rising discontent from the clergy. The US Ambassador reinforced the reality of this dissatisfaction to the Shah on numerous occasions in 1972, and warned privately to the Department of State back home of "the considerably sharper edge" of discontent and that "[t]he clergy, which is always antigovernment, is much more so today than in the past three years."[29]

The Shah additionally faced rising and audible unpopularity with the uneven pace of his modernization campaign, from both his militant opponents and even among his own rubber-stamp political cadres. On July 22, 1972, for instance, the head of the pseudo-opposition *Mardom* party, Alinaghi Kani, for the first time publicly denounced the government at a political rally for its election rigging and suppression of the opposition. When the Shah privately fumed about the matter – and that *Mardom* could not win even if the elections were not rigged – to his court minister Asadollah Alam, Alam replied to the Shah that he

---

[27] FRUS Volume XXVIII, Documents on Iran and Iraq, 1973–1976: "Airgram from the Embassy in Iran to the Department of State, January 9, 1973, A-4 P10."

[28] FRUS Volume E–4, Documents on Iran and Iraq, 1969–1972: "Airgram 217 from the Embassy in Iran to the Department of State, July 7, 1970."

[29] FRUS Volume E–4, Documents on Iran and Iraq, 1969–1972: "Situation Report, February 28, 1972."

of all people should know that "the government is just as unpopular as [Kani's] own party" (Alam, 1991, 232). Just three weeks later, two events would prove Alam right about the level of dissatisfaction. On August 10th, the top two evening papers (*Ettela'at* and *Kayhan*) publicly pressed the regime for a transition to Western-style democracy; on August 13th, one of the Shah's top generals was gunned down in his home by the militant revolutionary opposition *Mojahedin*. Indeed, attacks by domestic opponents like the *Mojahedin* in 1972 had reached their highest levels since the early 1960s, with frequent raids and open street battles with the police and gendarmerie (Abrahamian, 1992). And it was clear such events – which were not covered by the state-run media – were felt personally by the Shah and "added to [his] burden of woes" (Alam, 1991, 235).[30] Perhaps the most visible of these attacks occurred during President Nixon's visit to Iran in May 1972, when numerous explosions went off at sites that the president was scheduled to visit. The CIA's postmortem on the situation emphasized the growing problem facing the Shah if his modernization efforts did not succeed:

The bombings in Tehran during President Nixon's visit highlight the existence of internal dissidence in Iran. In itself, such dissidence is nothing new. For many years it did not pose a serious problem for SAVAK, the Iranian National Security and Intelligence organization. However, dissident activities over the past two years show that a violence-inclined "youth underground" has taken root in Iran with possibly serious consequences for the country's long-term stability.[31]

As for fiscal pressures, the Shah's grandiose spending habits, coupled with promises like the Great Civilization, were already straining the public purse by January 1973. Government expenditures expanded nearly fivefold in real terms from 1963 to 1972, with the largest increases coming in the 1969–1972 period.[32] And a declassified US study showed the same patterns for the Shah's military spending habits, concluding that Iran's "armaments requirements for 1974–78 would be about *$5 billion in excess* of projected oil revenues for the period" (cited in

[30] The US diplomatic record also raised red flags about increasing terrorist activity in the summer of 1972, likely as a result of the lack of government efforts and policies that were "responsive to at least some of the political, economic and social complaints which form basis of guerrilla dissatisfaction." See FRUS Volume E–4, Documents on Iran and Iraq, 1969–1972: "Telegram 4789 from the Embassy in Iran to the Department of State, August 10, 1972, 0400Z."

[31] FRUS Volume E–4, Documents on Iran and Iraq, 1969–1972: "Intelligence Note RNAN–18, Prepared by the Bureau of Intelligence and Research Washington, June 12, 1972."

[32] Bank-i Markazi-i Iran [The Central Bank of Iran]. 1975. *National Income of Iran, 1338–1350 (1959–1972)*. Table 72, p. 77. Expenditures rose from 34.4 billion rials in 1963 to 159.3 in 1972.

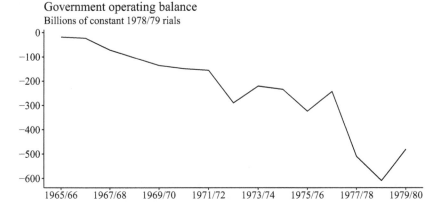

Government operating balance
Billions of constant 1978/79 rials

Figure 6.1 Iranian government budget operating balance, 1965–1979
Note: Figures are reported in billions of constant 1978/79 rials. The Iranian calendar year runs from March 21st to March 20th. For example, the Iranian year 1344 corresponds to the period from March 21, 1965, to March 20, 1966. Data source: Central Bank of Iran, Economic Research and Policy Department

Cooper, 2012, 141 (emphasis added)).[33] Government revenues clearly could not keep up, even with rising oil prices and production compared to the late 1960s. Between the start of the White Revolution programs (1963) and the last year before operational nationalization (1972), Iran's balance of payments were "almost permanently in deficit" every fiscal year (Katouzian, 1981, 265) (see Figure 6.1). This fact was not lost in US diplomatic reports on the state of Iran's financing, given that deficits "were covered mainly by long-term foreign borrowing."[34] And by March 1973, deficits had ballooned to 53 billion (nominal) rials or roughly 785 million US dollars.[35]

The archival record on conversations between the Iranian government and the oil consortium illustrates these pressures as well. As early as 1970, members of the consortium knew that the Shah's finances were starting to teeter and needed an outside injection. In May 1970, for instance, the Shah's Minister of Finance, Jamshid Amouzegar, pleaded

[33] Cooper (2012, 71–72) earlier notes that $2 billion of this excess was spent on eighty F-14 fighters purchased from US-based Grumman, a key benefactor to the Nixon–Agnew ticket that was on the verge of bankruptcy if not for the Shah's massive purchase. It should be noted that the F-14 was exclusively designed for aircraft carriers, which at the time were completely lacking in Iran's navy.

[34] FRUS Volume E–4, Documents on Iran and Iraq, 1969–1972: "Intelligence Memorandum, ER IM 72-23, February, 1972."

[35] Bank-i Markazi-i Iran, 1975.

with consortium executives to assist Iran in receiving a much-needed bank loan of $100 million – the equivalent of one month's worth of total imports to Iran – that the consortium would pay back.[36]

While we cannot observe the Shah's mental state and personal perceptions of his time horizons, we can intimate that the combination of fiscal pressures and perceived threats to his rule influenced the Shah's calculations of surviving in power during the period leading up to operational nationalization in 1973. The Shah's cancer diagnosis likely played a smaller role given the uncertainty as to when he definitively knew of the severity of his condition, which was more likely to have been known in the years that followed operational nationalization. Nonetheless, while the case does not offer smoking gun evidence that short time horizons were the cause of nationalization, it does show how factors that indirectly affected the Shah's survival calculations had coalesced in the months prior to his decision. Iranian politics was no stranger to each factor on its own in the 1960s and early 1970s: staunch opposition from the clergy as well as secular militants like the *Mojahedin* and the *Fedayan-e Islam*, growing fiscal deficits, uneven social and economic development, and regional instability had all reared their heads at one time or another in the decade prior to nationalization. But it was the confluence of these events in 1972 – rather than weak evidence of the Shah's knowledge of his fatal illness – that narrowed the Shah's time horizon to plant the seeds of doubt for what he thought would be a long and lasting regime.

6.3.5   Summary of Archival Findings

The factors of international diffusion in revenue sharing fit in with the broader chain of events that led to operational nationalization. Beginning with the immediate need for more revenues to make up for the country's increased expenditures on economic and military development, the Shah's reaction to the Arab states' 1972 agreements triggered his own renegotiation for a greater share of oil revenues (see Dietrich, 2017). The consortium's response with a fifty-five–forty-five percent split in favor of Iran, with no agreement to increasing production levels, was not enough to satisfy the Shah's demands. This desire was compounded by initial estimates of $32 billion of expenditures in the ambitious Fifth Five Year Plan (1973–1978), a whopping 13 times larger than the preceding

---

[36] BP 247667. P. Note No. 1210 dated August 28, 1970, "Bank Loan to Iran" from J Addison to Mr Van Reeven and other members, including DEC Steele.

Fourth Five Year Plan.[37] In an attempt to fill this expenditure gap quickly, in July 1973 the Shah implemented his vision for a NIOC with full control over operations and the ability to set posted prices, which for nearly seventy years had been controlled by the West.

As a matter of course, these events led to the outright control of production by NIOC in a manner consistent with hypothesis 1. The Shah reformed NIOC into an operator because of his dissatisfaction with revenue-sharing arrangements in comparison to his neighbors' own agreements. Based on archived conversations and direct corre-spondences, we know that (1) the Shah was fluent in the terms of revenue-sharing arrangements struck by his competition in 1972; (2) this knowledge explicitly prompted not only better terms for sharing revenues but also higher production levels; and (3) that, absent the companies' willingness to increase production, the Shah would take over the means to do so himself.

6.4   Did Operational Nationalization Increase Revenues?

In April 1974, the Shah was so enthused about the outcome of increased oil income that he bragged about it while holding court. "We have the money," he exclaimed, in reference to new projected flows of $22 billion for the fiscal year, "Now we must use it to fashion 'The Great Civilization'."[38] To assess whether nationalizing operations was the cause for this windfall, I use data collected from the BP Archives to construct counterfactual oil revenues and compare these to actual state revenues collected from the consortium. The effect that I seek to estimate, in other words, is how much more oil revenue the Iranian government collected because of operational nationalization compared to a counterfactual world in which NIOC continued to play a nonoperational role in the oil sector.

6.4.1   Estimating and Assessing Counterfactual Oil Revenues

Counterfactual oil revenues are computed using different monthly pro-jections from BP from December 1970 to April 1975. These projections were made in November 1970 by two separate divisions of the company:

---

[37] Revisions to the Fifth Plan in 1974, after the price shock, would later quadruple planned expenditures to $122.8 billion. See Fesharaki (1976) for a discussion of how operational nationalization impacted these revisions.

[38] Alam, p. 365.

the Valuations team[39] and the Capital Development team.[40] Based on financial statements,[41] the consortium made monthly revenue payments to the Iranian government based on the following formula:

$$\underbrace{\pi_t}_{\text{Revenue}} = \underbrace{(p_t * q_t * \gamma)}_{\text{Royalty}} + \underbrace{\left((p_t * q_t * (1 - \gamma)) - c_t\right) * \tau}_{\text{Income tax}}$$

where π_t is total government revenue in month t; p_t is the posted price per barrel in month t; q_t is the number of barrels produced in month t; and c_t is the total operating cost of production in month t. The royalty rate γ is fixed at 12.5 percent and the tax rate τ is fixed at 55 percent.[42] The two bracketed components refer to the monthly royalty payment and monthly income tax payment, respectively. Monthly revenues from this approach are plotted in Figure 6.2, along with monthly production for comparison.

The effect of the July 1973 agreement is calculated by comparing actual monthly revenues π_t to projected monthly revenues π_t^*. The formulae for four such projections are described in the Appendix (Section 6.7). The most relevant projections are calculated by inputting BP's projected production quantities q_t and operating costs c_t and using actual values for posted prices p_t. This allows us to focus solely on production decisions, since projecting posted prices beyond one month leads to high uncertainty – and in this case, there is no reason why we would expect BP's projection team to have foreseen the Arab oil embargo and its impacts on international oil prices.

This effect is estimated using a difference-in-difference (DID) design. Following notation from the potential outcomes framework (Rubin, 1974), the DID estimand of the average causal effect is given by

$$\tau_{DID} = (E[Y(1)|D = 1] - E[Y(1)|D = 0])$$
$$- (E[Y(0)|D = 1] - E[Y(0)|D = 0])$$

where Y is the outcome (oil revenues) and D is a binary status indicator for treatment (nationalization). The fundamental problem of causal

---

[39] BP 4413. "Valuations of 100 percent crude exports from Kuwait, ADMA, and Iran." Pages 4–5 and Attachment 3. Data used are reproduced with permission from the BP Archive, © BP plc.

[40] BP 247666. "Draft capital development plans 1971–1975." Appendix 1-D. Data used are reproduced with permission from the BP Archive, © BP plc.

[41] BP 247672. "Advance payments to NIOC and the Iranian government." Memorandum no. 200. Data used are reproduced with permission from the BP Archive, © BP plc.

[42] The income tax rate was changed on November 14, 1970, from 50 percent to 55 percent. See BP 247672. "Advance payments to NIOC and the Iranian government." Memorandum no. 200.

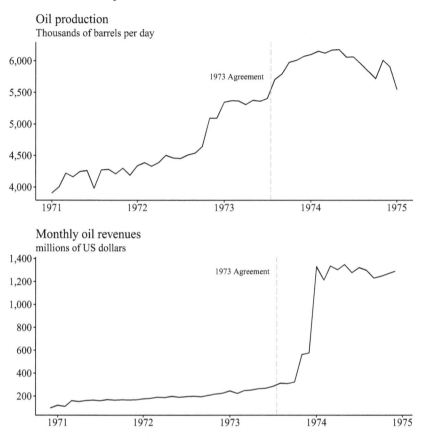

Figure 6.2 Monthly oil production and revenues in Iran, 1970–1975
Note: production in thousands of barrels per day (top) and government revenues from oil in nominal US dollars (bottom). The vertical dashed line marks the month of the signing of the nationalization agreement in July 1973. Data source: Reproduced from the BP Archive © BP plc

inference is that while we observe $E[Y(1)|D=1]$ (expectation of the outcome of the treatment group when assigned to treatment) and $E[Y(0)|D=0]$ (expectation of the outcome of the control group when assigned to control), we do not observe their counterparts $E[Y(1)|D=0]$ and $E[Y(0)|D=1]$. The technique I propose here uses corporate projections as counterfactuals to estimate missing potential outcomes. Specifically, I use the average projected outcomes for the post-July 1973 period to estimate $E[Y_1(0)|D=0]$, or the post-intervention outcome for the treated group in the absence of the treatment. I use average pre-July 1973 projected outcomes to estimate $E[Y_0(0)|D = 0]$, or the pre-intervention outcome in the absence of the treatment.

For a causal effect to be identified, two key assumptions need to be satisfied. First, we have to assess whether we are observing the potential outcomes associated with treatment and control (referred to as the stable unit treatment value assumption). In this case, we assume that these projections, made in November 1970, were developed without the expectation that operational nationalization would occur. Archival evidence affirms this assumption: as late as December 1972 (one month before the Shah announced his decision to renationalize), the consortium predicted that the outcome of any negotiations with the Shah would *not* result in outright loss of control over operations and prices. Instead, private correspondences between BP and other members of the consortium show that the expected worst-case scenario was a new purchase agreement, similar to the 1954 agreement but with different terms for royalty and tax rates.[43] It was not until early January 1973 that the Shah presented the consortium with multiple options as to the restructuring of the 1954 Agreement, one of which included the complete management of production and exports by NIOC.[44] But until then, neither the consortium nor NIOC itself could have anticipated the turn of events culminating in nationalization of operations.

How can we assess the assumption of so-called parallel paths in treated and untreated groups? In this case, this assumption requires that absent the Shah's nationalization, actual revenues would follow the same trajectory as projected revenues. This implies that no other events besides nationalization affected or altered revenue trajectories over time for both groups. Since we assume the same price and tax rate for both groups, the only remaining potential factors for determining revenues other than the treatment are production quantity and production cost. Although prices impact both in the medium run, quantities and operating costs in the oil sector change only incrementally from one month to the next in response to price shocks.

There are two exceptions to this rule. The first is in the event of damage to existing fields, such as could be incurred either due to destruction during a war or conflict, or due to natural disaster. The historical record indicates that neither was the case in the months before or after nationalization in Iran: there were no wars from January through

[43] BP 4779. "Iran negotiations." Letter from Cole to Steel dated January 19, 1973.
[44] BP 113502, "Telegram from van Reeven to Manson," PT 0112 dated January 23, 1973. See also FRUS 1969–1976, Volume XXXVI: "Paper Prepared by the National Security Council Staff, Washington, February 16, 1973."

June 1973, nor were there any major earthquakes in the producing regions of southwest Iran.[45]

The second exception is a major discovery, which would cause a sharp increase in production and sharp change in operating cost (in either direction, depending on the geology of the new field). The timeline from verified discovery to commercial production varies, but does not typically exceed three years. This would mean that for a discovery to have impacted production or operating cost in June 1973, a new field would had to have been discovered no later than June 1970. A review of major discoveries in Iran confirms this was not the case: the latest "supergiant" discovery (>5 trillion barrels estimated reserves) was the Parsi field in 1964 and the latest "giant" discovery (>100 billion barrels) was the Lab-e-sefid field in 1969 (Arezki et al., 2017).[46] The lack of evidence for either damage to existing fields or a new discovery suggest (but do not confirm) that the parallel paths assumption is justified.

6.4.2   Results: Higher Oil Revenues after Operational Nationalization

I begin by comparing actual revenue trends to projected revenues with a visualization. Figure 6.3 provides a simple look at this comparison by showing the difference in actual revenues and counterfactual revenues using four of BP's projections. In December 1970, when these projections were first made, the difference is 0 as expected. The difference remains minimal until all four trends begin rising in late 1972. This shift upwards is entirely due to changes in production. As Figure 6.2 depicts, starting in November 1972, monthly crude oil output from the consortium rose from 4,632,000 barrels per day to 5,090,000 barrels per day – the first time in Iran's history that monthly average oil production exceeded 5 million barrels per day. By November 1973, four months after nationalization, production passed the 6 million mark with a monthly average of 6,008,000 barrels per day. By contrast, the projected production levels for November 1973 were only 4,830,000 barrels per day.

With these differences in mind, it is clear that the Shah's decision to vest NIOC with control over production led to an overall increase in government capture of oil revenues. Six months following the implementation of the 1973 agreement, actual revenues outpaced counterfactual revenues by roughly $160 to $270 million in January 1974, depending on which projection is used. With actual revenues in

---

[45] *Earthquake Hazards Program: Earthquake Catalog.* United States Geological Survey. Accessed from https://earthquake.usgs.gov/earthquakes/search/.

[46] The next major discovery would not be made until the Zeloi field in 1976.

Net projected monthly change in oil revenues
Millions of US dollars

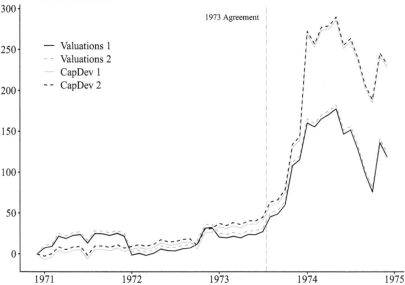

Figure 6.3 Actual minus counterfactual monthly oil revenues in Iran
Note: The vertical dashed line marks the month of the signing of the nationalization agreement in July 1973. The four trends plotted correspond to actual revenues minus projected revenues from four different projections: two from the Valuations team and two from the Capital Development team at BP

January 1974 of $1.3 billion, this puts the effect at somewhere between 14 percent and 26 percent higher than projected. The cumulative effect of operational nationalization – calculated by summing the monthly differences between predicted and actual revenues – amounted to an increase in government oil revenues by $2.8 billion from August 1973 to December 1974. The average effect – calculated by taking the mean difference between predicted and actual revenues – is $164 million.

Because it takes into account differences prior to nationalization, the DID estimand shows a slightly more conservative result. Using a regression framework for the DID,[47] the results show that the causal effect of nationalization is $147.5 million. There is, however, much uncertainty in this effect: the 95 percent confidence interval is bounded by $3.3 million and $291.7 million, just barely not including 0

---

[47] The specification is given by $Y \sim \beta_0 + \beta_1 P + \beta_2 D + \beta_3 P \times D + \epsilon$, where β_3 provides an unbiased estimate of the average causal effect on the treated, τ_{DID}.

($p = 0.0462$). The full statistical table for these results, plus results from the less conservative approach of using fixed posted prices, are included in the Appendix (Section 6.7).

Given the largely deterministic formula for how the Iranian government collected oil revenues, this finding is not surprising. The whole point of operational nationalization was to increase production, while the cost in terms of lost efficiency would not be realized for several years. Absent immediate changes in the tax and royalty rates, it would be impossible for revenues *not* to increase. But what is surprising is that the shift to an operational NOC did in fact lead to levels of production that were higher compared to the case when NIOC had no prominent role in operations. This point, which may seem trivial, is indeed quite remarkable: roughly 30 years after first nationalizing the industry, Iran's government was able to reform the industry to further increase both production and revenues. Any ceiling effect for production under NOC control (Victor et al., 2012) was seemingly absent in the two years following the Shah's operational nationalization.

6.4.3   Increased Capture Amidst the 1974 Oil Price Shock

Of course, the price shock of the Arab oil embargo of October 1973 to March 1974 benefited not just Iran but nearly all petrostates. But a key point is that not all states benefited equally. That the Shah happened to have changed the institutional structure and fiscal terms of oil extraction right before the shock meant that he could fully reap the dramatic upswing in oil prices. Not only did higher posted prices allow the Shah to capture greater oil revenues, but the ability to control production meant he could maximize extraction and therefore maximize overall revenues. Recall that before the 1973 Agreement, the consortium had full control over production levels and refused the Shah's requests to increase production (indeed, this was one of the grievances that led to nationalization).

By seizing control over operations only months before the Arab embargo and the subsequent price shock, the Shah had put himself in a position to fully control Iran's oil revenue stream. This structure was still lacking in exporters like Oman and Angola, which followed suit in 1974 and 1978, respectively. Indeed, the price shock by itself is often regarded as a key determinant of the wave of nationalizations in 1974–1979, not only because higher prices masked the costs of expropriation (Guriev et al., 2011), but also because they incentivized oil-producing governments to go back to the negotiating table for a larger share of rising profits (Manzano and Monaldi, 2009).

This injection would prove crucial to the Shah's strategy of holding onto power. At the onset of the nationalization process in January 1973, the Shah announced a grandiose plan to commemorate the tenth anniversary of the White Revolution. Ownership in industrial corporations would be opened up to employees and to the general public; civil servants and workers would receive interest-free loans; and all citizens would receive access to nationwide free education and free health care. His fears of popular unrest had been, at least temporarily, allayed "all thanks to the Shah's own magnanimous endeavor" (see Alam, 1991, 11–12).

6.5   And Yet He Fell

In spite of this dramatic increase in revenues and subsequent social expenditures in 1973–1975, the Shah was stunningly ousted a mere three years later, ushering in the Islamic Republic. This naturally raises the question, why didn't operational nationalization strengthen the Shah?

6.5.1   Reversal of Fortunes in 1976

Tensions grew with the consortium in November 1975 when, as Iran's oil income began declining, it became clear to the Shah that Iran's global petroleum sales did not match its production output. By January 1976, the Shah spared no formalities in meeting with company representatives when he exclaimed that "the consortium was in breach of the 1973 agreement" for its failure to export as much Iranian oil as promised.[48] At the heart of the problem was a disagreement over "liftings" – which refer to the amount of crude oil produced *and* sold on the market by the consortium – and that NIOC and the consortium were producing more oil than was being exported and distributed for consumption. Even though NIOC had full control over production vis-à-vis the 1973 agreement, it did not have control over selling the oil to the world's consumers.

The Shah thus blamed the consortium for his declining oil income – roughly $2.85 billion in foregone revenues – because of BP, Shell, and the American companies' deliberate reduction in liftings.[49] Outwardly, the consortium blamed the post-1973 global recession for reduced demand for crude oil and therefore reduced sales to their consumers

---

[48] "Record of the conversation between the Foreign & Commonwealth Secretary and Mr. David Steel, chairman of BP: 1 March 1976." FCO 96/537. British National Archives. Document 51.

[49] "Iran starts new talks with the oil companies." *The Washington Post* 23 April 1976.

in the US and Europe. But internally, conversations among consortium members painted a different picture: while it was true that demand had slumped, the bigger reason for the underlifting of Iranian oil was that the American companies had "allowed their liftings to fall to low levels partly as a way of exerting pressure in the negotiations for a new agreement."[50] Exxon, Texaco, Mobil, and Socal had effectively cut liftings to zero in late 1975 and had displaced Iranian crude with oil from Saudi Arabia, which was more profitable to the Americans based on their latest deal with the Saudis. BP even knew that this action by members of the consortium was in violation of the 1973 agreement, but it was reluctant to admit as much and instead preferred "to bluff the matter out with the Iranians."[51] In short, the Shah was right in his suspicions for why the Iranian government was receiving less revenue than was dictated by prices and production levels.

But why didn't the Shah secure control over the sale and distribution of his oil? During negotiations with the Shah in 1972, it became clear to the consortium that the Shah knew that NIOC could not handle marketing for the foreseeable future.[52] Without strong ties to refiners and consumers in Japan, Europe, and the US, there was simply no way that NIOC could secure sales contracts for its own exports. Nor could the Shah turn to the Eastern Bloc, given his strongly anticommunist ideologies (see, however, Alvandi, 2014, for a contrasting view).[53]

Indeed, when the Shah publicly threatened to take over marketing and direct sales to foreign consumers in April 1976, the consortium knew it was all a bluff. NIOC, the consortium asserted to journalists covering the matter, "presently lacks the capability to take on such a vast operation."[54] Even though neither the Shah's time horizons had grown longer nor had his perceptions of state intervention in the international scene grown any less bullish, the technical capabilities of NIOC were

---

[50] "Mr. Dell's visit to Iran: 31 December 1976." FCO 96/537. British National Archives. Document 73.

[51] "Iran: Negotiations with the consortium." FCO 96/537. British National Archives. Document 46.

[52] BP 4779. "Letter to Julius Cole from Harry F. Kern." Dated February 9, 1972. Note that while operations management by NIOC could be successfully outsourced to expatriates, outsourcing sales would once again increase the information gap between the Shah and the consortium; as such, outsourcing was never considered as a viable option if NIOC were to take over marketing.

[53] An interesting comparison is the Libyan 1971–1973 nationalizations, whereby Libya's NOC took on not only production but also liftings. Via Qaddafi's partnerships with the Eastern Bloc, Libya's NOC successfully marketed and delivered oil to consumers in the USSR and Eastern Europe amidst an informal embargo by Western states to purchase Libyan oil. See Bamberg (2000, 469).

[54] "Iran starts new talks with the oil companies." *The Washington Post* 23 April 1976.

constrained enough such that the reversal to a nonoperational SOE was inevitable. Although NIOC was indeed skilled in production and extraction, it could not successfully lift its oil and sell it on the international market. And the lack of a major spot market at the time made it unlikely that NIOC could find a suitable middleman to process sales.

There is, of course, some historical irony in the Shah's inability to foresee this impediment. The inability to secure customers was a key reason why Iran's first attempted nationalization in 1951 by Mohammad Mossadegh did not succeed. Indeed, US President Nixon hinted as such in a press conference just two months after the Shah's renationalization, when addressing the issue of Arab countries seeking to use oil as a political weapon via expropriation and cartelization: "Oil without a market, as Mr. Mossadeq learned many, many years ago, does not do a country much good."[55]

All in all, this ensured a decline in oil revenues despite NIOC's new powers over production and prices – especially once the global market cooled off and international oil prices turned sour. After years of consecutive growth, oil revenues dropped 4.6 percent in real terms from their peak in the 1974–1975 Iranian calendar year of $18 million to $17.1 million the following year.[56] By 1978, state expenditures continued to increase – based on the Fifth Five Year Plan which presumed oil revenues would monotonically increase indefinitely.[57] And because the Shah could do nothing to counter the drop in prices by increasing sales, deficits continued to widen (see Figure 6.1). Public expenditures tripled from 1973 to 1976, and deficits subsequently hit $2.64 billion in 1977 and $1.74 billion in 1978 (Razavi and Vakil, 1984, 82,91). Iran would thus not be spared the scenario that is all too familiar to oil-producing countries once booms turn to busts.

6.5.2 Why Not Weather the Storm?

Scholarly explanations for the 1979 Iranian Revolution comprise nothing short of a cottage industry. Theories of why the Shah collapsed

---

[55] Richard Nixon: "The President's News Conference," September 5, 1973. Online by Gerhard Peters and John T. Woolley, *The American Presidency Project*. www.presidency.ucsb.edu/ws/?pid=3948.

[56] Bank Markazi *Annual Reports and Balance Sheets*.

[57] A postmortem evaluation of the cabinet discussions during the 1973 revisions of the Fifth Five Year Plan concluded that the new plan "contained promises that could not possibly be kept" based on "optimistic assumptions on annual oil-price increases, as well as oil-export growth." In particular, it noted that "in every sector, oil money was to be spent on bigger projects and more wide-ranging social programs." See Razavi and Vakil (1984, 73–75).

range from the suppression-induced mobilization of religious leadership (Bakhash, 1984; Arjomand, 1989); the alienation of the merchant class (Parsa, 1989; Keshavarzian, 2005; Mazaheri, 2016); economic crisis, inflation, and discontent (Bashiriyeh, 1984; Razavi and Vakil, 1984); the repression of protesters, which sparked cycles of even larger protests (Chelkowski and Dabashi, 2000); activism as an opportunistic result of limited liberalization (Amuzegar, 1991); the lack of institutional capacity to foster civil society linkages (Smith, 2007); and the disconnect between economic modernization and political development (Keddie, 1981; Abrahamian, 1982). Few of these explanations, of course, pretend to posit a monocausal process for what was indeed a complex, multifaceted political metamorphosis. And as sociologist Charles Kurzman is keen to remind us, revolutions as a whole may be ultimately unpredictable – further casting doubt on scholarly attempts to systematically explain idiosyncratic events (Kurzman, 2004). While I do not wish to revisit this vast debate in great detail here, one aspect of these theories that merits discussion is that the Shah was unable to survive because he lacked an apparatus capable of preventing would-be supporters from turning into members of the opposition. As Smith (2006, 66) argues:

By the summer of 1978, the Iranian army and the much-feared secret police organization SAVAK were increasingly unable to control the growth of the crisis into a genuinely revolutionary movement. The regime's early inability to limit the scope or to co-opt critical elements of the opposition grew directly out of its experience in party building, taxing, and local government. Even through a generally consistent policy of attempting to quell social dissent through repression, the lack of social and institutional resources ultimately led to the shah's abdication and flight into exile in January 1979.

This could still be the case; the inability to quell revolutionaries could have been the product of weak early development of state-citizen linkages. What certainly made matters worse was the loss of oil revenues that the Shah had previously relied on to buy support. With greater revenues, perhaps he could have overcome limited institutional capacity by diverting increasing amounts of wealth to the merchant class and to the clergy, just as he did in 1973–1975. That oil revenues began to decline starting in 1976 because of the consortium's reactions to the 1973 agreement meant less money for repression, less money for cooptation, and less money to buy the support necessary to prolong his rule.[58]

---

[58] This, of course, presumes that support for the monarchy was purchasable, an assumption that likely did not hold for many of the Shah's opponents, whose grievances were not based on financial needs but rather ideological ones. See Kurzman (2004).

But it is important to keep in mind that government revenues did not plummet. Indeed, compared to the pre-1973 period, state coffers were significantly richer. So it is not that the state ran out of money to maintain the status quo; rather, it is that the state could not keep up with increasing demands from upwardly mobile social classes. This conforms with existing theories of the Iranian Revolution as a result of unfulfilled expectations. The political theorist and sociologist Hossein Bashiriyeh, for example, explains the revolution from the theoretical lens of the Marxist James Davies that "Revolutions are most likely to occur when a prolonged period of objective economic and social development is followed by a short period of sharp reversal" (cited in Bashiriyeh, 1984, 85).

There is no doubt that the 1960s and early 1970s in Iran were marked by rapid economic development. This was not merely an edict-like decree from the Shah acting "from above"; rather, the push for broad programs like the 1963 White Revolution reforms came from outside the palace. In particular, the Shah's government was reacting to demands from the elite – industrialists, the intelligentsia, and the urban aristocracy. The result of the 1961–1963 land reforms and the massive infrastructural investments of the 1960s was not to improve the plight of the peasant class, but instead to reward the powerful layers of society that had viewed the Shah's return in 1953 with skepticism (Harris, 2017). To win them over, the Shah's government turned to top-down cooptation policies that were motivated from below.

As is often the case with rapid modernization, such reforms cultivate a rising middle class that places ever-increasing demands on the state (Lipset, 1959). With Iran, the reforms of the 1960s paved the way for a growing urban working class as well as a professional stratum of society (Katouzian, 1981). The initial investments in higher education and a social-insurance program were both targeted to Iran's urban centers, where salaried workers and civil servants benefited from welfare policies like worker profit sharing, free schooling, and low-interest loans (Harris, 2017, 68–70). This fostered a powerful new middle class that became increasingly critical of the Shah in the mid- to late-1970s as state policies failed to satisfy the mass public. Despite the doubling and tripling of state budgets in the years of the Fifth Five Year Plan (1973–1978), most of the realized expenditures went to defense and infrastructure, not health, education, or agriculture.[59] And as demands

---

[59] Indeed, even in the 1974 revisions to the Fifth Five Year Plan after oil revenues skyrocketed after nationalization, total public expenditures for agriculture only amounted to a meager 6.6 percent compared to 28.5 percent for industry and transport and 28.4 percent for "other" – presumably defense-related – expenditures. See Razavi and Vakil (1984, 71).

rose for more effective and inclusive bureaucracies, the government would not spare resources to enable further upward mobility for the urban middle class. Many began turning instead to nonstate groups like the *hayāt* (council) neighborhood organizations. In the words of sociologist Kevan Harris, "formal corporatist welfare measures looked generous from the perspective of state ministries, but many individuals were excluded from concretely visible links to the 'Great Civilization' that the monarchy was building" (Harris, 2017, 70).

The promises of the White Revolution failed to materialize for the rural poor in particular. Where they had expected the delivery of clean water, reliable electricity, durable roads, and well-staffed schools and clinics, they had instead been left with hollowed-out towns and fallowed lands. Previously absentee provincial landlords were replaced with absentee farmers (Abrahamian, 1982, 429). Construction shortages in energy infrastructure led to rolling power blackouts in the winter and spring of 1977 (Looney, 1982). Programs like the Social Insurance Organization and the subsequent Social Security Organization never made it to the countryside (Harris, 2010). Although these social initiatives were often included in planned budgets, they were first on the chopping block when expenditures outpaced actual revenues in favor of greater military and capital-intensive spending.

It is in some ways ironic that it was not the clergy, but instead these groups – the rural poor, the urban workers, and the professional class – that were on the frontlines of the initial protests in 1977 that would eventually topple the monarchy (Parsa, 1989). The latter two in particular benefitted greatly from the White Revolution and subsequent modernization reforms at their outset, but the state could not sustain the momentum into the next decade. This intimates a "rising expectations" explanation (Tocqueville, 1955), such that the dissatisfaction with the Shah was less about absolute deprivation – that is, that his government failed to deliver *any* development-enhancing services and provisions – but rather about the relative deprivation felt by urban and professional classes (Davies, 1962).[60] On top of these unkept promises was the conspicuity of inequality as rapid modernization clearly did not touch all citizens equally. The juxtaposition of ostentatious spending by the highest stratum of society against the crumbling of agrarian life and the struggles of the urban working class was as clear a reminder as any of the Shah's failures to bring Iran into the realm of developed nations. The "Great Civilization," as summarized by economists

---

[60] This account of social movements is famously challenged by Theda Skocpol, although it is considerably rolled back for the specific case of the Iranian Revolution (Skocpol, 1979, 1982).

Hossein Razavi and Firouz Vakil, "did not seem so great any more, at least in its actual experience up to the end of 1978" (Razavi and Vakil, 1984, 96). In the Shah's waning days in 1979, Khomeini perfectly swept in to promise an end to many of society's grievances and, as historian Ervand Abrahamian describes, "rekindle[d] the hopes the earlier revolution had raised but failed to realize" (Abrahamian, 1982, 533). In effect, the Shah's version of rentierism failed not because of its ineffectiveness in economic development writ large, but rather because of its fiscal inability to satisfy growing expectations from a rapidly modernizing society. By contrast, his deposers promised – and ultimately delivered – a "populist, welfare-oriented rentier state" (Skocpol, 1982, 280), one that would be backed by oil revenues after the postrevolution return of operational nationalization in 1980.[61]

Despite my reading of events, I do not wish to impart to the reader yet another missing piece that explains the puzzle of the Iranian Revolution. It was a complex transition that may in fact lack a unified, systematic explanation. As Kurzman aptly notes, the only way to make sense of the Shah's fall is from the lens of an "anti-explanation," one that "attempt[s] to understand the experience of the revolution in all its anomalous diversity and confusion" (Kurzman, 2004, 5–6). But what is clear is that the government was unable to satisfy a growing appetite from below, in part because the top-down approach that had worked for the Shah up until the 1970s could no longer be financially sustained. And while previous research attributes this fiscal "slow down" to poor planning or to lukewarm global demand for oil in the late 1970s (see Looney, 1982), a key factor has hitherto gone unnoticed: by the end of 1976, the Iranian government no longer effectively controlled oil operations, allowing profits to once again be captured by the Western consortium of companies that the Shah tried so valiantly but unsuccessfully to break.

6.6   Conclusion

Drawing on the case of prerevolutionary Iran, this chapter shows that the Shah's decision to reform NIOC into an operational company was motivated by the desire to increase government take of oil revenues beyond the levels of his long-time adversaries across the Persian Gulf. The game of leapfrog being played between host governments and

---

[61] After the revolution, the government cancelled all existing foreign oil contracts and placed all operations in the hands of NIOC, with regulatory authority vested in a newly established Ministry of Petroleum. In practice, however, the SOE and ministry were one and the same – and were staffed with the same individuals who, as one former international oil company manager put it, "held two cards – one for NIOC and one for the Ministry." See Mahdavi (2012, 255).

MNCs was thus taken to the ultimate level by the Shah in response to his scorn for the better deals granted to his competitors. This choice had direct consequences for the fiscal strength of Pahlavi Iran. The operational nationalization of production by BP and the consortium provided immediate benefits to the Shah and the Iranian treasury. In the first six months after the passage of the new purchase-and-sales agreement in July 1973, revenues increased to $950 million, roughly 14 to 26 percent higher than projected. From July 1973 to December 1974, oil revenues increased by $2.8 billion more than expected when compared to a counterfactual world in which operations were not nationalized.

The results from this in-depth case analysis corroborate the cross-national findings from Chapters 4 and 5. The diffusion of information provided a clear spark for the Shah's decision to nationalize operations, just as countries exposed to information diffusion through their involvement in OPEC were more likely to nationalize operations. Fiscal and social pressures in the pre-1973 period combined to narrow the Shah's time horizons, pushing him toward nationalization rather than maintaining private operations. The consequence of this decision was an immediate windfall to the Iranian treasury, through both the reduced information asymmetry between the government and NIOC (compared to between the government and BP) and the ability to increase production levels at will. Consistent with theoretical expectations and with the cross-national results from Chapter 5, operational nationalization in Iran increased the government's short-term fiscal strength.

However, I cannot directly assess whether this decision would have increased the Shah's durability, since the nationalization was effectively reversed in 1976. But my argument would imply that *without* the sustained influx of oil revenues through 1978, the Shah failed to sufficiently consolidate power when he needed to most. In the face of a popular revolution sparked in part by broken economic promises, the Shah was unable to ward off his many challengers and ultimately succumbed to his rivals by fleeing the country in January 1979.

6.7 Appendix: BP Projections and Difference-in-Difference Results

Operating costs c_t are projected by the Val team on an annual basis; an alternative is to take the fixed operating cost assumed by BP in November 1970 of $0.1077 per barrel. The Val team and CapDev team each reported different projections for production q_t. Prices p_t are inputted using actual monthly posted prices for both light and heavy Iranian crude.

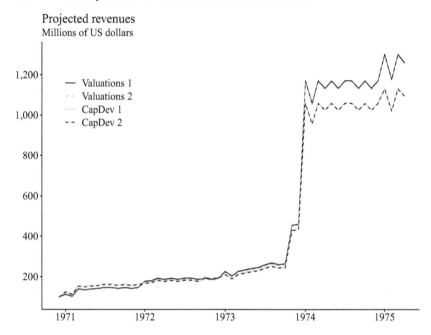

Figure 6.4 Trajectory of four different BP projections of monthly Iranian oil revenue

Data source: Reproduced from the BP Archive © BP plc

There are thus four different projected revenues based on different values of q_t and c_t:

- Projection 1: q_t based on Val; c_t based on Val.
- Projection 2: q_t based on Val; c_t based on fixed BP.
- Projection 3: q_t based on CapDev; c_t based on Val.
- Projection 4: q_t based on CapDev; c_t based on fixed BP.

These projections are plotted in Figure 6.4 from December 1970 to April 1975. The biggest difference between the projections is that the CapDev team was more aggressive in forecasting 1971 production while being more conservative in forecasting 1972 and 1973 production, with an exception to projecting a strong fourth quarter in 1972. By April 1975 (the final month in the comparison), Projection 2 anticipated the greatest increase in government revenue, while Projection 4 anticipated the lowest increase. Note that the slight jaggedness of the trends is primarily due to the difference in the number of days per month.

Cross-Validating the Revenue Formula

To assess the validity of the monthly revenue formula in the text, I compare the aggregated annual revenues from this formula to annual revenue assessments of government oil revenue from the online record of the British Foreign and Commonwealth Office (FCO).[62] Differences between the two amount to less than 0.5 percent in the 1971–1973 period.

Year	Formula revenue	Reported revenue	Difference
1971	1,875,560,049	1,869,600,000	−0.3 percent
1972	2,369,740,621	2,380,000,000	0.4 percent
1973	3,879,917,580	3,900,000,000	0.5 percent

Table 6.1. *Difference-in-difference results using OLS*

	Dependent variable:	
	Oil revenues (millions of US dollars)	
	(1)	(2)
Period dummy	693.56***	24.60
(post-nationalization = 1)	(32.91)	(16.39)
Treatment dummy	16.26	64.13***
(actual revenue = 1)	(43.34)	(21.58)
Period × Treatment	147.48**	816.44***
	(73.58)	(36.64)
Constant	175.53***	127.66***
	(19.38)	(9.65)
Observations	245	245
R^2	0.717	0.814
Adjusted R^2	0.714	0.812
Residual Std. Error (df = 241)	219.28	109.20
F Statistic (df = 3; 241)	203.76***	352.51***

***$p < 0.01$, **$p < 0.05$, *$p < 0.1$
The period dummy is 1 for all months after July 1973 and 0 for all months prior to and including July 1973. The treatment dummy is 1 for the actual revenue figures and 0 for all projected revenue figures. The average causal effect of nationalization on government revenues, τ_{DID}, is estimated by the coefficient on the interaction term Period × Treatment. Column 1 shows the results from projections using actual posted prices. Column 2 shows the results from projections using projected posted prices; these projections therefore do not capture the unexpected price shock during the Arab oil embargo of 1973–1974

---

[62] Files accessed from the United States Library of Congress in August 2017: FCO 8/1964 (1973). "Oil Affairs in Persian Gulf." File number NBP 12/1 Part A. See page 19. FCO 8/2074 (1973). "Oil in Iran." File number NBP 12/2 Part B. See page 201. FCO 8/2516 (1975). "Oil in Iran." File number NBP 12/4. See page 112.

7   Conclusion
The Implications of Nationalization

The concept of state intervention in the economy is one that has plagued political economists from Aristotle to Adam Smith to Paul Krugman. The role of government in the market has been concurrently endorsed and criticized. On the one hand, the state is viewed as the market-clearing panacea for the ailments of a purely capitalist economy; on the other, state control of private firms is derided as corrupt, inefficient, and a hindrance to positive economic growth. Yet, when it comes to the production of natural resources, state intervention is popular and often the norm. Why do states intervene in the private sector of natural resource industries? Specifically, why do leaders nationalize natural resource operations?

This book demonstrates that leaders nationalize operations to increase their survival prospects. Operational nationalization – whereby states take de facto control over the extraction and development of natural resources – is a route for governments to capture revenues that would otherwise flow to foreign agents through multinational corporations (MNCs). Just as governments devised land titling as a means to seize agricultural revenues earned by domestic citizens, governments crafted operational nationalization to capture natural resource revenues earned by foreign firms. I argue that where a state-owned enterprise (SOE) has operational control over natural resource production, the government is able to fully capture resource revenues (i.e., rents and quasi-rents) but forfeits future gains, given the inefficiencies of state-run entities, the loss of long-run cost recovery, and the risks of international retaliation to expropriation. Where the state vests operational control in nonstate companies, the bulk of these revenues is instead pocketed by MNCs, but the production efficiencies of these firms ensures a long-term positive revenue stream for host governments (see Chapter 2).

For weaker leaders who perceive a low probability of future survival, the influx of revenues from nationalization is sorely needed to buy political support and thwart challengers to their rule. Conversely, stronger leaders who perceive higher odds of political survival can justify giving up these short-term windfalls in favor of the long-term efficiency of private operations. But when the gamble of nationalization pays off, initially weaker leaders who nationalize can use the resulting revenue infusion to increase their duration in power and become stronger as a result. Initially strong leaders who eschew nationalization pass up this opportunity and forfeit revenues that could be used to consolidate rule if their strength ever wains.

Chapter 4 shows that the diffusion of information about agreements negotiated by other host governments provides a spark for the decision to nationalize operations. Upon learning of the viable possibility of achieving higher returns from resource extraction, leaders will seek to renegotiate their existing contracts with nonstate operating firms. This spark, importantly, prompts leaders to update their beliefs about the probability of their own survival in power. For those who perceive a long and stable future ahead, this choice-point leads to renegotiations to maintain operations by nonstate firms but at higher tax rates. But for those who perceive that their days in office are numbered, this choice-point leads to renegotiations that result in nationalization of extractive operations.

Applying this theory to the book's original cross-national, time-series data on operational nationalizations in the oil industry (see Chapter 3), I find that leaders are more likely to nationalize operations when they are exposed to diffused information – through their membership and attendance at OPEC meetings and other forums like the Nonaligned Movement – and when they rule within the context of a young, unestablished political regime. The case comparison of Iran and Saudi Arabia in the 1945–1951 period corroborates this finding with a more precise look at how information about agreements is diffused from one country to the next. Because of his successful consolidation of power and perceptions of a lasting dynastic monarchy, King Ibn Saud chose to continue allowing American-owned Aramco to operate Saudi Arabia's oil fields instead of opting for nationalization. By contrast, the Shah of Iran was in the midst of a political crisis with the rise to power of the charismatic and oft-adversarial prime minister Mohammad Mossadegh in 1951. Faced with mounting government debts and a parliament that had sworn in its first prime minister without the Shah's approval, the Shah capitulated to nationalize the operations and assets of the British-owned AIOC.

If nationalization is a decision made to increase a leader's duration in office, then it must be the case that nationalization indeed ensures the survival of initially weak leaders. Chapter 5 revisits the cross-national, time-series oil nationalizations data in Chapters 3 and 4 to find support for this implication of the book's argument. Not only does nationalization increase government capture of resource revenues that had previously flowed to outside firms, but leaders who nationalize operations are more likely to survive in office than those who eschew this choice. Beyond leadership survival, I also find that operational nationalization increases the survival of political regimes among autocracies. This provides additional support to proponents of a conditional resource curse, whereby natural resource wealth prolongs regimes under some conditions but not others. In this case, the results indicate that more oil income corresponds to lower regime failure but only in states with operational NOCs.

Chapter 6 evaluates the causal mechanisms of how information diffusion sparks the decision to nationalize and how operational nationalization increases government revenues in the context of 1970s Iran. Drawing on archival records from the BP Archive in Coventry, UK, I find that knowledge about better terms reached between the oil companies and the Arab states prompted the Shah to go one step further by nationalizing BP's operations in 1973. To assess how this decision impacted the actual collection of oil revenues, I compare monthly oil receipts paid directly to the Iranian treasury to various projections of monthly payments that would have been paid had the Shah not nationalized operations. These projections – which I obtained by again drawing from archival records at BP – help to establish a credible counterfactual to the "treatment" of nationalizing operations in July 1973. This technique shows a dramatic increase in revenues after nationalization: roughly $2.8 billion higher between August 1973 and December 1974, compared to projections if operations had not been nationalized.

But the Shah could not reap the benefits of nationalization for long. His gamble failed when BP and the other members of the consortium reversed operational nationalization in 1976 by effectively blocking NIOC's ability to sell oil on the open market. As a result, oil revenues collected by the Iranian government plummeted. And as matters worsened for the Shah politically in 1977 and 1978, this foregone wealth meant less money to satisfy expectations of a rising middle class, to shore up support from loyalists, to fend off would-be challengers, and to repress his opponents. One year later, the Shah fled the country and opened the door for the Islamic Revolution of 1979. These findings, in conjunction with the cross-national evidence from Chapters 4 and 5, support the argument's implications that nationalization and perceptions of survival

are mutually endogenous: weaker leaders choose operational nationalization and, if they can pull it off, this action provides the revenue windfall
to consolidate power and to increase their survival in office.

The empirical evidence in this book has largely drawn on nationalizations in one industry – petroleum. In addition to the cross-national
analysis of oil nationalizations over the past 100 years, I highlight the
decisions facing leaders in 1940s Iran and Saudi Arabia, 1960s Iraq,
and 1970s Iran. As I review in Chapters 1 and 3, oil nationalizations
provide an excellent testing ground for my theory, given the prominence
of oil as the world's most traded commodity and the rich variation
in nationalizations over time and across countries. But the proposed
theory is just as salient for understanding oil nationalizations in the
modern era and nonoil nationalizations of the future, as well as other
instances of opportunistic behavior by political leaders. The remainder
of this concluding chapter considers the implications of the argument
for opportunism in general, the nationalization of oil operations in the
twenty-first century, and the potential nationalizations of precious metals
and minerals in the decades to come.

7.1   Nationalization as Opportunism

Before assessing the argument's predictions for the modern era of extractive resources, it is useful to consider how the theory I advance relates to
political behavior in other contexts. Extractive resource nationalization
is but one tool in the leader's arsenal to increase survival in office.
The action of appropriating privately held wealth is a specific case of
a general pattern of acquiring more power at the expense of another
party. Within the context of dictatorships, for instance, the balance of
power sharing between dictators and their ruling coalitions is tilted in
favor of leaders when they opportunistically use national resources to
recruit supporters loyal directly to themselves rather than to the ruling
regime writ large (Svolik, 2009). Elites can also engage in opportunistic
behavior to stay within the governing coalition, such as manipulating
the economy with expansionary policy prior to elections to bolster their
reelection prospects – in both democratic and electoral authoritarian
contexts alike (Nordhaus, 1975; Magaloni, 2006; Blaydes, 2010). At
the extreme, opportunism can entail aggressive behavior in the form
of inciting conflict. Initiating and perpetuating war, for example, can
help to increase a leader's survival prospects at the enemy's expense
(Bueno de Mesquita et al., 2003; Debs and Goemans, 2010).

The argument I put forth throughout this book would imply that
opportunism in general is the product of leaders adjusting their odds

of survival based on factors affecting their own time horizons. Where there are credible challenges to their rule and few barriers to successfully follow through on opportunistic behavior, leaders will be more likely to exploit existing circumstances to reap short-term gains at the expense of not only those that are exploited but also of long-term gains. The diffusion of information regarding the behavior of one's competitors, for instance, is one factor I show that reduces barriers to behave opportunistically and impacts the decision calculus of leader survival prospects. The promise of immediate returns that can be used to consolidate power is another such factor, even when such behavior imposes high future costs.

From this perspective, actions like Saddam Hussein's invasion of Kuwait in 1990, Vladimir Putin's annexation of Crimea in 2014, and the PRI's repeated appropriation of Pemex's revenues in the 1980s and 1990s all make sense despite their significant economic costs in the long run. Economic arguments might view these actions as irrational, given the negative net present value of their consequences, namely the costs of military occupation, accumulation of massive debt, and long-term reputational damage from aggressive foreign policy. Yet, such explanations fail to incorporate the short-term political benefits from opportunism that allow leaders to survive rather than lose their grip on power. The Iraqi invasion of Kuwait, for example, was a clear military failure that cost the Ba'athist government hundreds of billions of dollars in reconstruction and reparations (Caron, 2004), but enabled Hussein to retain power for more than a decade thereafter. One of the more persuasive arguments to explain Hussein's decision is based on his perceptions that international enemies were "conspiring with his domestic opponents against him" and that war was the only way to project strength – despite knowing that August 1990 was not "the ideal time to launch a war" given the weak position of the Iraqi military (Gause III, 2002, 57,61). The war may indeed have had a low probability of outright military success a priori. But with Hussein's perceived time horizons and his belief that aggression was the only way to stay alive, opportunism was a logical choice despite its long-term costs.

Consider the Olsonian standpoint in which opportunistic behavior is not revenue-maximizing when taking into account the long-run costs of predatory actions (see Olson, 1993, 2000). Repeated opportunism would deprive the market of strong property rights, stable regulations, and steady investment that drive long-term economic growth that can be sustainably taxed to maintain healthy government fiscal balances over time. But this perspective underestimates the value that opportunism provides to a leader who, without a short-term injection of capital to build a loyal governing coalition, credibly faces removal from power via coup d'état, imprisonment, or even assassination. Incorporating these threats to survival into the leader's decision calculus, opportunism is indeed revenue-maximizing despite its long-run costs because it strengthens the leader and increases the leader's duration in power. Compared to the counterfactual in which the leader does not engage in appropriation – and faces the possibility of ouster and therefore zero long-term revenues – opportunism today allows the leader to stay in power to collect revenues down the road.

This logic applies to postnationalization decision making as well. After deciding to nationalize oil operations, for instance, a leader will be faced with the choice of whether to continue appropriating rents from the operational NOC. Recall from Chapter 2 that some leaders opt for the state-as-steward model of SOE governance, in which the government allows the NOC to recover long-run costs and to reinvest profits to ensure sustainable production in the future. Such is the story of Norway's Equinor (petroleum) or Chile's Codelco (copper), both of which have successfully maintained stable operations over time and are widely considered to be the leading SOEs of their industries. Other leaders instead opt for the state-as-appropriator model, in which the government continues to appropriate rents and quasi-rents from the SOE in an attempt to maximize government take of resource revenues in the short run. The most infamous case of this approach is the Venezuelan petroleum industry that, at the time of writing, is in complete shambles. In general, choosing the opportunistic state-as-appropriator approach will, in all likelihood, have damaging long-term consequences. But if behaving opportunistically can improve the survival prospects of leaders up front, then it will be the strategy of choice for leaders who perceive their days in power will be numbered without taking such aggressive and damaging actions.

7.2   Oil Nationalizations in the Twenty-First Century

The narrative constructed here is not only useful for understanding historical oil nationalizations in the heydays of the post–World War II era and amidst the 1973 Arab oil embargo. Operational nationalizations of oil resources continue to be relevant in the modern era. The methods used to establish state control of production, however, differ from the nationalizations of yesteryear.

Argentina's failed and costly seizure of the private Spanish oil firm Repsol-YPF in 2012 produced a blueprint for future would-be nationalizers on how *not* to expropriate operations. The government's takeover of Repsol-YPF was intended to, in the words of President Cristina

Fernández de Kirchner, "recuperate sovereignty and control of hydro-carbons" from the hands of a private firm that was blamed for the country's lackluster production rates because of underinvesting in exploration and development.[1] The nationalization came at a time when new shale discoveries in the Vaca Muerta fields of northern Patagonia in 2010 promised future riches for the cash-strapped government. The idea was for state-owned YPF to develop these new fields in tandem with technically capable firms, such as Chevron and Total, even though production at commercial levels had not yet been firmly established in 2012. But within two years of nationalization, YPF failed to make progress on developing the Vaca Muerta and had trouble producing from existing fields. To make matters worse, the Argentine government was forced to pay $5 billion to Repsol as court-ordered compensation for the expropriation.[2] Faced with mounting debts and development failures, petroleum production continued to decline and the state was worse off fiscally than before nationalizing Repsol.

The risks of investor retaliation after expropriations and the extractive failures of SOEs in the postdiscovery phase have prompted a different tactic for leaders seeking greater state involvement in the extractive sector. Instead of full-blown expropriation, emerging producers like Kenya and Ghana have opted for what is called back-in participation. Here, the state pays off costs incurred by operating companies after discoveries are made, in exchange for shares of new production. This kind of indirect expropriation allows firms more flexibility in negotiating the terms of state involvement, but questions remain as to the legality of such actions in international courts.[3]

Some producers are using these indirect expropriation methods to establish national oil companies with de facto control over operations locked-in to their petroleum legislation. In Lebanon, for instance, the government is considering the establishment of the Lebanese National Oil Company through a reform to its existing legislative framework for natural resource extraction.[4] As of 2019, the Lebanese oil and gas sector is in the prediscovery phase. With one major exploration contract awarded for development of offshore blocks by France's Total, Italy's ENI, and Russia's Novatek in January 2018, production will

---

[1] "Las frases más destacadas del discurso de Cristina Kirchner." *La Nacion*. April 16, 2012. Translated from Spanish and accessed 26 October 2017 from www.lanacion.com.ar/1465470-cristina-somos-el-unico-pais-que-no-maneja-sus-recursos-naturales

[2] "Repsol in $5 Billion settlement with Argentina." *The New York Times* February 25, 2014.

[3] I thank Marc Busch for raising this point.

[4] *Offshore Petroleum Resources Law number 132/2010*. Accessed from www.lpa.gov.lb/pdf/OPRL%20-%20English.pdf on 14 March 2018.

optimistically begin in ten years. If an NOC is indeed established, Article 11 of the draft NOC bill states that

[t]he company has the option to participate in production activities by investing, using the Back-in-Rights method adopted worldwide, in accordance with Item 1 / Article 6 of the Offshore Petroleum Resources Law (number 132/2010) and provisions of the Onshore Petroleum Resources Law. This method guarantees the rights of the State to purchase a share in oil wells without having to contribute to the expenses during the exploration phase until first revenues are generated during the production phase.[5]

Lebanon's plan is to have an NOC that will be operationally focused and technically capable, with clear and defined objectives for an autonomous, independent company by the time production begins. This kind of capacity building includes investing in training programs for the NOC's minimal staff; requiring outside firms to employ NOC personnel through secondment programs; observing exploration decisions made by outside firms; and managing geological data during the exploration phase. This will allow the NOC to hit the ground running, so to speak, when the government exercises its future legal right to indirectly expropriate operations.[6]

As with operational nationalizations of the past, the establishment of the Lebanese NOC is still a fiscal gamble for Lebanon's leaders. Putting operations in the hands of an NOC early in the extraction stage may jeopardize production success, as with the case of YPF in Argentina. But if successful, it will keep the bulk of future oil and natural gas revenues within the government's grasp rather than see these profits sent off to the shareholders of MNCs. One Lebanese bank estimated that the government's share of the Total–ENI–Novatek contract to be operated jointly with the NOC could be as large as $200 billion, potentially "turn[ing] the public deficit into a surplus five years after the start of extraction."[7] Such an influx of wealth would be a welcome event for the tenuous governing coalition's efforts to maintain popular support in the face of economic crisis, aging and underdeveloped basic infrastructure, and rampant unemployment.[8]

---

[5] *Lebanese National Oil Company Draft Bill 173/2017.* Draft bill provided to the author on 21 December 2017 by the Lebanese Parliamentary Committee on Public Works, Transportation, Energy, and Water.

[6] Ibid., Article 3: Establishment of the Company.

[7] "Audi: Lebanon's share from gas over $200 billion." *The Daily Star (Lebanon).* February 8, 2018. Accessed from www.pressreader.com/lebanon/the-daily-star-lebanon/20180208/281608125887635 on 14 March 2018.

[8] For more on these issues, see "Lebanon and its Multiple Challenges" *Brookings* www.brookings.edu/events/lebanon-and-its-multiple-challenges/.

The short-sighted nature of government policy in Lebanon is in many ways a product of its factional democracy. The country's consociational structure deliberately divides power across sectarian lines, with each group legally entitled to representation in the Lebanese government. The division of power between three major sects – Marionite Christians, Sunni Muslims, and Shi'a Muslims – has fostered unstable coalitions, which in turn promote a high degree of uncertainty regarding the holders of future political leadership (see Fakhoury, 2014; Rizkallah, 2016). This type of political system lends itself to procyclical expenditures like temporary welfare programs to the general public or clientelistic distributions of rents to loyal partisans to secure either broad or narrow backing, respectively (Cammett, 2014; Corstange, 2016). In the context of oil and gas development, opportunism in the form of operational nationalization should not be surprising, given the shorter time horizons that factionalism entails (Eifert et al., 2003). Constant political instability provides incentives for incumbent parties to maximize expenditures (and the revenues to sustain this spending) so as not to leave money on the table for future parties that may or may not include them in their governing coalitions (see Dunning, 2010). But, if successful, operational nationalization could entrench the ruling coalition and break the cycle of instability. By increasing the revenue base from which to finance patronage as well as welfare spending, the parties in power can build the foundations for lasting political support (and endanger long-term electoral competitiveness in the process).

Although operational nationalization is the predominant ownership strategy in the modern pool of major oil-producing countries (recall Figure 3.2), it is not an inevitability for new entrants to the producers' club. Petroleum discoveries in Guyana in 2015–2017 prompted the government to reconsider its existing extractive resource policies. Under the renegotiated terms of a contract with ExxonMobil, the state is expected to receive only 52 percent of the lifetime profits, a rate that is far lower than the industry standard of 60 to 80 percent in similar frontier countries.[9] Despite these low returns, President David Granger and his People's National Congress (PNC) coalition have no plans to vest operations in a newly developed NOC. Instead, the government has opted for the nonoperational NOC route, and is seemingly content with its choice of maintaining operations in the hands of a capable major MNC.

---

[9] "Guyana's oil deal is outlier low: government takes just over half." *OpenOil* briefing. March 15, 2018. Accessed from http://openoil.net/2018/03/15/guyanas-oil-deal-is-outlier-low-government-takes-just-over-half/.

To the current Guyanese government, the risks of nationalization do not outweigh its fiscal benefits. As I have argued, the gamble of nationalization is worth taking for leaders and governments whose days in office appear to be numbered, but not for those who perceive higher odds of political survival. Compared to Lebanon, Guyana's political system has witnessed far less factional instability despite the country's rich mix of ethnoreligious diversity and the competing power dynamic between its urban Afro-Caribbean and rural Indian constituencies (see Brown, 1999).[10] Both political groups in government – the ruling PNC and the opposition People's Progressive Party (PPP) – are cohesive and unified coalitions that have been in place since before Guyana's independence in 1966.[11] Such institutionalized parties tend to have long time horizons given their expectations of indefinitely retaining power in some form or another – whether as the ruling party or the credible opposition – through overlapping generations of party members that keep the coalition intact over time (Simmons, 2016b). Viewed from this perspective, neither the PNC nor the PPP is likely to engage in opportunistic appropriation of the oil sector for fear that it would hinder the long-term financial strength of the Guyanese government.

Perhaps the most institutionalized party system within the oil world is the United States, which has never nationalized oil operations in its 160-year history as a producer. Yet, party institutionalization may not be the only reason why the US has eschewed nationalization. Consider the case of Alaska in 2007, when newly elected governor Sarah Palin publicly threatened to revoke ExxonMobil's natural gas leases and privately floated the possibility of a state-owned natural gas enterprise to operate undeveloped gas fields on state lands (Leonard, 2008).[12] The apparent motivation was the failure by Alaska's Big Three – BP, ExxonMobil, ConocoPhillips – to develop North Slope gas fields as well

---

[10] This is not to say that Guyanese discourse has not been marred by ethnopolitical conflicts; indeed, violent protests along ethnic lines have been commonplace, even after the 1992 democratic reforms (Mars, 2001).

[11] The PNC party held what is effectively considered to be unchecked single-party power for the first twenty-six years of Guyana's postindependence political history. Nineteen ninety-two was the first year of certified competitive elections and the first year a PNC member did not hold the executive office (prior to 1980, de facto power was held by the prime minister; the presidency was largely a ceremonial office). While the PPP held the presidency continuously from 1992 to 2015, elections throughout the period were considered to be free and fair. See Bynoe et al. (2006) and Freedom House (Various Years) *Freedom in the World*. For a contrasting view of Guyanese political stability in the post–1992 period, see Hinds (2005).

[12] The option of nationalization was never, to the best of my knowledge, stated in public in those terms. This perspective is based on an interview with Clifford Groh, a former Alaska State Legislative Director, which I conducted by phone on September 28, 2017.

as the desire to capture greater revenues for the state during a time of booming commodity prices (Conn, 2008). But Palin's government instead ended up increasing taxes on MNC profits and allowed them to continue privately extracting the state's oil and gas reserves. Why didn't Palin follow through? What made Alaska different than, say, the case of Canada in 1976 or Norway in 1981?

The incentives and preconditions for nationalization were certainly present: after forty years' worth of experience with petroleum, Alaska had both the human capital and the technical knowledge to sustain a successful SOE. And with the clock ticking on Palin's reelection campaign in 2010 (had she not later decided to run for vice president, of course), the governor's time horizons in 2007 were tight enough to justify seeking the short-term means to finance ambitious expenditures for expanding her political base. Yet two factors precluded operational nationalization that are unique to the Alaskan case. The first is the possibility of exit by the oil companies in response to gas nationalization, given both the relatively high extraction costs of Alaskan oil and, more important, the fluidity of capital across US state borders.[13] Palin knew that capital flight was a credible threat to state opportunism and could seriously damage the oil industry in the short term.[14]

The second is a more general factor that explains why extractive resource nationalization has never occurred in the United States writ large.[15] Dating back to its early postcolonial policies, mineral ownership in the US consists of a mixed public-and-private property-rights system that is absent almost everywhere else in the world. The federal government manages approximately 30 percent of the country's minerals, with the remainder split between state and private property management. Accordingly, the US government lacks the monopoly on resource rights that exists in the United Kingdom, Norway, and other advanced-market

[13] The ease with which ExxonMobil could divert financial resources away from Alaska to its operations in Texas, for example, stands in contrast to its ability to relocate from one country to another.

[14] This did not turn out to be the case after taxes were increased; rather than witness an oil company exodus, new investors entered the market, such as Italy's ENI and its proposed $1.4 billion North Slope development. On the issue of capital flight fears and the lack of exodus after the tax reform, see Milkowski (2008) and Knapp (2012).

[15] Aside from the Alaska case, oil nationalization has been floated on a number of occasions in US political history. Two notable instances occurred during the 1912–1920 period on the grounds of national defense to ensure security of supply for the navy, and again in 1943, when Secretary of the Interior Harold Ickes pushed President Franklin D. Roosevelt for the creation of an American NOC that would exploit oil reserves overseas, primarily in Saudi Arabia. See Nash (1968).

economies (all of which have pursued operational nationalization at some point or another).[16]

Any attempts at complete nationalization, then, would have to entail forced acquisition of private property on a massive scale. But as the Tennessee Valley Authority eminent domain seizures during the New Deal Era showed, such appropriation is not only costly from a compensation standpoint but can also lead to economic stagnation and a complete loss of trust in government (Kitchens, 2013; Kline and Moretti, 2013). Moreover, nationalization would not just involve a seizure of assets and operations; it would also entail an entire overhaul of the country's property-rights system. Even in times of short time horizons and diffused information about revenue sharing or cost misreporting, the short-term net present value of nationalization would be negative, given the larger economic costs incurred from a large-scale violation of property rights (see North, 1994; Acemoglu and Robinson, 2008). In short, the US is an outlier case, one in which the incentives for opportunism have existed over time but where unique institutional constraints have been strong enough to prevent nationalization of extractive resources.

7.3   Resource Nationalizations of the Future: Precious Metals, Minerals, and the Energy Transition

In addition to the cases of oil-market governance discussed throughout the book, the study of why leaders nationalize extractive operations has broader implications for the next generation of extractive resources beyond oil. The world's energy production, consumption, and transportation system is in the midst of a profound transformation. This energy transition will shift the future shape of the energy system from one that is predominantly powered by fossil fuels to one composed of renewable energy and decarbonized resources (World Economic Forum, 2018).

The rise of renewables like solar and wind power promises a near-zero emissions solution to address both rising demand from emerging markets and the mitigation of anthropogenic climate change. But both technologies are dependent on advanced nonrenewable raw materials for manufacturing of parts and for storage of electricity to maintain

---

[16] One exception to the system of state monopoly over resource rights is Canada's Alberta, where private landowners hold the leasing rights to roughly one sixth of all oil and gas fields, with the remainder held by the Federal government or the Alberta provincial government. See the International Comparative Legal Guide *Oil and Gas Regulation 2018: Canada*, accessed from https://iclg.com/practice-areas/oil-and-gas-laws-and-regulations/canada.

reliability. Because these energy sources are naturally intermittent, they require large-scale rechargeable batteries to harness energy – generated when the sun is shining or when the wind is blowing – to supply electricity to the market when it is dark or when the winds are calm. The current state-of-the-art systems for energy storage are lithium-ion batteries, comprised not only of their mineral namesake but also materials like cobalt, manganese, phosphate, and titanate. Cobalt is also used in the generators of large-scale wind turbines.

These materials tend to be highly concentrated geographically: Chile and China together hold two-thirds of the world's lithium reserves; two-thirds of global manganese reserves are located in South Africa, Ukraine, and Brazil; and the DRC alone holds half of the world's cobalt.[17] As of 2019, these resources are predominantly produced by nonstate firms like Glencore, Albemarle, SQM of Chile, and Rio Tinto.

As demand for minerals and advanced materials rises with the demand for renewable energy worldwide, the potential rents from these reserves could increase significantly. At the moment, information asymmetries between host governments and operating firms are surprisingly large given the high-information context of the current era. Information on the price of minerals sold to the final consumer, for example, is not readily available to host governments; instead, these figures are closely guarded by MNCs. Extraction costs are similarly unknown by host states, making it almost impossible for governments to discern the true level of profits from the sale of minerals extracted by private firms within their own borders.

My argument would predict that the diffusion of information about these figures and the terms of agreements reached between firms and other states will spark leaders to consider operational nationalization as a means to increase government capture of mineral revenues. The likelihood of nationalization will be particularly pronounced in states with leaders who perceive lower odds of future survival. Firms like Katanga Mining (majority owned by Glencore) doing business in the DRC, for instance, will likely feel the pressure of operational nationalization as global demand for cobalt skyrockets and as threats arise to Joseph Kabila's continued grip over Congolese politics.

The energy transition will be a welcome event for creating a future system powered by renewable energy sources to mitigate the rising threat of climate change. With it, deep decarbonization of the energy

---

[17] "Lithium" (2018) *United States Geological Survey Mineral Commodity Summaries*; "Manganese" (2018) *United States Geological Survey Mineral Commodity Summaries*; O'Sullivan et al. (2017, 13).

system may indeed portend the denouement of petroleum as the world's primary fuel. But as long as there are extractive resources in the value chain that can provide states with sorely needed revenues, operational nationalization will continue to be a strategy by which leaders increase their survival in power.

7.4   Conclusion

The implications of my argument about nationalization and political survival extend beyond the natural resource sector. Nationalizing operations is one type of government behavior that on the surface appears counterintuitive from a conventional political economy standpoint. Because of its risks and long-term inefficiencies, operational nationalization has a negative expected value. By contrast, maintaining private operations (and periodically adjusting tax rates as needed) has a positive expected value, given the long-run efficiency and stability of production managed by MNCs. Leaders who choose to nationalize operations should therefore suffer in fiscal terms, while those who uphold strong property rights by not expropriating assets should benefit in the long run.

Yet this book argues and provides evidence that counters these claims. The logic of the long-term weakness of the predatory state (see Levi, 1989; Olson, 1993) cannot explain the survival of the "roving bandits" who violate property rights by nationalizing natural resource operations in lieu of building institutions to promote economic development. The argument presented here implies that such predation is crucial for those leaders who face impending collapse, by providing them with the financial means to secure their rule. Although this behavior has negative long-term consequences for development, weak leaders will happily accept these losses if it means they get to hold onto power – using the revenue infusion that nationalization provides. But by not incorporating this life-or-death struggle into a leader's decision calculus, conventional models will underestimate the political value of behavior that has clearly negative long-term economic consequences. I do not attempt to give definitive support for this claim across all types of predatory behavior, of which operational nationalization is only one example. Rather I offer a theory that future research can assess in other contexts of opportunistic behavior, such as corruption, excessive taxation, aggressive foreign policy, or any other activity that that offers high long-term risks but high short-term rewards at the cost of societal development.

Bibliography

Abrahamian, E. (1982). *Iran between Two Revolutions*. Princeton, NJ: Princeton University Press.

(1992). *The Iranian Mojahedin*. New Haven, CT: Yale University Press.

Acemoglu, D. and J. Robinson (2005). *Economic Origins of Dictatorship and Democracy*. New York: Cambridge University Press.

(2008). The role of institutions in growth and development. Working Paper 10, Commission on Growth and Development.

Addison, T. and A. R. Roe (2018). Introduction and ten main messages. In *Extractive Industries: The Management of Resources as a Driver of Sustainable Development*, WIDER Studies in Development Economics, Chapter 1, pp. 3–30. Oxford: Oxford University Press.

Afkhami, A. A. (2003). The sick men of Persia: The importance of illness as a factor in the interpretation of modern Iranian diplomatic history. *Iranian Studies 36*(36), 339–352.

Al-Obaidan, A. M. and G. W. Scully (1992). Efficiency differences between private and state-owned enterprises in the international petroleum industry. *Applied Economics 24*(2), 237–246.

Alam, A. (1991). *The Shah and I: The Confidential Diary of Iran's Royal Court, 1968–1977*. London: I. B. Tauris.

Albertus, M. and V. Menaldo (2012). If you're against them you're with us: The effect of expropriation on autocratic survival. *Comparative Political Studies 8*(45), 973–1003.

Alnasrawi, A. (1991). *Arab Nationalism, Oil, and the Political Economy of Dependency*. Westport, CT: Greenwood Press.

(2002). *Iraq's Burdens: Oil, Sanctions, and Underdevelopment*. Westport, CT: Greenwood Press.

Alvandi, R. (2014). The Shah's détente with Khrushchev: Iran's 1962 missile base pledge to the Soviet Union. *Cold War History 14*(3), 423–444.

Amuzegar, J. (1991). *Dynamics of the Iranian Revolution: The Pahlavis' Triumph and Tragedy*. Albany, NY: State University of New York Press.

Andersen, J. J. and M. Ross (2013). The big oil change: A closer look at the Haber-Menaldo analysis. *Comparative Political Studies 47*(7), 993–1021.

Arezki, R., V. A. Ramey, and L. Sheng (2017). News shocks in open economies: Evidence from giant oil discoveries. *The Quarterly Journal of Economics 132*(1), 103–155.

Arjomand, S. A. (1989). *The Turban for the Crown: The Islamic Revolution in Iran.* Oxford: Oxford University Press.

Arriola, L. R. (2009). Patronage and political stability in Africa. *Comparative Political Studies 42*, 1339–1362.

Aslaksen, S. (2010). Oil and democracy: More than a cross-country correlation? *Journal of Peace Research 47*, 421–431.

Bakhash, S. (1984). Sermons, revolutionary pamphleteering and mobilisation: Iran, 1978. In S. A. Arjomand (Ed.), *From Nationalism to Revolutionary Islam*, Chapter 9, pp. 177–194. London: Palgrave Macmillan.

Bamberg, J. (2000). *British Petroleum and Global Oil, 1970–1975: The Challenge of Nationalism.* Cambridge: Cambridge University Press.

Bashiriyeh, H. (1984). *The State and Revolution in Iran.* London: Routledge.

Bates, R. H. and D.-H. D. Lien (1985). A note on taxation, development, and representative government. *Politics & Society 14*(1), 53–70.

Baunsgaard, T. (2001). A primer on mineral taxation. Working Paper WP/01/139, International Monetary Fund.

Beblawi, H. and G. Luciani (1987). *The Rentier State.* London: Croom Helm.

Beer, S. and J. Loeprick (2017). Taxing income in the oil and gas sector: Challenges of international and domestic profit shifting. *Energy Economics 61*, 186–198.

Berrios, R., A. Marak, and S. Morgenstern (2011). Explaining hydrocarbon nationalization in Latin America: Economics and political ideology. *Review of International Political Economy 18*, 673–697.

Besley, T. and T. Persson (2014). Why do developing countries tax so little? *Journal of Economic Perspectives 28*(4), 99–120.

Blaydes, L. (2010). Electoral budget cycles under authoritarianism: Economic opportunism in Mubarak's Egypt. In *Elections and Distributive Politics in Mubarak's Egypt.* Cambridge: Cambridge University Press.

Blitzer, C. R., D. R. Lessard, and J. L. Paddock (1984). Risk-bearing and the choice of contract forms for oil exploration and development. *The Energy Journal 5*(1), 1–28.

Boardman, A. E. and A. R. Vining (1989). Ownership and performance in competitive environments: A comparison of the performance of private, mixed, and state-owned enterprises. *The Journal of Law and Economics 32*(1), 1–33.

Bohn, H. and R. T. Deacon (2000). Ownership risk, investment, and the use of natural resources. *American Economic Review* (90), 526–549.

Boix, C. (1997). Privatizing the public business sector in the eighties: Economic performance, partisan responses, and divided governments. *British Journal of Political Science.*

(2003). *Democracy and Redistribution.* Cambridge: Cambridge University Press.

Box, G. E. P. and G. C. Tiao (1973). *Bayesian Inference in Statistical Analysis.* Reading, MA: Addison-Wesley.

Brautigam, D., O.-H. Fjeldstad, and M. Moore (Eds.) (2008). *Taxation and State-Building in Developing Countries: Capacity and Consent.* Cambridge: Cambridge University Press.

Bremmer, I. and R. Johnston (2009). The rise and fall of resource nationalism. *Survival 51*(2), 149–158.

Brooks, S. M. (2009). *Social Protection and the Market in Latin America: The Transformation of Social Security Institutions*. Cambridge: Cambridge University Press.

Brooks, S. M. and M. J. Kurtz (2016). Oil and democracy: Endogenous natural resources and the political "resource curse." *International Organization 70*(2), 279–311.

Brown, D. R. (1999). Ethnic politics and public sector management in trinidad and guyana. *Public Administrative Development 19*(4), 367–379.

Brunnschweiler, C. N. and S. Poelhekke (2019). Pushing one's luck: Petroleum ownership and discoveries. University of East Anglia School of Economics Working Paper 2019–01.

Buchanan, J. M., R. D. Tollison, and G. Tullock (Eds.) (1980). *Toward a Theory of the Rent-Seeking Society*. College Station, TX: Texas A&M University Press.

Bueno de Mesquita, B. and A. Smith (2010). Leader survival, revolutions, and the nature of government finance. *American Journal of Political Science 54*(4), 936–950.

Bueno de Mesquita, B., A. Smith, R. Siverson, and J. Morrow (2003). *The Logic of Political Survival*. Cambridge, MA: MIT Press.

Bynoe, M., T. Choy, and M. A. Seligson (2006). The political culture of democracy in Guyana. Technical report, Latin American Public Opinion Project, Vanderbilt University.

Cammett, M. (2014). *Compassionate Communalism: Welfare and Sectarianism in Lebanon*. Ithaca, NY: Cornell University Press.

Carney, R. W. (2018). *Authoritarian Capitalism: Sovereign Wealth Funds and State-Owned Enterprises in East Asia and Beyond*. Cambridge: Cambridge University Press.

Caron, D. (2004). The reconstruction of Iraq: Dealing with debt. *U.C. Davis Journal of International Law and Policy 11*(123), 123–143.

Chang, R., C. Hevia, and N. Loayza (2010). Privatization and Nationalization Cycles. NBER Working Paper.

Chaudhry, K. A. (1997). *The Price of Wealth: Economies and Institutions in the Middle East*. Ithaca, NY: Cornell University Press.

Cheibub, J. A., J. Gandhi, and J. R. Vreeland (2009). Democracy and dictatorship revisited codebook. Technical report, University of Illinois at Urbana-Champaign.

(2010). Democracy and dictatorship revisited. *Public Choice 143*, 67–101.

Chelkowski, P. J. and H. Dabashi (2000). *Staging a Revolution: The Art of Persuasion in the Islamic Republic of Iran*. New York, NY: New York University Press.

Cheon, A. (2015). *On Whose Terms? Understanding the Global Expansion of National Oil Companies*. Ph.D. thesis, Columbia University.

(2019). Developing global champions: Why national oil companies expand abroad. *Economics & Politics 31*(3): 403–427.

Cheon, A., M. Lackner, and J. Urpelainen (2015). Instruments of political control: National oil companies, oil prices, and petroleum subsidies. *Comparative Political Studies 48*(3), 370–402.

Cohn, G. (1968). *Petroleo e nacionalismo.* Sao Paolo: Difusão Européia do Livro.

Colgan, J. D. (2013). *Petro-Aggression: When Oil Causes War.* Cambridge: Cambridge University Press.

(2019). Guns and Oil: The Politics of International Order. Brown University unpublished book manuscript.

Conn, S. (2008, September). Palin and the politics of big oil. *CounterPunch,* www.counterpunch.org/2008/09/17/palin-and-the-politics-of-big-oil/.

Cooper, A. S. (2012). *The Oil Kings: How the U.S., Iran, and Saudi Arabia Changed the Balance of Power in the Middle East.* New York, NY: Simon and Schuster.

Corstange, D. (2016). *The Price of a Vote in the Middle East: Clientelism and Communal Politics in Lebanon and Yemen.* Cambridge: Cambridge University Press.

Crystal, J. (1989). Coalitions in Oil Monarchies: Kuwait and Qatar. *Comparative Politics 21*(4), 427–443.

Cuaresma, J. C., H. Oberhofer, and P. A. Raschky (2011). Oil and the duration of dictatorships. *Public Choice 148,* 505–530.

Cukierman, A., S. Edwards, and G. Tabellini (1992). Seigniorage and political instability. *American Economic Review 82*(3), 537–555.

Davies, J. C. (1962). Toward a theory of revolution. *American Sociological Review 27*(1), 5–19.

de Alessi, L. (1974). An economic analysis of government ownership and regulation: Theory and the evidence from the electric power industry. *Public Choice 19,* 1–42.

de Oliveira, A. (2012). Brazil's Petrobras: Strategy and performance. In D. G. Victor, D. Hults, and M. C. Thurber (Eds.), *Oil and Governance,* pp. 515–556. Cambridge: Cambridge University Press.

Debs, A. and H. Goemans (2010). Regime type, the fate of leaders, and war. *American Political Science Review 104*(3), 430–45.

Devlin, J. F. (1991). The Baath party: Rise and metamorphosis. *American Historical Review,* 1396–1407.

Diamond, L., J. J. Linz, and S. M. Lipset (1989). *Democracy in Developing Countries.* Boulder, CO: Lynne Reiner.

Dietrich, C. R. W. (2017). *Oil Revolution: Anticolonial Elites, Sovereign Rights, and the Economic Culture of Decolonization.* Cambridge: Cambridge University Press.

Doran, C. F. (1980). OPEC structure and cohesion: Exploring the determinants of cartel policy. *The Journal of Politics 42*(1), 82–101.

Duncan, R. (2006). Price or politics? An investigation of the causes of expropriation. *The Australian Journal of Agricultural and Resource Economics 50*(1), 85–101.

Dunning, T. (2008). *Crude Democracy.* New York, NY: Cambridge University Press.

(2010). Endogenous oil rents. *Comparative Political Studies 43*(3), 379–410.

Eifert, B., A. Gelb, and N. B. Tallroth (2003). The political economy of fiscal policy and economic management in oil-exporting countries. In J. M. Davis, R. Ossowski, and A. Fedelino (Eds.), *Fiscal Policy Formulation and Implementation in Oil-Producing Countries*, Chapter 4, pp. 82–122. International Monetary Fund, Washington, DC.

Elkins, Z., A. T. Guzman, and B. A. Simmons (2006). Competing for capital: The diffusion of bilateral investment treaties, 1960–2000. *International Organization 60*(04), 811–846.

Eller, S. L., P. R. Hartley, and K. B. Medlock (2011). Empirical evidence on the operational efficiency of national oil companies. *Empirical Economics 40*(3), 623–643.

Fakhoury, T. (2014). Debating Lebanon's power-sharing model: An opportunity or an impasse for democratization studies in the middle east? *The Arab Studies Journal 22*(1), 230–255.

Farouk-Sluglett, M. and P. Sluglett (2001). *Iraq since 1958: From Revolution to Dictatorship*. London: I.B. Tauris.

Fearon, J. and D. Laitin (2003). Ethnicity, insurgency, and civil war. *American Political Science Review 97*, 75–90.

Feng, Y. (1997). Democracy, political stability and economic growth. *British Journal of Political Science 27*(3), 391–418.

Fesharaki, F. (1976). *Development of the Iranian Oil Industry*. New York, NY: Praeger Publishers.

First, R. (1975). *Libya: The Elusive Revolution*. New York: Africana Publishing Company.

Frankel, J. A. (2010). The natural resource curse: A survey. NBER Working Paper, Volume 15836.

Gandhi, J. (2008). *Political Institutions under Dictatorship*. New York: Cambridge University Press.

Garrido de Sierra, S. (2012). Eroded unity and clientele migration: An alternative explanation of Mexico's democratic transition.

Gause III, F. G. (2002). Iraq's decisions to go to war, 1980 and 1990. *The Middle East Journal 56*(1), 47–70.

Geddes, B. (2003). *Paradigms and Sand Castles*. Cambridge: Cambridge University Press.

Geddes, B., J. Wright, and E. Frantz (2014). Autocratic breakdown and regime transitions: A new data set. *Perspectives on Politics 12*(02), 313–331.

Gelb, A. H. (1988). *Oil Windfalls: Blessing or Curse?* Oxford: Oxford University Press.

Gelman, A., J. B. Carlin, H. S. Stern, D. B. Dunson, A. Vehtari, and D. B. Rubin (2013). *Bayesian Data Analysis*. Boca Raton, FL: Chapman and Hall/CRC.

Gelvin, J. (1994). Demonstrating communities in post-Ottoman Syria. *The Journal of Interdisciplinary History 25*(1).

Gillies, A. (2009). Reforming corruption out of Nigerian oil? *Chr. Michelson Institute U4 Brief 2*, 1–4.

Girod, D. M., M. A. Stewart, and M. R. Walters (2017). Mass protests and the resource curse: The politics of demobilization in rentier autocracies. *Conflict Management and Peace Science*.

Goemans, H., K. S. Gleditsch, and G. Chiozza (2009). Introducing Archigos: A data set of political leaders. *Journal of Peace Research 46*(2), 269–283.

Goldberg, E., E. Wibbels, and E. Mvukiyehe (2008, April). Lessons from strange cases: Democracy, development, and the resource curse in the U.S. states. *Comparative Political Studies 41*(4), 477–514.

Goldman, M. I. (2008). *Petrostate: Putin, Power, and the New Russia*. Oxford: Oxford University Press.

Grayson, L. (1981). *National Oil Companies*. New York, NY: Wiley Press.

Greene, K. F. (2008). *Why Dominant Parties Lose: Mexico's Democratization in Comparative Perspective*. New York, NY: Cambridge University Press.

Guriev, S., A. Kolotilin, and K. Sonin (2011). Determinants of nationalization in the oil sector: A theory and evidence from panel data. *Journal of Law, Economics, and Organization 27*(2), 301–323.

Haber, S. and V. Menaldo (2011). Do natural resources fuel authoritarianism? A reappraisal of the resource curse. *American Political Science Review 105*(1), 1–26.

Haggard, S. and R. R. Kaufman (1995). *The Political Economy of Democratic Transitions*. Princeton, NJ: Princeton University Press.

(2016). *Dictators and Democrats: Masses, Elites, and Regime Change*. Princeton, NJ: Princeton University Press.

Hajzler, C. (2012). Expropriation of foreign direct investments: Sectoral patterns from 1993 to 2006. *Review of World Economics 148*(1), 119–149.

Hansohm, D. (2007). Oil and foreign aid: Curse or blessing? The case of Sudan. In K. Wohlmuth (Ed.), *Reconstructing Economic Governance after Conflict in Resource-rich African Countries: Learning from Country Experiences*, pp. 117–150. Bremen: Institute for World Economics and International Management.

Harris, K. (2010). Lineages of the Iranian welfare state: Dual institutionalism and social policy in the Islamic Republic of Iran. *Social Policy & Administration 44*(6), 727–745.

(2017). *A Social Revolution: Politics and the Welfare State in Iran*. Berkeley, CA: University of California Press.

Hartley, P. and K. B. Medlock (2008). A model of the operation and development of a national oil company. *Energy Economics 30*(5), 2459–2485.

Heckman, J. J. and J. M. Snyder, Jr (1977). Linear probability models of the demand for attributes with an empirical application to estimating the preferences of legislators. *Rand Journal of Economics 28*, 142–189.

Heller, P. R. P. (2012). Angola's Sonangol: Dexterous right hand of the state. In D. G. Victor, D. Hults, and M. C. Thurber (Eds.), *Oil and Governance*, pp. 836–884. Cambridge: Cambridge University Press.

(2017). Doubling down: National oil companies as instruments of risk and reward. Technical report, UNU-WIDER Working Paper 2017/81.

Heller, P. R. P., A. Fleming, and D. Mihalyi (2019). *NRGI national oil company database: Key findings*. New York, NY: Natural Resources Governance Institute (NRGI).

Heller, P. R. P., P. Mahdavi, and J. Schreuder (2014). Reforming national oil companies: Nine recommendations. New York, NY: NRGI.

Heller, P. R. P. and D. Mihalyi (2019, April). Massive and misunderstood: Data-driven insights into national oil companies. New York, NY: NRGI.

Henisz, W. J. (2000). The institutional environment for multinational investment. *Journal of Law, Economics, and Organization 16*(2), 334–364.

(2004). Political Institutions and Policy Volatility. *Economics and Politics 16*(1), 1–27.

Herb, M. (1999). *All in the Family: Absolutism, Revolution and Democracy in the Middle Eastern Monarchies.* Albany, NY: State University of New York Press.

(2005). No Representation without taxation? Rents, development, and democracy. *Comparative Politics 37*(3), 297–316.

(2014). *The Wages of Oil: Parliaments and Economic Development in Kuwait and the UAE.* Ithaca, NY: Cornell University Press.

Herbst, J. (2000). *States and Power in Africa: Comparative Lessons in Authority and Control.* Princeton, NJ: Princeton Univ. Press.

Hertzmark, D. I. (2007). Pertamina: Indonesia's state-owned oil company. Technical report.

Hinds, D. (2005). Problems of democratic transition in Guyana: Mistakes and miscalculations in 1992. *Social and Economic Studies 54*(1), 67–82.

Hodges, T. (2004). *Angola: Anatomy of an Oil State.* Bloomington, IN: Indiana University Press.

Hogan, W. and F. Sturzenegger (Eds.) (2010). *The Natural Resources Trap: Private Investment without Public Commitment.* Cambridge, MA: MIT Press.

Hogan, W., F. Sturzenegger, and L. Tai (2010). Contracts and investment in natural resources. In W. Hogan and F. Sturzenegger (Eds.), *The Natural Resources Trap: Private Investment without Public Commitment,* Chapter 1, pp. 1–43. Cambridge, MA: MIT Press.

Horrace, W. C. and R. L. Oaxaca (2006). Results on the bias and inconsistency of ordinary least squares for the linear probability model. *Economics Letters 90*(3), 321–327.

Hotelling, H. (1931). The economics of exhaustible resources. *Journal of Political Economy 39*(2), 137–175.

Hughes, L. (2014). *Globalizing Oil: Firms and Oil Market Governance in France, Japan, and the United States.* Cambridge: Cambridge University Press.

Hults, D. R. (2012a). Hybrid governance: State management of national oil companies. In D. G. Victor, D. R. Hults, and M. C. Thurber (Eds.), *Oil and Governance,* pp. 62–120. Cambridge: Cambridge University Press.

(2012b). Petroleos de Venezuela, S.A. (PDVSA): From independence to subservience. In D. G. Victor, D. R. Hults, and M. C. Thurber (Eds.), *Oil and Governance,* pp. 418–477. Cambridge: Cambridge University Press.

Huntington, S. P. (1991). *The Third Wave: Democratization in the Late Twentieth Century,* Volume 4. Norman, OK: University of Oklahoma Press.

Hurwitz, J. C. (Ed.) (1956). *Diplomacy in the Near and Middle East: A Documentary Record.* Princeton, NJ: D. Van Nostrand Company.

Imai, K., L. Keele, and T. Yamamoto (2010). Identification, inference and sensitivity analysis for causal mediation effects. *Statistical science 25*(1), 51–71.

Jensen, N. M. (2006). *Nation-States and the Multinational Corporation: A Political Economy of Foreign Direct Investment*. Princeton, NJ: Princeton University Press.

(2008). Political risk, democratic institutions, and foreign direct investment. *The Journal of Politics 70*(4), 1040–1052.

Jensen, N. M. and N. P. Johnston (2011). Political risk, reputation, and the resource curse. *Comparative Political Studies 44*(6), 662–688.

Jensen, N. M., E. Malesky, and S. Weymouth (2014). Unbundling the relationship between authoritarian legislatures and political risk. *British Journal of Political Science 44*(3), 655–684.

Jensen, N. M. and L. Wantchekon (2004). Resource wealth and political regimes in Africa. *Comparative Political Studies 37*(7), 816–841.

Jensen, N. M., G. Biglaiser, Q. Li, E. Malesky, P. M. Pinto, S. M. Pinto, and J. L. Staats (2012). *Politics and Foreign Direct Investment*. Ann Arbor, MI: University of Michigan Press.

Jensen, N. M., N. P. Johnston, C. Y. Lee, and H. Sahin. (2019). Crisis and contract breach: The domestic and international determinants of expropriation. *The Review of International Organizations*, 1–30.

Jodice, D. A. (1980). Sources of change in third world regimes for foreign direct investment, 1968–1976. *International Organization 34*(2), 177–206.

Johnston, D. (2001). *International Petroleum Fiscal Systems Analysis*. Tulsa, OK: PennWell Publishing Company.

Jones Luong, P. and J. Sierra (2015). The domestic political conditions for international economic expansion: Lessons from Latin American national oil companies. *Comparative Political Studies 48*(14), 2010–2043.

Jones Luong, P. and E. Weinthal (2001). Prelude to the resource curse: Explaining oil and gas development strategies in the soviet successor states and beyond. *Comparative Political Studies 33*(4), 367–399.

(2006). Rethinking the resource curse: Ownership structure, institutional capacity, and domestic constraints. *Annual Review of Political Science 9*, 241–263.

(2010). *Oil Is Not a Curse: Ownership Structure and Institutions in Soviet Successor States*. New York: Cambridge University Press.

Karl, T. L. (1997). *The Paradox of Plenty: Oil Booms and Petro-States*. Berkeley, CA: University of California Press.

Katouzian, H. (1981). *The Political Economy of Modern Iran*. London: Macmillan Press.

Keddie, N. R. (1981). *Roots of Revolution: An Interpretive History of Modern Iran*. New Haven, CT: Yale University Press.

Kemp, A. (1992). Petroleum policy issues in developing countries. *Energy Policy 20*(2), 104–115.

Keohane, R. O. (1984). *After Hegemony: Cooperation and Discord in the World Political Economy*. Princeton, NJ: Princeton University Press.

Keshavarzian, A. (2005). Contestation without Democracy: Elite Fragmentation in Iran. In M. Posusney and M. Angrist (Eds.), *Authoritarianism in the Middle East*. Boulder, CO: Lynne Reinner.

Kitchens, C. (2013). A dam problem: TVA's fight against malaria 1926–1951. *Journal of Economic History 73*(3), 694–724.

Klapp, M. G. (1987). *The Sovereign Entrepreneur: Oil Politics in Advanced and Less Developed Capitalist Countries*. Ithaca, NY: Cornell University Press.

Klein, B., R. G. Crawford, and A. A. Alchian (1978, October). Vertical integration, appropriable rents, and the competitive contracting process. *Journal of Law and Economics 21*(2), 297–326.

Kline, P. and E. Moretti (2013). Local economic development, agglomeration economies and the big push: 100 years of evidence from the TVA. University of California Berkeley working paper.

Knapp, G. (2012). Alaska's experience with arctic oil and gas development: History, policy issues, and lessons. Presented at Energies of the High North – Arctic Frontiers 2012, Tromso, Norway, January 25, 2012.

Kobrin, S. J. (1979). Political risk: A review and reconsideration. *Journal of International Business Studies 10*(1), 67–80.

   (1980). Foreign enterprise and forced divestment in LDCs. *International Organization 34*, 65–88.

   (1984). Expropriation as an attempt to control foreign firms in LDCs: Trends from 1960 to 1979. *International Studies Quarterly 28*, 329–348.

   (1985). Diffusion as an explanation of oil nationalization: Or the domino effect rides again. *Journal of Conflict Resolution 29*, 3–33.

Kohli, A. (1986). Democracy and Development. In J. Lewis and V. Kallab (Eds.), *Development Strategies Reconsidered*. New Brunswick, NJ: Transaction Books.

Kretzman, S. and I. Nooruddin (2011). *Drilling into Debt: An Investigation into the Relationship between Debt and Oil*. Washington, DC: Oil Change International.

Kretzschmar, G., A. Kirchner, and L. Sharifzyanova (2010). Resource Nationalism: Limits to Foreign Direct Investment. *Energy Journal 31*(2), 27–52.

Kugler, J. and R. Tammen (2012). *Performance of Nations*. Lanham: Rowman and Littlefield.

Kurtz, M. J. and S. M. Brooks (2011). Conditioning the 'resource curse': Globalization, human capital, and growth in oil-rich nations. *Comparative Political Studies 44*(6), 747–770.

Kurzman, C. (2004). *The Unthinkable Revolution in Iran*. Cambridge, MA: Harvard University Press.

Kyle Cohen, J. (2015). *Essays on the Effects of Political Institutions on Development Policies*. Ph.D. thesis, Columbia University.

Lederman, D. and W. Maloney (2008). In search of the missing resource curse. *Economia 9*, 1–57.

Lenczowski, G. (1949). *Russia and the West in Iran*. Ithaca, NY: Cornell University Press.

Leonard, A. (2008, September). Sarah Palin: The Hugo Chavez of Alaska. *Salon*.

Levi, M. (1981). The predatory theory of rule. *Politics & Society 10*(4), 431–465.

   (1989). *Of Rule And Revenue*. Berkeley, CA: University of California Press.

Li, Q. (2009). Democracy, autocracy, and expropriation of foreign direct investment. *Comparative Political Studies 42*(8), 1098–1127.

Liou, Y.-M. and P. Musgrave (2014). Refining the oil curse: Country-level evidence from exogenous variations in resource income. *Comparative Political Studies 47*(11), 1584–1610.

(2016). Oil, autocratic survival, and the gendered resource curse: When inefficient policy is politically expedient. *International Studies Quarterly 60*(3), 440–56.

Lipset, S. M. (1959). Some social requisites of democracy: Economic development and political legitimacy. *American Political Science Review 53*(1), 69–105.

Loewenstein, G. and D. A. Moore (2004). When ignorance is bliss: Information exchange and inefficiency in bargaining. *The Journal of Legal Studies 33*(1), 37–58.

Looney, R. (1982). *Economic Origins of the Iranian Revolution*. New York: Pergamon Press.

Lopez, L. (2012). Petronas: reconciling tensions between company and state. In D. G. Victor, D. Hults, and M. C. Thurber (Eds.), *Oil and Governance*, pp. 809–835. Cambridge: Cambridge University Press.

Luciani, G. (1990). Allocation vs. production states: A theoretical framework. In G. Luciani (Ed.), *The Arab State*, pp. 65–84. Berkeley, CA: University of California Press.

Magaloni, B. (2006). *Voting for Autocracy: Hegemonic Party Survival and its Demise in Mexico*. New York, NY: Cambridge University Press.

Mahdavi, P. (2012). Oil, monarchy, revolution, and theocracy: A study on the National Iranian Oil Company (NIOC). In D. G. Victor, D. Hults, and M. C. Thurber (Eds.), *Oil and Governance*, pp. 234–279. Cambridge: Cambridge University Press.

(2014). Why do leaders nationalize the oil industry? The politics of resource expropriation. *Energy Policy 75*(C), 228–243.

Mahdavy, H. (1970). The patterns and problems of economic development in rentier states: The case of Iran. In M. A. Cook (Ed.), *Studies in Economic History of the Middle East*. London: Oxford University Press.

Makki, H. (1950). *Kitabe Siah (The Black Book)*. Tehran: Elmi Press.

Manley, D. (2017). *Ninth Time Lucky: Is Zambia's Mining Tax the Best Approach to an Uncertain Future?* New York, NY: NRGI.

Manzano, O. and F. Monaldi (2009). The political economy of oil production in Latin America. *Economia 9*, 59–98.

Manzano, O. and R. Rigobon (2001). Resource curse or debt overhang? NBER Working Paper 8390.

Marcel, V. (2006). *Oil Titans: National Oil Companies in the Middle East*. Baltimore, MD: Brookings Institution Press.

(2016). *The Cost of an Emerging National Oil Company*. Energy, Environment and Resources. London: Chatham House.

Mars, P. (2001). Ethnic politics, mediation, and conflict resolution: The Guyana experience. *Journal of Peace Research 38*(3), 353–372.

Marshall, A. (1961 [1890]). *Principles of Economics* (8th ed.). New York: Macmillan.

Marshall, M. G., K. Jaggers, and T. R. Gurr (2011). *Polity IV Project: Dataset Users' Manual*. Arlington, VA: Polity IV Project.

Martz, J. D. (1987). *Politics and Petroleum in Ecuador*. New Brunswick, NJ: Transaction Books.

Marx, K. (1981 [1894]). *Capital*, Volume 3. London: Penguin Books.

Maurer, N. and G. Herrero (2013). YPF: The Argentine oil nationalization of 2012. Harvard Business School Case Study 9-713-029, 1–28.

Maxwell, P. (2015). Transparent and opaque pricing: The interesting case of lithium. *Resources Policy 45*, 92–97.

Mazaheri, N. (2016). *Oil Booms and Business Busts: Why Resource Wealth Hurts Entrepreneurs in the Developing World*. Oxford: Oxford University Press.

McDermott, R. (2008). *Presidential Leadership, Illness, and Decision Making*. Cambridge: Cambridge University Press.

McPherson, C. (2003). National oil companies: Evolution, issues, outlook. In J. M. Davis, A. Fedelino, and R. Ossowski (Eds.), *Fiscal Policy Formulation and Implementation in Oil-Producing Countries*. International Monetary Fund.

(2010). State Participation in the Natural Resource Sectors: Evolution, Issues and Outlook. In P. Daniel, M. Keen, and C. McPherson (Eds.), *The Taxation of Petroleum and Minerals: Principles, Problems, and Practice*, pp. 263–288. New York: Routledge.

Mead, W. J. (1994). Toward an optimal oil and gas leasing system. *Energy Journal 15*(4), 1–18.

Meade, J. E. (1955). *Trade and Welfare*. Oxford: Oxford University Press.

Mearsheimer, J. J. and S. M. Walt (2013). Leaving theory behind: Why simplistic hypothesis testing is bad for international relations. *European Journal of International Relations 19*(3), 427–457.

Menaldo, V. (2012). The Middle East and North Africa's Resilient Monarchs. *The Journal of Politics 74*(3), 707–722.

(2016). *From Institutions Curse to Resource Blessing*. New York: Cambridge University Press.

Meseguer, C. (2005). Policy learning, policy diffusion, and the making of a new order. *The ANNALS of the American Academy of Political and Social Science 598*(1), 67–82.

Mikdashi, Z. (1966). *A Financial Analysis of Middle Eastern Oil Concessions: 1901–65*. New York: Praeger Publishers.

(1972). *The Community of Oil Exporting Countries: A Study in Government Cooperation*. Ithaca, NY: Cornell University Press.

Mikesell, R. F. (1971). Foreign investment in the petroleum and mineral industries. *The International Executive 13*(4), 3–6.

Milkowski, S. (2008, January). Eni petroleum takes on Alaska project. *Fairbanks Daily News-Miner*.

Miller, M. K. (2012). Economic development, violent leader removal, and democratization. *American Journal of Political Science 56*(4), 1002–1020.

Minor, M. S. (1994). The Demise of Expropriation as an Instrument of LDC Policy, 1980–1992. *Journal of International Business Studies* (25), 273–287.

Mitchell, T. (2011). *Carbon Democracy: Political Power in the Age of Oil*. London: Verso Books.

Mommer, B. (2002). *Global Oil and the Nation State*. Oxford: Oxford University Press.

Moran, T. H. (1973). Transnational strategies of protection and defense by multinational corporations: Spreading the risk and raising the cost for nationalization in natural resources. *International Organization, 27*(2), 273–287.

Morrison, K. M. (2009). Oil, nontax revenue, and the redistributional foundations of regime stability. *International Organization 63*(1), 107–138.

   (2015). *Nontaxation and Representation*. New York: Cambridge University Press.

Mu'assasat al-Naqd al-Arabi al-Saudi, Saudi Arabian Monetary Agency (1960). Annual report.

Mufti, M. (1996). *Sovereign Creations: Pan-Arabism and Political Order in Syria and Iraq*. Ithaca, NY: Cornell University Press.

Nash, G. D. (1968). *United States Oil Policy, 1890–1964: Business and Government in Twentieth Century America*. Pittsburgh, PA: University of Pittsburgh Press.

Nolan, P. A. and M. C. Thurber (2010). On the state's choice of oil company: Risk management and the frontier of the petroleum industry. *PESD Working Paper 99*.

Noori, H. S.-H. (1965). *A Study on the Nationalization of the Oil Industry in Iran*. Ph.D. thesis, Colorado State College.

Nooruddin, I. (2008). The political economy of national debt burdens, 1970–2000. *International Interactions 34*(2), 156–185.

Nordhaus, W. D. (1975). The political business cycle. *Review of Economic Studies 42*(2), 169–190.

North, D. C. (1994). Economic performance through time. *American Economic Review 84*(3).

North, D. C. and B. R. Weingast (1989). Constitutions and commitment: The evolution of institutions governing public choice in seventeenth-century England. *The Journal of Economic History 49*(4), 803–832.

OECD (2015). *OECD Guidelines on Corporate Governance of State-Owned Enterprises*. Paris: Organization for Economic Cooperation and Development Publishing.

Olivetti, E. A., G. Ceder, G. G. Gaustad, and X. Fu (2017). Lithium-ion battery supply chain considerations: Analysis of potential bottlenecks in critical metals. *Joule 1*, 229–243.

Olson, M. (1993). Dictatorship, democracy, and development. *American Political Science Review 87*(3), 567–576.

   (2000). *Power and prosperity: Outgrowing communist and capitalist dictatorships*. New York: Basic Books.

O'Sullivan, M., I. Overland, and D. Sandalow (2017, June). The geopolitics of renewable energy. Columbia SIPA Center on Global Energy Policy Working Paper.

Pargeter, A. (2012). *Libya: The Rise and Fall of Qaddafi*. Cambridge: Cambridge University Press.

Parsa, M. (1989). *Social Origins of the Iranian Revolution*. New Brunswick, NJ: Rutgers University Press.

Philip, G. (1982). *Oil and Politics in Latin America*. Cambridge: Cambridge University Press.

(1999). The political constraints on economic policy in post-1982 Mexico: The case of Pemex. *Bulletin of Latin American Research 18*(1), 35–50.

Philip, K. (2002). The quest for rural enterprise support strategies that work. *Small Enterprise Development 13*(1), 13–25.

Pindyck, R. S. (1999). The long run evolution of energy prices. *Energy Journal 20*, 1–27.

Posner, R. A. (1975). The social costs of monopoly and regulation. *Journal of Political Economy 83*(4), 807–27.

Post, J. M. and R. S. Robins (1995). *When Illness Strikes the Leader: The Dilemma of the Captive King*. New Haven, CT: Yale University Press.

Pratt, J. A. (2013). *Exxon: Transforming Energy, 1973–2005*. Austin, TX: University of Texas Press.

PriceWaterhouseCoopers (2016). *Oil and Gas in Indonesia: Investment and Taxation Guide*. PwC Indonesia.

Prichard, W., A. Cobham, and A. Goodall (2014). The ICTD Government Revenue Dataset. ICTD Working Paper 19.

Prichard, W., P. Salardi, and P. Segal (2014). Taxation, non-tax revenue and democracy: New evidence using new cross-country data. ICTD Working Paper 23.

Przeworski, A. (2000). *Democracy and Development: Political Institutions and Well-Being in the World, 1950–1990*. New York, NY: Cambridge University Press.

Rai, V. and D. G. Victor (2012). Awakening Giant: Strategy and Performance of the Abu Dhabi National Oil Company (ADNOC). In D. G. Victor, D. Hults, and M. C. Thurber (Eds.), *Oil and Governance*, pp. 478–514. Cambridge: Cambridge University Press.

Ramsay, K. (2011). Revisiting the resource curse: Natural disasters, the price of oil, and democracy. *International Organization 65*(3), 507–529.

Razavi, H. and F. Vakil (1984). *The Political Environment of Economic Planning in Iran, 1971–1983: From Monarchy to Islamic Republic*. Boulder, CO: Westview Press.

Readhead, A. (2016). *Preventing Tax Base Erosion in Africa: A Regional Study of Transfer Pricing Challenges in the Mining Sector*. New York, NY: NRGI.

Readhead, A., D. Mulé, and A. Op de Beke (2018). *Examining the Crude Details: Government Audits of Oil and Gas Project Costs to Maximize Revenue Collection*. Oxford: Oxfam International.

Ricardo, D. (1976[1871]). *The Principles of Political Economy and Taxation* (3rd ed.). London: J.M. Dent and Sons.

Rizkallah, A. T. (2016). *Coffins and Castles: The Political Legacies of Civil War in Lebanon*. Ph.D. thesis, University of California Los Angeles.

Robinson, C. (1993). *Energy Policy: Errors, Illusions and Market Realities*. London: Institute for Economic Affairs.

Robinson, J. A., R. Torvik, and T. Verdier (2006). Political Foundations of the Resource Curse. *Journal of Development Economics 79*(2), 447–468.

Ross, M. L. (1999). The political economy of the resource curse. *World Politics 51*(2), 297–322.

(2001). Does oil hinder democracy? *World Politics 53*(3), 325–361.

(2004). Does taxation lead to representation? *British Journal of Political Science 34*(02), 229–249.

(2012). *The Oil Curse: How Petroleum Wealth Shapes the Development of Nations.* Princeton, NJ: Princeton University Press.

(2015). What Have We Learned about the Resource Curse? *Annual Review of Political Science 18*(1), 239–259.

Ross, M. L. and P. Mahdavi (2014). *Oil and Gas Data, 1932–2014.* Harvard Dataverse, v2.

Rubin, D. B. (1974). Estimating causal effects of treatments in randomized and nonrandomized studies. *Journal of Educational Psychology 6*, 688–701.

Sarbu, B. (2014). *Ownership and Control of Oil: Explaining Policy Choices across Producing Countries.* New York, NY: Routledge.

Sayne, A., A. Gillies, and C. Katsouris (2015). *Inside NNPC Oil Sales: A Case for Reform in Nigeria.* New York, NY: NRGI.

Schwartz, E. S. and A. B. Trolle (2010). Pricing expropriation risk in natural resource contracts. In W. Hogan and F. Sturzenegger (Eds.), *The Natural Resources Trap: Private Investment without Public Commitment,* Chapter 8, pp. 263–287. Cambridge, MA: MIT Press.

Selley, R. C. and S. A. Sonnenberg (2014). *Elements of Petroleum Geology* (3rd ed.). Cambridge, MA: Academic Press.

Shahri, N. N. (2010). The petroleum legal framework of Iran: History, trends and the way forward. *China and Eurasia Forum Quarterly 8*(1), 111–126.

Shawcross, W. (1988). *The Shah's Last Ride: The Fate of an Ally.* New York, NY: Simon and Schuster.

Simmons, J. (2016a). *The Politics of Technological Progress: Parties, Time Horizons and Long-Term Economic Development.* Cambridge: Cambridge University Press.

(2016b). Resource wealth and women's economic and political power in the U.S. states. *Comparative Political Studies 49*(1), 115–152.

Simons, G. (1993). *Libya: The Struggle for Survival.* London: Macmillan Press.

Singh, C. (1989). *Multinationals: The State and the Management of Economic nationalism.* Praeger Publishers.

Skocpol, T. (1979). *States and Social Revolutions: A Comparative Analysis of France, Russia and China.* Cambridge: Cambridge University Press.

(1982). Rentier state and Shi'a Islam in the Iranian revolution. *Theory and Society 11*(3), 265–283.

Slaski, A. (2019). *Bargaining Power and State Capacity: Evidence from Multinational Investment in the Oil Sector.* Princeton University unpublished manuscript.

Smith, A. (1776). *An Inquiry into the Nature and Causes of the Wealth of Nations.* Oxford: Clarendon Press.

Smith, B. (2004). Oil wealth and regime survival in the developing world, 1960–1999. *American Journal of Political Science 48*(2), 232–246.

(2005). Life of the party: The origins of regime breakdown and persistence under single-party rule. *World Politics 57*(3), 421–451.

(2006). The wrong kind of crisis: Why oil booms and busts rarely lead to authoritarian breakdown. *Studies in Comparative International Development 40*(4), 55–76.

(2007). *Hard Times in the Land of Plenty: Oil Politics in Iran and Indonesia.* Ithaca, NY: Cornell University Press.

Soares de Oliveira, R. (2007). *Oil and Politics in the Gulf of Guinea.* London: Hurst and Company.

Solberg, C. E. (1979). *Oil and Nationalism in Argentina: A History.* Stanford, CA: Stanford University Press.

Stevens, P. (2003). National oil companies: Good or bad? World Bank Working Paper.

(2007). Investing in oil in the Middle East and North Africa: Institutions, incentives and the national oil companies. Technical report.

(2008). Resource nationalism and the role of national oil companies in the Middle East. *Journal of World Energy Law and Business 1*(1), 5–30.

(2012). Assessing NOC performance and the role of depletion policy. In D. G. Victor, D. Hults, and M. C. Thurber (Eds.), *Oil and Governance,* pp. 940–45. Cambridge: Cambridge University Press.

(2018). The role of oil and gas in the economic development of the global economy. In *Extractive Industries: The Management of Resources as a Driver of Sustainable Development,* WIDER Studies in Development Economics, Chapter 4, pp. 71–89. Oxford: Oxford University Press.

Stigler, G. J. (1971). The theory of economic regulation. *The Bell Journal of Economics and Management Science,* 3–21.

Stojanovski, O. (2012). Handcuffed: An assessment of PEMEX's performance and strategy. In D. G. Victor, D. Hults, and M. C. Thurber (Eds.), *Oil and Governance,* pp. 280–333. Cambridge: Cambridge University Press.

Stokes, S. C. (2005). Perverse accountability: A formal model of machine politics with evidence from Argentina. *American Political Science Review 99*(03), 315–325.

Stokes, S. C., T. Dunning, M. Nazareno, and V. Brusco (2013). *Brokers, Voters, and Clientelism: The Puzzle of Distributive Politics.* Cambridge: Cambridge University Press.

Stroebel, J. and A. van Benthem (2013). Resource extraction contracts under threat of expropriation: Theory and evidence. *Review of Economics and Statistics 95*(5), 1622–1639.

Sulaimani, M. O. (2018). Saudi Aramco's IPO: An interaction between a national oil company and international stock markets. Master's thesis, The Pennsylvania State University.

Suleiman, A. (2008). *The Petroleum Experience of Abu Dhabi.* Abu Dhabi: ECSSR Publishing.

Svolik, M. (2009). Power-sharing and leadership dynamics in authoritarian regimes. *American Journal of Political Science 53,* 477–494.

(2012). *The Politics of Authoritarian Rule.* New York, NY: Cambridge University Press.

Takin, M. (2009). Iran's oil century: Review of oil and gas operations. *Middle East Economic Review 52*(1).

Thompson, L. and G. Loewenstein (1992). Egocentric interpretations of fairness and interpersonal conflict. *Organizational Behavior and Human Decision Processes 51*(2), 176–197.

Thurber, M. C., I. M. Emelife, and P. R. P. Heller (2012). NNPC and Nigeria's Oil Patronage Ecosystem. In D. G. Victor, D. Hults, and M. C. Thurber (Eds.), *Oil and Governance*, pp. 701–752. Cambridge: Cambridge University Press.

Tilly, C. (1975). *The Formation of National States in Europe*. Princeton, NJ: Princeton University Press.

Tocqueville, A. d. (1955). *The Old Regime and the Revolution, Volume II: Notes on the French Revolution and Napoleon*. New York, NY: Doubleday.

Tomz, M. (2007). *Reputation and International Cooperation: Sovereign Debt across Three Centuries*. Princeton, NJ: Princeton University Press.

Tordo, S., B. Tracy, and N. Arfaa (2011). National oil companies and value creation. World Bank Working Paper 218.

Treisman, D. (2007). Putin's silovarchs. *Orbis 51*(1), 141–153.

   (2015). Income, democracy, and leader turnover. *American Journal of Political Science 59*(4), 927–942.

Tripp, C. (2000). *A History of Iraq*. Cambridge: Cambridge University Press.

Tsebelis, G. (2002). *Veto Players: How Political Institutions Work*. Princeton, NJ: Princeton University Press.

Tsui, K. K. (2011). More oil, less democracy: Evidence from worldwide crude oil discoveries. *The Economic Journal 121*(551), 89–115.

Ulfelder, J. (2007). Natural-Resource Wealth and the Survival of Autocracy. *Comparative Political Studies 40*(8), 995–1018.

United States Geological Survey (1932). *Minerals Yearbook, Area Reports: International*. Multiple volumes.

van der Linde, C. (2000). *The State and the International Oil Market: Competition and the Changing Ownership of Crude Oil Assets*. New York, NY: Springer.

Vandewalle, D. (1995). *Qadhafi's Libya, 1969–1994*. New York, NY: St. Martin's Press.

   (1998). *Libya since Independence: Oil and State-Building*. Ithaca, NY: Cornell University Press.

Vernon, R. (1971). *Sovereignty at Bay: The Spread of U.S. Enterprises*. New York, NY: Basic Publishing.

Victor, D. G. (2009). The politics of fossil-fuel subsidies. Global subsidies initiative (GSI) of the International Institute for Sustainable Development (IISD), Available at SSRN 1520984.

   (2013). National oil companies and the future of the oil industry. *Annual Review of Resource Economics 5*, 445–462.

Victor, D. G., D. Hults, and M. C. Thurber (eds.) (2012). *Oil and Governance: State-owned Enterprises and the World Energy Supply*. New York, NY: Cambridge University Press.

Victor, N. M. (2007). On measuring the performance of national oil companies (NOCs). Working Paper 64, Program on Energy and Sustainable Development, Stanford University.

Vining, A. R. and D. L. Weimar (1990). Government supply and government production failure: A framework based on contestability. *Journal of Public Policy 10*(1), 1–22.

Vives, X. (2000). Corporate governance: Does it matter? In X. Vives (Ed.), *Corporate governance: Theoretical and Empirical Perspectives*, pp. 1–22. Cambridge: Cambridge University Press.

Vivoda, V. (2009). Resource nationalism, bargaining and international oil companies: Challenges and change in the new millennium. *New Political Economy 14*(4), 517–534.

Vreeland, J. R. (2007). *The International Monetary Fund: Politics of Conditional Lending*. New York, NY: Routledge.

Vreeland, J. R., B. P. Rosendorff, and J. R. Hollyer (2017). Information, democracy, and autocracy: Transparency and political (in)stability. Cambridge: Cambridge University Press.

Waddams, F. C. (1980). *The Libyan Oil Industry*. Baltimore, MD: Johns Hopkins University.

Warshaw, C. (2012). The political economy of expropriation and privatization of national oil companies. In D. G. Victor, D. Hults, and M. C. Thurber (Eds.), *Oil and Governance*, pp. 35–61. Cambridge: Cambridge University Press.

Weiner, R. J. and R. W. Click (2010). Resource nationalism meets the market: Political risk and the value of petroleum reserves. *Journal of International Business Studies, 41*(5), 783–803.

Weinthal, E. and P. Jones Luong (2006). Combating the resource curse: An alternative solution to managing mineral wealth. *Perspectives on Politics 4*(1), 35–53.

Weiss, R. E. (2005). *Modeling Longitudinal Data*. New York, NY: Springer.

(2012). *Bayesian Methods for Modeling Data*. Unpublished manuscript.

Wenar, L. (2007). Property rights and the resource curse. *Philosophy and Public Affairs 36*(1), 2–32.

(2015). *Blood Oil: Tyrants, Violence, and the Rules that Run the World*. Oxford: Oxford University Press.

Williamson, J. (1990). What Washington means by policy reform. In J. Williamson (Ed.), *Latin American Adjustment: How Much Has Happened?* Peterson Institute for International Economics.

Williamson, O. E. (1979). Transaction-cost economics: The governance of contractual relations. *Journal of Law and Economics 22*(2), 233–261.

Wilson, M. C. and J. Wright (2017). Autocratic legislatures and expropriation. *British Journal of Political Science 47*(1), 1–17.

Wolf, C. (2009). Does ownership matter? The performance and efficiency of state oil vs. private oil (1987–2006). *Energy Policy 37*(7), 2642–2652.

World Bank (2011). *Overview of State Ownership in the Global Minerals Industry*. Extractive Industries for Development Series no. 20. Washington, DC: The World Bank Group – Oil, Gas, and Mining Unit.

World Economic Forum (2018). *Transformation of the Global Energy System*. Global Future Council on Energy 2016–2018. Geneva, Switzerland: World Economic Forum.

Wortley, B. A. (1956). Observations on the public and private international law relating to expropriation. *The American Journal of Comparative Law*, 577–594.

Wright, J., E. Frantz, and B. Geddes (2015). Oil and autocratic regime survival. *British Journal of Political Science 45*(2), 287–306.

Wright, M. L. J. (2002). Reputations and sovereign debt. Stanford, CA: Stanford University manuscript.

Yergin, D. (1991). *The Prize*. New York, NY: Simon and Schuster.

Zahlan, R. S. (1998). *The Making of the Modern Gulf States: Bahrain, Kuwait, Qatar, the United Arab Emirates, and Oman*. Reading: Garnet Publishing Limited.

Zonis, M. (1991). *Majestic Failure: The Fall of the Shah*. Chicago, IL: University Of Chicago Press.

Index

Abdul Aziz, King of Saudi Arabia
  (ibn-Saud), 106, 126–129, 132
Abrahamian, Ervand, 208
Abu Dhabi National Oil Company
  (ADNOC), 67, 77, 92
  see also United Arab Emirates
Afghanistan, 97, 132, 191
al-Bakr, Ahmed Hassan, 34, 85–89
al-Nahyan dynastic monarchy, 77
al-Rahman 'Arif, 'Abd, 86–89
al-Salim 'Arif, 'Abd, 86–89
Alam, Asadollah, 186n, 189n, 190, 191
Alaska, 221–223
Albania, 33, 115n
Alberta, 96, 223n
Algeria
  commercialization of SOEs in, 8
  information diffusion and
    nationalization in, 22
  joint ventures in, 107
  oil nationalization (1969) in, 33, 177
  resource curse in, 43
Algiers Agreement (1975), 88
aluminum, 5, 97
American Revolution, 41
Amouzegar, Jahangir, 185
Amouzegar, Jamshid, 193
Anglo Platinum, 5
Anglo-Iranian Oil Company (AIOC)
  Agreement (1933) with Iran and, 129
  Iranian nationalization (1951) of, 106,
    126–132, 144, 213
  Supplemental Agreement (1949) with
    Iran and, 56, 130, 131
  see also British Petroleum (BP); Iran;
    Great Britain
Angola
  civil war in, 61
  fiscal autonomy of SOEs in, 25,
    66, 146n
  Law 13/78 of, 61
  oil nationalization (1978) in, 33, 61, 177

People's Movement for the Liberation of
    Angola (MPLA) party, 61
  regime stability in, 42
  resource curse in, 43
  use of SOE revenues for regime
    strengthening in, 39
Arab oil embargo (1973), 50, 121, 178,
    184, 196, 201, 211, 217
Arabian American Oil Company
    (Aramco), 59, 126–129, 213
  see also Saudi Arabia; Saudi Aramco
Archigos measure of leader exit, 153–155,
    158, 161
Argentina
  expropriation of Repsol in, 33, 76,
    108–109, 124n, 217, 219
  formation of YPF (1911) in, 33, 109
  nationalization backsliding in, 76
  shale oil in, 76
Aristotle, 212
Austria, 33
authoritarianism
  breakdown of, 36, 153, 168, 172
  electoral institutions within, 215
  endurance of, 31, 41, 44, 141–143
  increased likelihood of nationalization
    and, 48, 111–113
  lack of institutional checks and, 46n, 48
  puzzling cases of, 30
  varieties of, 115, 124, 137, 138
  weak fiscal regimes and, 44
  see also dictatorships; elite co-optation;
    leader survival; regime type;
    revolution
Azerbaijan, 33, 98, 191
Azienda Generale Italiana Petroli
    (AGIP), 30
  see also Ente Nazionale Idrocarburi
    (ENI)

back-in participation, 218, 219
Bahrain, 33, 114

244

Baker Hughes, 144
bargain theory, 21, 47, 60
  bargaining constraints and, 51
Bashiriyeh, Hossein, 206
batteries, 3, 5, 224
bauxite, 47
Bayesian statistics
  elicited priors for, 106, 126, 134
  frequentist results versus, 116–117,
    125, 126, 135
  hierarchical logistic regression results,
    117–123, 161–163
  longitudinal discrete outcomes and,
    106, 157
  Markov Chain Monte Carlo estimation
    and, 116, 157
  mixed-method designs using, 35
  small sample sizes and, 32
Bayesian updating, 58, 59
Belize, 31, 132
bin-Musaid, Faisal, 167
Bolivia, 13, 97, 114
  nationalization of Standard Oil (1936)
    in, 33, 92, 109
  nationalization of YPFB (2007) in,
    33, 124n
  privatization of YPFB (1996) in, 8
Botswana, 14, 115n, 151
Bouterse, Desi, 165
Brazil
  joint ventures in, 107
  oil nationalization (1938) in, 13, 33,
    92, 109
  partial privatization of Petrobras in, 8
  resource blessing in, 42, 43
  SOE governance in, 97
British National Archives, 82n, 182, 187n
British Petroleum (BP), 144
  Archive, 36, 82n, 177n, 178, 182,
    195–197, 214
  Emirati nationalization of, 77
  expectations of Iranian nationalization
    by, 198
  Iranian consortium led by, 34, 35, 82,
    86, 90, 178, 180, 182, 184
  Iranian nationalization (1973) of, 34,
    36, 170, 179, 209, 214
  Iranian negotiations (1971) with, 187
  Iraqi consortium and, 86
  joint partnerships in Abu Dhabi with, 67
  joint partnerships in Canada with, 96
  Libyan nationalization of, 1n
  production in Alaska by, 221
  projections of revenue from Iranian oil
    by, 179, 183, 195–202, 209, 210, 214

revenues from Iranian oil of, 83, 202
revenues from Iraqi oil of, 89
reversal of 1973 Iranian nationalization
  by, 202–204, 209, 214
settlement with the Libyan government
  (1974) by, 180
Seven Sisters and, 22n
Statistical Review of Energy, 31n, 114n
supply inelasticity and, 27
see also Anglo-Iranian Oil Company
  (AIOC); Iran

Côte d'Ivoire, 132, 151
Cairn (India), 144
Cairn Energy (UK), 121n
Cameroon, 33, 98, 124n
Canada
  institutional pathways in, 96
  oil nationalization (1976) in, 33, 113
  oil privatization in, 95, 113
  resource blessing in, 42, 43
Cardenas, Lázaro, 5, 95
Chávez, Hugo, 2–4, 12, 168
Chad, 7n, 65, 148
Chemetall, 5
Chevron, 5, 27, 76, 218
Chile
  copper nationalization (1971) in, 62
  copper production in, 23, 97
  lithium production in, 5, 23, 97, 224
  oil nationalization (1950) in, 13, 33
  state capacity of, 23
  state capture of revenues in, 151
China
  iron production of, 5, 97
  lithium reserves of, 224
China National Offshore Oil Corporation
  (CNOOC), 144
Chinese National Petroleum Company
  (CNPC), 98
clean energy transition, 3, 37, 223, 224
  see also cobalt; lithium; palladium; wind
    power; solar power
clientelism, 48, 57, 78, 142, 220
coal, 5, 19, 31, 35, 40, 61, 97
cobalt, 35, 97, 224
  consequences of potential
    nationalization of, 3
  contract negotiations over, 56
  geographic concentration of, 3, 224
  global demand for, 3, 224
  multinational corporation production of,
    3, 37, 56
Cold War, 12
Colombia, 13, 33

colonialism
  see Great Britain; postcolonialism
Compagnie Française des Pétroles (CFP),
    52
  see also Total (French oil company)
Congo, Democratic Republic of
  cobalt mining in, 56, 97
  oil nationalization (2010) in, 33, 124n
  potential nationalization of cobalt in, 3
ConocoPhillips, 27, 98n, 221
Conselho Nacional do Petróleo (CNP),
    109
  see also Petrobras
contract theory, 29, 49–50
  see also bargain theory; natural resources
    trap; transaction cost theory; rents
copper, 31
  complex extraction of, 11, 62
  information asymmetries in, 23, 64
  multinational corporation production
    of, 5
  nationalization of, 47, 217
  resource nationalism and, 108
  varieties of nationalization of, 10, 35, 97
Corporación Estatal Petrolera Ecuatoriana
    (CEPE), 95, 101, 125
  see also Petroecuador
Corporación Nacional del Cobre de Chile
    (Codelco), 23, 62, 75, 217
corporate income tax
  see taxation
Cox proportional hazards model, 157n,
    162–165
Cuba, 33
Cyprus, 132

Dana Energy, 101
Davies, James, 206
de la Madrid, Miguel, 78
deep-shaft mining, 11, 19, 51, 61, 72
  see also copper; extractive resource
    exploration/production
democracy
  factionalism in, 220
  nationalization probabilities across
    varieties of, 109–110, 112–114
  natural resource effects on, 14, 41–43
  pressures for transition to, 142n, 142,
    192
  statistical results for nationalization and
    transition to, 168
  see also leader survival; regime survival;
    regime type
Denmark, 33

depletion rate
  see production elasticity
dictatorships
  balance of power sharing with elites in,
    215
  economic growth and endurance in,
    142n
  elites in democracies compared to, 110
  instability and time horizons of, 19
  institutions as information providers in,
    48
  land expropriation by, 15
  nationalization and the rise and fall of,
    30, 35
  nationalization and time horizons in, 105
  nationalization probabilities across
    varieties of, 48, 109–110, 112–115,
    124, 138
  natural resource wealth and endurance
    of, 41
  puzzling cases of, 30
difference-in-difference model
  design, 196–199
  results from, 200–201, 211
discoveries
  see extractive resource
    exploration/production; oil
    exploration
distributional conflict, 45, 143
distributive institutions, 2
dividends, 56, 65
dos Santos, José Eduardo, 29

Ecuador
  military dictatorship in, 124–125
  NOC formation versus nationalization
    in, 33, 95, 101
  oil nationalization probabilities of, 121
Egypt, 33
electric cars, 3
Elf-Aquitaine, 52, 94
  see also Total (French oil company)
elite co-optation, 57, 142, 153
  see also authoritarianism; clientelism;
    dictatorships; resource curse
Empresa Nacional del Petroleo (ENAP),
    151
endogeneity of survival
  leader beliefs and, 17, 57
  to nationalization decision-making, 4, 8,
    14, 20, 30, 46, 57, 215
  resource revenues and, 20, 31
  see also leader survival; nationalization
Energie Beheer Nederland (EBN), 97–98
energy storage, 5, 37, 224

Ente Nazionale Idrocarburi (ENI), 218, 219, 222n
Entreprise Tunisienne d'Activités Pétrolières (ETAP), 97
Equatorial Guinea, 33
Equinor, 52, 59, 75, 144, 217
exploration
see extractive resource exploration/production; oil exploration
expropriation
see nationalization
Extractive Industries Transparency Initiative (EITI), 22n
extractive resource exploration/production
complexity of, 19, 61, 62, 72
consequences of failure to invest in, 10, 76
cost recovery and investment in, 73
costs of, 11
different stages of, 11, 27, 39, 51, 54, 72, 73, 114, 165, 170
human capital and, 61
initial contracts and, 49, 53, 144
operating firms' leverage during, 47, 54
operational SOEs and, 6, 97
risks of, 19, 47
see also geological complexity; oil exploration; oil production
ExxonMobil, 7, 15, 27, 30, 67, 144, 186, 220–222

Faisal, King of Saudi Arabia, 167
Federal Trade Commission, 129
Fernández de Kirchner, Cristina, 218
fiscal pressure
in Iran, 192–195
information asymmetry and, 64–66
leader survival and perceptions of, 8, 51, 190, 194
oil busts and, 23, 52
privatization as a result of, 10
production elasticity and, 79
rapid modernization and, 52, 84, 190, 192, 194
technical inefficiencies of extraction and, 10
fiscal regimes, 16, 17, 38, 44, 46, 53
fiscal strength
counterfactual estimates and analysis of, 195–202
definition of, 16
effects of nationalization on, 23–29, 63–73, 179–182
effects on leader survival of, 73–74

fiscal regimes compared with, 16, 102
hypothetical levels of, 72–73
measures of, 148–151
statistical results for leader survival and, 168, 176
statistical results for nationalization and, 151–153, 158–161
theoretical expectations of, 80
see also oil revenue; rents
FMC Lithium, 5
Foreign and Commonwealth Office (FCO), 82n, 182
foreign direct investment (FDI)
expropriation of, 15, 45–46
loss of as a result of nationalization, 9, 47, 55
see also nationalization
foreign exchange reserves, 2, 16
Foreign Relations of the United States (FRUS), 1, 182
foreign-imposed regime change, 34, 109, 132n, 153
France, 33, 52, 93, 95
FreeportMcMoRan, 3

Gabon, 33
Gazprom, 7, 66n
Geddes-Wright-Franz Autocratic Regime Data, 137, 153–154
gender equity, 40
geological complexity, 61–63
see also extractive resource exploration/production; human capital
Ghana, 33, 97, 132, 159, 218
Ghana National Petroleum Corporation (GNPC), 98, 132
Glencore, 3, 38, 56, 64, 224
gold, 97
Granger, David, 220
Great Britain
end of protectorate over Kuwait of, 119n
involvement in overthrow of Mossadegh (1954) by, 132
involvement with AIOC in Iran by, 130
Middle East colonialism and, 12
retaliation against Iranian nationalization by, 132n, 180
revenue sharing between Iran and, 129–131
withdrawal of armed forces from the Persian Gulf by, 190
see also United Kingdom
Greater Nile Operating Company, 121
Gulf of Mexico, 147
Gulf Oil, 22n, 61n, 101

Guyana
  A Partnership for National Unity
    (APNU) of, 221
  People's National Congress (PNC) of,
    220, 221n, 221
  petroleum discoveries in, 132, 220
  political system of, 221
  private operation of oil in, 37, 220–221

Hakim, Ayatollah Seyed Mohsen, 191
Halliburton, 144
Harris, Kevan, 207
Hassan II, King of Morocco, 119
Holland Sea Search, 121n
Hughes, Llewelyn, 52
human capital
  domestic fostering of, 62
  emigration of, 62
  extractive resource operations and, 19,
    61, 189, 222
  lack of, 20, 62
  see also geological complexity
Hussein, Saddam, 12, 34, 85, 88, 89, 216
hydrogen fuel cells, 5

Idris al-Sanusi, King of Libya, 2, 17, 30,
  123, 153
Impala, 5
Imperial Oil Development Corporation, 52
independent oil contractors, 83, 144, 184
  see also international oil companies
    (IOCs)
India, 33, 97
Indonesia, 6, 33, 43, 85, 92
information asymmetry
  between BP and the Iranian
    government, 36, 185, 203n, 209
  in the precious metals sector, 224
  leader perceptions of, 21, 78, 108
  overview of, 25–26, 63–67
  between government and SOE, 25, 66,
    67, 77, 146n
  as reduced by operational SOEs, 39, 63,
    65, 80, 146, 182
  regarding production costs, 54–55
  regarding production levels, 25, 64
  regarding profit-sharing, 21, 63, 108
  because of weak institutional capacity,
    55, 64
  see also revenue-sharing agreements; oil
    revenue; rents
information diffusion
  absence of, 60
  archival analysis of nationalization and,
    180–182, 186–188

case-comparison analysis of
  nationalization and, 126–132
culmination of, 61
domino effects and, 21–22
effects on nationalization, overview of,
  20–23
international competitors and, 58
international media and, 59
misreported profit-sharing and, 58
operationalization of, 23, 60, 61
opportunism and, 215, 216
proxies for, 105, 111, 114
renegotiation as a result of, 39, 54
as a spark for nationalization, 58–63
statistical results for nationalization and,
  117–119
survival probability updating and, 20,
  58, 131
theoretical expectations for
  nationalization and, 60, 78–79, 111
Initial Public Offering (IPO), 8, 52, 95n
  see also privatization
institutional quality, 14, 16, 48, 53, 167n
  see also relative political capacity
institutions curse theory, 16, 43
international arbitration, 76, 180, 218
International Monetary Fund (IMF), 53,
  149
international oil companies (IOCs)
  conflict and flight of, 61
  definition of, 4n
  information asymmetries and, 63–67,
    105, 185
  long-term gains of, 8, 58, 71–73, 75,
    127
  OPEC, information diffusion, and, 111
  operational control by, 97–98, 100
  operational efficiency of, 71
  participatory contracts with, 92, 100,
    101n
  partnerships between NOCs and, 71
  portfolio diversification by, 49
  resource nationalism and, 107–109
  social efficiency of, 71
  taxation of, 29, 50, 97, 98, 144–145,
    222
  see also multinational corporations
    (MNCs); taxation
Iran
  agricultural expenditures in, 206 81, 89
  Baluchestan province of, 190
  case selection of, 183, 184
  Central Bank of, 192n, 193
  clerical discontent in, 191, 194, 205

conflict over oil liftings in, 83–84,
  202–203
election rigging in, 191
energy infrastructure of, 207
explanations for revolution in, 84, 204,
  208
Fedayan-e Islam, 130, 194
Fifth Five Year Plan of, 83, 84, 194,
  204n, 204, 206n, 206
Fourth Five Year Plan of, 83, 195
Great Civilization, 83, 189, 192, 195,
  207, 208
income inequality in, 207
information diffusion of Saudi Arabian
  1950 Agreement to, 131
Islamic Revolution (1979) of, 83, 84,
  202–208, 214
Islamic theocracy in, 154, 183
as the "island of stability," 34, 81, 89
Mardom Party of, 191
Mojahedin in, 192, 194
National Front Party of, 130, 132
oil nationalization (1951) in, 33, 34, 86,
  106, 129–132, 204
oil nationalization (1973–74) in, 33,
  82–83, 184–195
oil nationalization reversal (1976) in,
  83–85, 202–204
Petroleum Act (1974) of, 82, 184
Petroleum Act (1987) of, 101
political media reporting in, 192
private ownership of zinc in, 97
problems with marketing oil in, 83, 84,
  203n, 203, 204
protests in, 207
regime instability in, 43
relative deprivation explanations for
  discontent in, 207
revenue-sharing in, 131
SAVAK apparatus in, 192, 205
Social Insurance Organization of, 207
socioeconomic discontent in, 206–209
Tehran Agreement (1971) between
  BP-led Consortium and, 187
time horizons and nationalization (1951)
  in, 128
Treasury of, 209, 214
varieties of nationalization in, 81, 97
welfare policies of, 206–208
White Revolution, 82, 184, 193, 202,
  206, 207
see also Anglo-Iranian Oil Company
  (AIOC); British Petroleum (BP);
  Mossadegh, Mohammad; Pahlavi,
  Mohammad Reza, Shah of Iran

Iraq
  Ba'athist consolidation (1968) of, 34,
    81, 85–89
  Ba'athist opposition to the Shah of Iran,
    190, 191
  Free Officers coup (1958) in, 85
  invasion of Kuwait by, 12, 216
  Kurdistan Democratic Party (KDP) in,
    88
  Law no. 80 (1961) of, 86
  National Guard of, 88
  oil nationalization (1972) in, 33, 35, 87,
    88
  oil revenues and political instability in,
    85, 86, 88
  patronage networks in, 88
  Ramadan Revolution (1963) of, 85
  varieties of nationalization in, 81
Iraq Petroleum Company (IPC), 35,
  86–88
iron, 5, 62n, 97, 108
Israel, 27, 69, 132, 178
Italy, 30, 33, 93, 218, 222n

Jamieson, J. Kenneth, 186
Japan, 52, 203
Japanese National Oil Company (JNOC),
  52
Jarrin Ampudia, Cpt. Gustavo, 125
Jones Luong, Pauline, 14, 44, 47
Jordan, 33

Kabila, Joseph, 3, 56, 224
Kani, Alinaghi, 191
Karl, Terry Lynn, 41
Katanga Mining, 224
Kazakhstan, 33
Kenya, 115n, 132, 218
Khatami, Mohammad, 154
Khomeini, Ayatollah Ruhollah, 191, 208
Kobrin, Stephen, 13, 109
Krugman, Paul, 212
Kurdistan
  see Iran; Iraq
Kuwait, 33, 119n, 148, 216
Kuwait Petroleum Corporation (KPC),
  148

land expropriation, 15, 48
land titling, 15, 18, 212
lead mining, 47
leader survival
  case-comparison analysis of
    nationalization and, 81–89, 126–132
  fiscal pressures and, 8, 51, 190, 194

leader survival (cont.)
  income inequality and, 142
  increased spending and, 141–143
  leader perceptions of, 8, 15, 20, 38, 39,
    46, 56, 57, 77, 79
  measures of, 153–155
  nationalization reversal and, 204,
    208, 209
  opportunism and, 48, 77, 78, 189,
    215–217
  puzzling cases of, 17, 30, 31, 35, 81
  resource revenues and, 41, 42, 143
  statistical results for nationalization and,
    161–167
  updated probabilities of, 18, 20, 60,
    63, 131
  see also endogeneity of survival;
    nationalization; operational
    nationalization theory; regime survival
leapfrogging effect in oil negotiations, 21,
  186, 188, 208
Lebanon
  consociationalism in, 220
  petroleum discoveries in, 132, 218
  Petroleum Resources Laws of, 219
  potential nationalization in, 37, 218–220
Liberia, 115n
Libya
  control over oil liftings in, 203n
  dispute over posted prices in, 145
  first wave of oil expropriations (1971) in,
    22, 203n
  militarization of, 30
  military republicanism (jamahiriya) in,
    2, 30, 123
  oil nationalization (1973) in, 1, 33, 123,
    145, 203n
  oil partnerships with foreign firms in, 30
  Petroleum Law (1965) of, 2, 30n
  revolution (1969) of, 1, 153
  Revolutionary Command Council
    (RCC) of, 1, 2
  settlment with BP and, 180
Libyan National Oil Company (Linoco), 1,
  30, 203n
lithium
  geographic concentration of, 224
  information asymmetries in production
    of, 23
  lack of nationalization of, 10
  market concentration of, 50
  multinational corporation production of,
    5, 35, 37, 97
  role in energy storage of, 5, 224

Mahdavy, Hussein, 41
Makki, Hossein, 130
Malaysia, 33, 42, 65, 97, 111
manganese, 224
Meade, James, 145
mediation analysis, 167, 174–176
Mexico
  as a case of early oil nationalization, 92,
    96, 98, 103
  energy reforms (2015) of, 77
  international retaliation against
    nationalization in, 109, 114
  as a nonmember of OPEC, 111
  oil nationalization (1938) in, 5, 33, 95
  Partido Revolucionario Institucional
    (PRI) party of, 77, 143, 216
  regime instability in, 43, 143
  regime stability (pre-2000) in, 78, 85,
    110, 143
  resource blessing in, 43
  state-as-appropriator model of
    governance in, 75, 78
military dictatorship, 85, 114, 124, 138
Minerals Marketing Corporation of
  Zimbabwe (MMCZ), 62n
Mobil
  see ExxonMobil
Mohammad bin Salman, Crown Prince of
  Saudi Arabia, 8
Mohammad VI, King of Morocco, 119
Morocco, 97, 119
Mossadegh, Mohammad
  British-American coup (1953) of, 86,
    132n
  effect on the Shah's time horizons of,
    127, 132
  nationalization of AIOC and, 106, 213
  passage of nationalization bill of, 130
  post-coup repercussions of, 191, 204
  rise of pro-nationalization campaign of,
    56, 106, 130
  time horizons of National Front Party
    and, 132
Mozambique, 115n
Mugabe, Robert, 153
Mulroney, Brian, 113
multinational corporations (MNCs)
  anticipation of expropriation by, 49
  control of minerals markets by, 5
  control of petroleum markets by, 22
  control over resource revenues by, 4, 24,
    38, 57, 89, 212, 219
  front-loading of resource profits by, 49
  information asymmetries compared to
    SOEs, 25, 66

information asymmetries in agreements
with, 23, 75, 224
information asymmetries in production
costs with, 25
long-run efficiency of, 73, 80, 212, 225
overview of operational efficiency
compared with SOEs, 27–28
participatory contracts with, 32n, 62,
220
portfolio diversification by, 49
postnationalization negotiations with,
50, 76
prenationalization operational control
by, 39, 49, 86
production of cobalt by, 3
production-sharing contracts with, 6,
100, 101n
quasi-rent expropriation of, 10n, 28
retaliation to nationalization by, 50
tax evasion by, 56, 64, 65
taxation of, 29, 50, 97, 98, 144, 222
withholding of technology by, 9n
see also international oil companies
(IOCs); taxation
Myanmar, 75

Namibia, 97, 115n
Nasser, Gamal Abdel, 12, 86, 88
National Iranian Oil Company (NIOC),
82–85, 98, 101, 184–195, 199–204
national oil companies (NOCs)
autonomy of (state-within-a-state), 25,
66, 77
endurance of, 32
establishment of with or without
expropriation, 91–92
global importance of, 7–9
in advanced economies, 52
instruments of control, 48
internationalization of, 144
leader survival rates before and after
establishment of, 154–156, 161–168
as a measure of oil nationalization,
31–32, 91–96
monitoring/oversight capacities of,
65–67
noncommercial activities of, 49, 96,
148n
nonoperational to operational reform of,
184–186
nonoperational-nonregulatory type of,
73n, 97–98
nonoperational-regulatory type of, 98
operational inefficiencies of, 27–28,
69–73

operational versus nonoperational, cases
of, 97–98
operational versus nonoperational,
definition of, 92–97
production elasticity and, 68–69
reserves-to-production conversion
inefficiency of, 71
revenues before and after establishment
of, 151–153, 158–161
taxation of, 65, 107, 144–149, 151
technical capacity-building of, 218–219
varieties of, 96–99
see also nationalization; state-owned
enterprises (SOEs); taxation
nationalization
as an alternative to taxation, 54–55
in advanced economies, 52, 221–223
asset seizure and, 28, 50, 54, 75, 107
bargain theory and, 21, 47, 51, 60
by first-movers, 112
case-comparison analysis for
determinants of, 126–132
coding of, 31–32
costs, overview of, 9–10, 109–110
counterfactual results for fiscal strength
and, 195–202
de jure versus de facto, 5–7, 100–102
definition of, 4–5, 91
determinants, overview of, 9–13,
107–110
elite backlash to, 39, 48, 112–113
endogeneity of survival and, 4, 8, 14, 20,
30, 46, 57, 215
failed attempts of, 76, 217–218,
221–223
fiscal strength and varieties of, 23–29,
144–147
indirect expropriation and, 218
information asymmetry and, 63–67
information diffusion and, 20–23, 58–63
institutions curse theory and, 16
international retaliation against, 9–10,
13, 55, 109, 180–181
leadership survival and, overview of,
29–31, 73–74
left-leaning ideologies and, 13, 48, 116n
measures of, 91–96, 113
as a measure of domestic ownership
structure, 32, 92, 99
as a second-best option absent Pareto
optimality, 145
oil nationalization database, as
compared to existing data, 99–102
oil nationalization database, overview of,
31–32

nationalization (cont.)
    oil versus nonoil types of, 31, 97–98,
        223–225
    operational versus nonoperational,
        definition of, 7, 96–97
    petroleum geology and, 62, 114, 117
    political consequences, overview of,
        13–17
    political constraints on, 54–57, 109–110
    postnationalization pathways and, 74–78
    preconditions for, 61–63, 185–186
    predicted probabilities of, 119–122
    privatization versus, 52–53, 218–219
    production cycle and, 18, 73
    production elasticity and, 68–69
    production inefficiency and, 69–73
    public regulation theory and, 69–71
    reputation costs of, 47, 50, 78, 216
    resource curse and, 14, 144
    single-case analysis for determinants of,
        184–195
    statistical determinants of, 117–126
    statistical results for fiscal strength and,
        158–161
    statistical results for leader survival and,
        161–168
    technical constraints on, 20, 61–63,
        180–181
    transaction costs and, 10–11, 28, 73
    varieties of, 5–6, 51–53, 96–99
    see also national oil companies (NOCs);
        privatization; state-owned enterprises
        (SOEs)
natural gas, 31
    failed nationalizations of, 221–222
    revenue-sharing contracts and, 59, 219
    SOE control over, 4, 7
    SOEs for, 8, 98n
Natural Resource Governance Institute
        (NRGI), 64
natural resources trap, 49–50
Netherlands, 98, 121n
nickel, 47
Nigeria
    de jure versus de facto operational
        control in, 6
    military dictatorship in, 124
    nationalization of nonoperational
        functions in, 31
    nonoperational SOE governance in, 5,
        97, 98, 100, 101
    production-sharing contracts in, 100
    regime instability in, 43
    resource curse in, 44
    shuffling of SOE management in, 66n

Nigerian National Petroleum Corporation
        (NNPC), 5, 6, 66n, 98, 100
Nixon, Richard Milhous, 188, 192, 193n,
        204
nonrenewable materials needed for
        renewable energy, 223
nonresource nationalizations, 48
nonresource taxes, 16, 29n
NorNickel, 5
North Africa, wave of oil nationalizations
        in, 13
Norway
    oil nationalization (1981) in, 33
    resource blessing in, 14
    SOE governance in, 97, 222
Novatek, 218, 219

obsolescing bargain, 9, 11, 14n, 18, 47n,
        47, 49
Occidental Petroleum, 1n, 30, 121n
oil exploration
    active involvement of NOCs in, 93
    comparison of IOCs to NOCs regarding
        success of, 71
    complexity of, 95, 125
    consequences of failure to invest in, 3,
        10, 28, 65, 218
    cost recovery and investment in, 65, 147
    cost-production dynamics and, 199
    different stages of, 181, 199
    endogeneity of political institutions and,
        16, 43, 167n
    expropriation's effects on, 50
    frontier cases of, 61
    initial contracts and, 144, 219
    nationalization prior to, 115n, 132
    quasi-rents and, 28
    risks of, 11, 61, 71
    see also extractive resource
        exploration/production
oil income
    see oil revenue
oil nationalization
    see national oil companies (NOCs);
        nationalization
oil prices
    attempted OPEC control over, 105
    boom-and-bust cycles of, 10, 23, 24, 43,
        84, 204
    collapse (1986) of, 78
    cooling (1975–1978) of, 84, 204
    detrended measure of, 114
    identifying competing revenue effects
        between nationalization and, 184,
        201, 202

nationalization amidst low levels of, 10, 170

renegotiation because of increases in, 108, 201

shock (1973–1974) of, 89, 177, 184, 196, 201

statistical results for nationalization and, 117–119, 121

theoretical expectations for nationalization and, 10, 47, 107, 112, 177, 201

oil production

aging fields and risks of, 11, 114

different stages of, 114

global share of across intervention types, 99

information asymmetries in, 21, 25, 64

measures of, 114, 115

before and after nationalization, 69, 70, 152

nationalization prior to, 165

statistical results for nationalization and, 114, 117, 119

see also extractive resource exploration/production; oil revenue

oil revenue

counterfactual results for nationalization and, 199–202

counterfactuals as projections of, 178, 179, 182, 183, 195–199

diffused information of, 105

information asymmetries in, 25–26, 64

Iranian maximization of, 83, 184

Iraqi maximization of, 86, 87

long time horizons and, 77

maximization through nationalization of, 23–29, 73–75, 217

measuring government take of, 148–151

modeling nationalization's effects on, 156–158

before and after nationalization, 152

perceived forfeiture to IOCs of, 30, 64, 81, 105, 108

perceived unfairness in sharing between Iran and Britain of, 129–131

repression and, 2, 7, 29, 205

social expenditures and, 3

statistical results for nationalization and, 158–161

statistical results for nationalization, survival, and, 161–169

taxation of, 144–147

theoretical expectations for nationalization and, 80, 182

theoretical expectations for survival and, 143, 147

see also information asymmetry; fiscal strength; nationalization; oil prices; oil production; rents

oil subsidies, 49, 96, 148n

oligopolistic market structure, 7, 11, 22, 50, 103

see also Organization of the Petroleum Exporting Countries (OPEC); Seven Sisters

Oman, 33, 201

OpenOil initiative, 22n

operational nationalization theory

case study selection and, 34, 82, 182–184

institutions curse theory and, 16

intellectual roots of, 9–17, 44–50

obsolescing bargain and, 47

opportunism and, 215–217

overview of, 17–31, 53–74

predatory state and, 57, 216–217

resource curse and, 44, 90

testable implications of, 78–81

time-inconsistency and, 49–50

opportunity costs, 18, 20, 108, 181

Organization of the Petroleum Exporting Countries (OPEC)

Charter of, 104

determinants of joining, 111

as a determinant of nationalization, 60, 111, 117

information-sharing characteristics of, 22, 60, 105, 209

overlap with Non-Aligned Movement members and, 126

production quotas of, 27, 68, 69

as a proxy for information diffusion, 22, 60, 79, 111

proxy error and, 111

statistical results for nationalization and, 117–121

Tehran and Tripoli meetings (1971) of, 22

see also information diffusion

Ottoman Empire, 12

Pahlavi, Mohammad Reza (Shah of Iran)

anticommunist ideologies of, 203

attempted assassination of, 130

backing of Iraqi Kurds by, 88

case selection and, 35, 81

debate over cancer diagnosis timing of, 188–190

failed co-optation efforts of, 206–207

Pahlavi, Mohammad Reza (Shah of Iran) (cont.)
friendship between Nixon and, 188
Great Civilization vision of, 83, 189, 192, 195
information diffusion and renegotiations by, 21, 37, 186–188
international reactions to overthrow of, 89
nationalization motives (1971–1973) of, 185–187
nationalization reversal as explanation for collapse of, 85, 202–204, 208
nationalization speech to National Congress (1973) by, 82, 184
negotiations between BP and, 34, 185–188
perceptions of relations with Western oil firms by, 187
popular dissatisfaction of reforms by, 191–192, 206–208
reinstatement (1954) of, 132
short time horizons of, 188–194
tensions between BP-led consortium and, 83–84, 185–188, 202–204
time horizons relative to King Abdul Aziz of, 129–132
unexpected overthrow of, 34, 81, 83, 204–208
vision of the oil industry (1973) of, 82
vocalized criticism (1950) of, 55
Pakistan, 33, 190, 191
Palin, Sarah, 221, 222
palladium, 5, 10, 23, 37
Pan-Arab movement, 13, 85
Panarctic, 113
Papua New Guinea, 97
Pareto optimality, 145
Pargeter, Alison, 30
Pasargad, 101
Patagonia, 218
Patrushev, Nikolay, 7
Persian Gulf, 35, 188, 190, 208
personalist dictatorship, 48, 110, 124, 168
Pertamina, 6
Peru, 33, 97
Petróleos de Venezuela, S.A. (PdVSA), 3, 6n, 12n, 75, 121
Petro-Canada, 95, 96, 113
Petrobras, 8
Petrochina, 7n
petrodollars
see oil revenue
Petroecuador, 95, 125

petroleum
see oil production; oil exploration; oil revenue
Petronas, 4n, 65, 75
PetroPars, 101
petrostate, 44, 74, 201
Petrotin, 148
Petróleos Mexicanos (Pemex), 5, 75, 77, 78, 95, 96, 98, 216
phosphate, 97, 224
platinum, 97
Poland, 33, 115n
Polity scores, 115, 123, 153–154, 168
postcolonialism
in the Middle East, 13, 190
nationalization after independence and, 12, 13
remnants of imperialism and, 12, 35, 130
revolutionary leaders and, 12
postnationalization pathways, 74–78, 217
see also nationalization
predatory state theory, 38, 42, 57, 77, 216, 225
Prichard, Wilson, 149
private domestic ownership of extractive resources, 44, 100, 101
privatization
amidst low commodity prices, 10
backsliding of, 32, 33
coding of, 33, 95, 113, 118n
as a form of opportunism, 8
indirect versus partial, 8
in later stages of resource production, 51, 62
partial, 8, 51, 52, 94
transition to nonoperational SOEs and, 98n
use of golden shares and, 94
waves of, 103
production elasticity
by operational SOEs, 80, 146
discount rates and, 26, 68
leader perceptions of, 26, 68, 180
to minimize production volatility, 26, 68
optimal rate of depletion and, 68
overview of, 26–27, 68–69
property rights
see land titling; land expropriation; nationalization
public regulation, as compared to state intervention, 70
Publish What You Pay (PWYP), 22n
puppet regimes, 12, 166
Putin, Vladimir, 7, 17, 42, 66n, 216

Qaddafi, Muammar
    endurance of, 2, 17
    militarization of Libya by, 30
    nationalization motives of, 145
    oil nationalization (1973) and, 1, 30,
        145
    partnerships with the Soviet Union of,
        203n
    perceptions of instability of, 2
    power consolidation of, 2, 30
    revolutionary leadership of, 123
    rise to power of, 1, 153
Qatar, 33, 92, 121
Qatar Petroleum Company (QPC), 92
quasi-rents
    see rents

Randgold, 56
rate of return (ROR), 107, 146
Razavi, Hossein, 208
Razmara, Ali, 130
redistribution, 15, 142, 147
regime survival
    authoritarian regimes and, 36
    democratic regimes and, 36
    increased spending and, 142n
    resource revenues and, 41, 42
    statistical results for nationalization and,
        167–169
    see also authoritarianism; democracy;
        dictatorship; leader survival
regime type, 41, 115, 154, 157, 158
relative political capacity, 115, 126, 137
    see also institutional quality
rentier state theory
    allocative strategy of, 42, 142, 143
    authoritarianism and, 74
    definition of, 41
    l'état providence and, 41
    patronage and praetorianism aspects of,
        177
    welfare spending and, 208
rents
    appropriation of, 24, 28–29, 56–57
    differential rents and, 10–11, 49, 63, 75
    government take and information
        diffusion of, 21
    quasi-rents, overview of, 10–11
    quasi-rents, perceived magnitude of,
        18–19, 63, 73
    quasi-rents, postnationalization seizure
        of, 28n, 74–78, 217
    state collection of, 29, 41–42, 143
Repsol, 76, 109, 217, 218
resource curse theory

authoritarianism and, 41
conditional effects of civil-society
    linkages on, 43
conditional effects of income inequality
    on, 14, 43
conditionality of, 14, 214
endogeneity of resource extraction and,
    43
existing critiques of, 43
leader survival aspects of, 42, 177
overview of, 14
role of ownership structure in, 14
in the post-1980 period, 14, 44, 143
revenue-sharing agreements, 18, 79
    in Iran, 182, 186–188
    international diffusion of, 35, 60, 61,
        111, 114, 182, 187
    leader perceptions of, 59, 79, 182
revolution
    irregular leader exit by, 153
    Marxist theory of, 206
    precursors in Iran of, 183, 205, 207, 208
    unpredictability of, 205
    see also leader survival
revolutionary leaders
    aggressive behavior and, 12, 109
    coding of, 115, 123
    database coverage of, 124
    foreign policy of, 12
    increased nationalization probabilities
        and, 122, 136
    Pan-Arabism and, 13
    short time horizons of, 19
    statistical results for nationalization and,
        123, 124
revolutionary republicanism, 2
Rio Tinto, 24, 224
Romania, 33
Rosneft, 7, 66n
Ross, Michael, 41
Royal Dutch Shell, 24, 38
    Emirati nationalization of, 77
    fifty-fifty agreement (1948) in Venezuela
        with, 128
    Iranian negotiations (1971) with, 187
    joint partnerships in Abu Dhabi with, 67
    joint partnerships in Canada with, 96
    Libyan nationalization of, 1n
    Mexican nationalization of, 5, 95
    operational control in Nigeria by, 5
    operational control in pre-Ba'athist Iraq
        by, 86
    postnationalization operations in
        Argentina by, 76
    production in Netherlands by, 98n

Royal Dutch Shell (cont.)
  Qatari nationalization of, 92
  revenues from Iranian oil of, 83, 202
  revenues from Iraqi oil of, 89
  Seven Sisters and, 22n, 105
  Surinamese nationalization of, 165
royalties
  accurate payments of, 59
  in Congo, 56
  in Ecuador, 101
  for exploration activities, 53
  in Iran, 129, 185
  for production activities, 54, 144
  renegotiations of, 54, 108, 129
  in Saudi Arabia, 128
  underpayment of, 64
  see also information asymmetry; taxation
Russia
  annexation of Crimea by, 216
  oil nationalization as means for regime
    endurance of, 7
  palladium production of, 5
  partial nationalization of operations in,
    31, 33
  political consolidation in, 7
  regime stability in, 42
  repression in, 7
  siloviki in, 7
  SOE governance in, 7, 97

Saudi Arabia
  considerations of oil privatization in, 8
  decision not to nationalize (1950) in,
    106, 127, 144
  diffusion of contract information to Iran
    from, 21, 23, 59, 187
  discovery of oil (1938) in, 128
  displacement of Iranian oil (1975) by,
    203
  dynastic monarchy of, 167
  ease of extracting oil in, 128
  fifty-fifty agreement (1950) of, 128
  global oil market importance of, 114
  information diffusion as motivation for
    renegotiations in, 128, 129
  lack of technical capacity as reason not
    to nationalize in, 129
  long time horizons of rulers in, 127, 132
  oil nationalization (1974) in, 31, 33, 145
  oil nationalization as means for regime
    endurance of, 7
  oil nationalization probabilities of, 121
  operational SOE governance in, 97, 98
  participation agreement (1972) between
    Aramco and, 187
  perceptions of leader survival in, 127
  regime stability in, 42

reliance on SOE revenues in, 7
renegotiation of oil agreements (1950)
  in, 127, 128
revenue-maximization in, 128–129
revenue-sharing in, 131
taxation of SOEs in, 65
use of the oil weapon by, 27, 69
Saudi Aramco, 7n, 7, 8, 65, 98
Sechin, Igor, 7
Senegal, 97
Serrano, Jorge Diaz, 78
Seven Sisters, 21, 22, 50, 60, 103
Shell
  see Royal Dutch Shell
Sierra Leone, 64
silver, 47
Sinclair Oil, 144
single-party dictatorship, 34, 77, 115, 143,
    221n
  long time horizons of, 19
  nationalization probabilities in, 124, 138
  rent-sharing with elites in, 110
Sinopec, 98
Smith, Adam, 70, 212
Smith, Benjamin, 43
Société des Hydrocarbures du Tchad
    (SHT), 7n, 65, 148
Société Nationale d'Opérations Pétrolières
    de la Côte d'Ivoire (Petroci), 151
Société Nationale des Hydrocarbures
    (SNH), 98
social programs
  oil revenues and, 3, 204
  SOEs and, 49, 96
socialist dictatorship, 3
Sociedad Química y Minera de Chile
    (SQM), 5, 23, 224
solar power, 223
Sonangol, 25n, 29, 61, 62, 66, 146n
Sonatrach, 8, 98, 148
South Africa, 33, 97
South America
  domino effects of nationalization in, 13
  early nationalizations in, 13
  emerging oil producers in, 132
  land expropriations in, 15
  resource nationalism in, 48, 108
  wave of democratization in, 43
sovereign debt defaults, 50
sovereignty over natural resources, 12, 45,
    56, 108, 218
sovereignty-maximization assumption of
    political leaders, 14, 45
Soviet Union
  see Union of Soviet Socialist Republics
    (USSR)
Sparrow, Cpt. Jack, 57

Staatsolie, 132
Standard Oil of California (Socal), 22n,
   84, 128, 129n, 144, 203
Standard Oil of New Jersey, 5, 22n, 95,
   109, 128, 129n, 177, 186
Standard Oil of New York, 22n, 129n
state employment, SOEs and, 49
State Oil Company of Azerbaijan Republic
   (SOCAR), 98
state-owned enterprises (SOEs)
   in advanced economies, 52
   autonomy of, 25n, 66, 77
   corporate governance of, 12
   cost-benefit analysis of, 180–182
   diversification of, 52
   expected outcomes across varieties of,
      79–81
   global importance of, 4–5, 7–9
   incentives to innovate of, 71
   information asymmetries and, 25–26,
      63–67
   monitoring/oversight capacities of,
      65–67
   as a measure of nationalization, 31–32,
      91–96, 113
   in the mining sector, 62, 97
   in the nonresource sector, 149
   operational inefficiencies of, 18, 27–28,
      69–73
   operational versus nonoperational, cases
      of, 97–98
   operational versus nonoperational,
      definition of, 6–7, 92–97
   optimal extraction rates and, 26
   optimal tax rates on, 54, 145–147
   partial privatization of, 8, 51, 52, 62
   political outcomes across varieties of,
      73–74
   production elasticity and, 68–69
   relative opacity of, 29
   state-as-appropriator versus
      state-as-steward models of, 74–78,
      217
   taxation of, 144
   varieties of, 51–53
   see also national oil companies (NOCs);
      nationalization
Statoil
   see Equinor
Sudan, 33, 121
Sudapet, 121
Suez Canal, 12
sunk costs, 9, 11, 47, 76
Suriname
   military dictatorship in, 165
   oil nationalization (1982) in, 33, 115n
   petroleum discoveries in, 132

Syncrude, 113
Syria, 33, 177

Talison, 5
Tanzania, 59, 115n, 132
taxation
   as an alternative to nationalization,
      54–55
   definitions of different types of, 144
   dividends as a form of, 65, 144
   effective tax rate and, 65, 104, 144,
      146–148
   enforcement of, 16, 55, 58
   of corporate income, 18, 45, 144
   royalties and, 25, 54, 59, 64, 144
   SOE oversight of, 7, 97, 100
   special taxes and, 144
   strength of institutions related to, 47
   variation in effective rates of, 149
   see also information asymmetry;
      international oil companies (IOCs);
      national oil companies (NOCs);
      state-owned enterprises (SOEs)
Tennessee Valley Authority, 223
Texaco, 22n, 84, 101, 128, 129n, 129, 203
Thailand, 33
time horizons
   see leader survival; operational
      nationalization theory
Timor-Leste, 97
tin, 5, 47, 97
titanate, 224
Total (French oil company), 5, 67, 77, 86,
   121n, 218, 219
transaction cost theory, 10, 28, 73
   see also rents
transparency of oil companies, 8, 22n, 22,
   29, 105, 131
Trinidad & Tobago, 14, 33, 121, 148
Tripp, Charles, 88
Tunisia, 33, 97, 98, 124
Turkey, 33
Turkmenneft, 98

Uganda, 115n, 132
Union of Soviet Socialist Republics
   (USSR)
   alliance between Libya and, 203n
   alliance between UAE and, 190
   as a case of early oil nationalization, 98
   collapse of, 99, 103
   exploration agreements between Iraq
      and, 88, 191
   former states of, 44, 98
   involvement in Ba'athist Iraq of, 190
   as a nonmember of OPEC, 111
   oil nationalization (1917) in, 33

Union of Soviet Socialist Republics
(USSR) (cont.)
relations between Shah of Iran and, 203
single-party regime of, 110
United Arab Emirates (UAE)
alliance between USSR and, 190
diffusion of contract information to Iran
from, 20
joint ventures in, 67, 107
long time horizons of rulers in, 77
oil nationalization (1971) in, 33, 77
participation agreements (1972) with,
187
postnationalization pathways in, 76
United Kingdom
bureaucratic institutions of, 52
effective tax rate on oil production in,
147
oil nationalization (1976) in, 33
oil privatization in, 93, 95
resource blessing in, 42
United States
boycott of Mexican oil (1938) by, 180
bureaucratic institutions of, 52
costs of producting oil in, 128
effective tax rate on oil production in,
147
eminent domain in, 223
expectations of Iranian stability by,
191–192
explanations for no nationalization in,
221–223
financial pressure of Argentina by, 76
foreign policy in Iran of, 188, 191,
193n, 204
invasion of Iraq (2003) by, 34
involvement in overthrow of Mossadegh
(1954) by, 132
lack of NOC in, 31, 99, 122
mineral property rights in, 222, 223
National Archives of, 182
National Security Council Files of, 187n
New Deal Era in, 223
oil nationalization probabilities of, 121
resource blessing in, 42, 43
revenue sharing between Saudi Arabia
and, 128–129
United States Geological Survey (USGS),
1, 32n, 70, 92, 93, 97, 114, 115
uranium, 97
Uruguay, 115n
Uzbekistan, 33
Uzbekneftegaz, 98

Vakil, Firouz, 208
Vargas, Getulio, 109
Vedanta, 64
Venezuela
collapse of oil sector in, 2, 3, 77
democratic failure in, 168
fifty-fifty agreement (1948) in, 127, 128
military dictatorship in, 124
oil nationalization (1960) in, 12n, 33,
119
oil nationalization probabilities of, 119
oil privatization in, 12
oil renationalization (2004–2007) in, 2,
12
political instability in, 2, 3
resource blessing in, 43
resource curse in, 44
state-as-appropriator model of
governance in, 75, 217
Vernon, Raymond, 9
Victor, David, 21
Vietnam, 33
Vivoda, Vlado, 108

Warshaw, Christopher, 63
Washington Consensus, 53
Weinthal, Erika, 14, 44, 47
wind power, 3, 223

xenophobia, impact on nationalization of,
108, 130

Yacimientos Petrolíferos Fiscales
Bolivianos (YPFB), 8, 109
Yahya, Tahir, 87
Yamani, Ahmed Zaki, 187
Yemen, 33

Zambia
copper production in, 23, 64
tax evasion by MNCs in, 64
tax rates on copper production in, 65
Zayed, Sheikh of the United Arab
Emirates, 76, 77, 92, 190
zero emissions, 223
see also clean energy transition
Zimbabwe
copper nationalization (1980) in, 62
copper production in, 97
leader failure in, 153
Zimbabwe Mining Development
Corporation (ZMDC), 62
zinc, 35, 47, 97